BURN
THE
BOATS

BURN THE BOATS

Toss Plan B Overboard and Unleash Your Full Potential

MATT HIGGINS

wm

WILLIAM MORROW

An Imprint of HarperCollinsPublishers

HarperCollins books may be purchased for educational, business, or sales promotional use. For information, please email the Special Markets Department at SPsales@harpercollins.com.

FIRST EDITION

Library of Congress Cataloging-in-Publication Data has been applied for.

ISBN 978-0-06-308886-3

23 24 25 26 27 LBC 5 4 3 2 1

CONTENTS

BURN THE
BOATS

———————

As I sat behind the desk on the set of a brand-new television pilot, I couldn't help but reflect on how I'd gotten to the point where I could be the host of my very own TV show. I didn't feel all that far removed from sleeping on a chewed-up mattress on the floor in a roach-infested apartment in the New York City borough of Queens, the youngest of four boys growing up with a single mother who cleaned houses on her hands and knees to pay our rent. My three older brothers were long gone by the time I realized just how desperate our situation was.

When I dropped out of high school at age sixteen, I'm pretty sure none of my classmates could have imagined they'd see me less than three decades later as a Guest Shark on *Shark Tank*, the top business television show in the world. Now I was leveling up once more, this time as host and executive producer of my own TV pilot developed by MGM's Mark Burnett, the visionary behind megahit reality TV franchises like *Shark Tank*, *The Apprentice*, *The Voice*, *Survivor*, and more.

I write these words before I know if the show will ever even air—but it doesn't matter. What excites me is the act of moving forward. Mark and his team saw the hunger in me that I still feel in my bones, and the sheer force of will I can recognize in the entrepreneurs we filmed who were right on the edge of buying their first business, making the biggest leap of their lives. The stakes are high. Almost half of all businesses fail in the first two years. That's where I come in, guiding their thinking in the same way that I guide the entrepreneurs I work with at RSE Ventures, the company I cofounded with Miami Dolphins owner Stephen Ross, where I've helped grow game-changing consumer businesses like David Chang's Momofuku food empire.

Through my own experience and through the hundreds of businesses and entrepreneurs I've worked with—many of whose stories appear in this book—I've realized that there is indeed a powerful formula for achieving never-ending progressive growth and sustained success: Toss your Plan B overboard and *burn the boats*.

What do I mean by "burn the boats"?

To accomplish something great, you have to give yourself no escape route, no chance to ever turn back. You throw away your backup plans and you push forward, no longer bogged down by the infinite ways in which we hedge our own successes. Over time, our primitive instincts have been supplanted by conventional wisdom that pushes us to make contingency plans. The words "You never know" echo in our brains on an endless loop. We are so out of practice tapping into our own internal navigation systems that when we're about to make a bold move, our first impulse is to undercut it with a backup plan. In other words, we no longer trust our instincts. Yet the act of building a safety net is precisely what forces you to need one. If you're someone who's worried you won't succeed, you've already failed.

I'm living proof that the universe sets no ceiling on ambition. If I've learned one thing over the past three decades—from dropping out of high school to get my GED in a bid to escape from poverty to landing on *Shark Tank* to help new entrepreneurs launch their careers—it's that you don't win when you give yourself the option to lose. Greatness doesn't emerge from hedging, hesitating, or submitting to the naysayers that skulk in every corner of our lives.

I wouldn't have accomplished anything if I hadn't lived the Burn the Boats philosophy. Now, with this book, I'm ready to arm *you* with all the tools and tips to do exactly the same.

◉ ◉ ◉

As a kid, I scratched and clawed my way out of that hellish Queens shoebox—to college, to law school, then on to becoming the youngest press secretary in New York City history, on the ground with Mayor Rudolph Giuliani during the horrors of 9/11. After that, I served as chief operating officer of the effort to rebuild the World Trade Center site, then executive vice president of business operations for the New York Jets, and then vice chairman of the Miami Dolphins and cofounder of RSE.

I'd always imagined myself in business, but I've also found myself succeeding in arenas far outside any initial plan, from appearing on *Shark Tank* to hosting my own TV pilot to becoming an executive fellow co-teaching one of the most popular intensive programs at Harvard Business School. I've met every US president who has served in the past three decades, and recently had a private audience with Pope Francis concerning our shared passion for human rights.

But I've also had my share of failures, big and small. I'd envisioned opening this book with the triumphant story of how in the fall of 2020, I stood on the podium of the New York Stock Exchange, looking out on bright-orange banners hanging from the rafters with the logo of a new public company I had created in the middle of global chaos. I raised $206 million to form the Omnichannel Acquisition Corp., whose mission was to identify an exceptional digitally fueled consumer business brimming with potential and merge with it, driving the company to new heights of success. I assembled a board of consumer giants and worked nonstop for months to get there, day and night, with a host of unexpected stresses on top of all of my other professional responsibilities. I rang the bell at the New York Stock Exchange, live on CNBC, only to end up the next day with COVID-19 and double pneumonia before there was even a glimmer of a vaccine.

A year and a half later, after so much more work, just as I was about to bring an incredible business called Kin Insurance public, the deal fell apart. I could blame the economic environment—inflation was soaring, high-growth stocks were getting crushed, and the company's biggest competitor (and comparison point) crashed and burned, casting a dark cloud on the entire insurance tech space—but the bottom line is that I failed.

I could have licked my wounds and decided to stick to safe projects that I knew would succeed. Instead, I doubled down on risk, putting *Shark Tank* in the rearview mirror to take a chance on a show of my own, launch a metaverse fund, and write this book. My philosophy informed my trust that the failure of Omnichannel would lead to something better, and I continued to press on in search of more freedom and more autonomy. I gave up my role with the Dolphins and I resigned from a number of boards, opening up opportunities to continue to burn the boats and seek even greater reward.

◉   ◉   ◉

This isn't just my story. It's every story, and it's all of history. Burning the boats as a strategy for success goes all the way back to the Old Testament. "In ancient times," writes Rabbi Naphtali Hoff, "Israelite armies would besiege enemy cities from three sides only, leaving open the possibility of flight . . . They understood that so long as the enemy saw that they had an escape route available, they would not fight with utmost earnestness and energy."[1]

Sun Tzu, the great Chinese general, military strategist, writer, and philosopher, echoes the same point. "The leader of an army . . ." he wrote in his classic guide to military strategy, *The Art of War*, "carries his men deep into hostile territory before he shows his hand. He burns his boats and breaks his cooking pots."[2] He gives his men no option to return, and the only way they will eat again is to eat the food of their enemy.

Five centuries later, Julius Caesar sailed his army from Rome to the Irish coast, looking to conquer England. As their ships arrived, and he and his men saw themselves greatly outnumbered, there was ample reason to retreat. But Caesar was set on completing his mission, and wanted to make sure his fighters—and the ones they would soon be up against—knew that there was no exit strategy. This would have to be a fight to the death. "Burn the boats!" Caesar ordered, and then there was no way home.

More recently, in 2022, Volodymyr Zelensky, the comedian turned president of Ukraine, was under siege from Russian invaders when the United States offered him a plan to evacuate. The entire free world had concluded that Ukraine had no chance of overcoming the full weight of the Russian army, and that if Zelensky didn't abandon Kyiv soon, he would meet his demise. But the Ukrainian president proved himself a student of both history and psychology when he took to the airwaves to reject the offer from US president Joe Biden. "I don't need a ride; I need weapons," he said.

Zelensky signaled to his Russian opponents—and to the world—that he had given himself no way out. He had burned the boats and was prepared to fight to the death. His defiance proved contagious, and with those simple words, he inspired his country—and ultimately all of NATO—to resist the invasion.

I was in a hotel in Pittsburgh with the New York Jets—their playoff hopes in the 2010–11 season quickly evaporating after two consecutive losses—when our emotive head coach, Rex Ryan, summoned fire and brimstone to awaken something deep inside his players. With his face bright red and his voice cracking, jowls animating every word, Rex told his team about the legend of Spanish conquistador Hernán Cortés, outnumbered as he tried to conquer the Aztecs in 1519, demanding his soldiers burn the boats and give themselves no chance to turn back. As the *New York Times* later reported, "'They burned their boats!' [Rex] shouted. 'I'm only asking you to give me seven weeks!'"[3]

"The Jets surged from the ballroom," the *Times* continued, "filled with adrenaline. Several said later that they could not sleep. The Jets went on to topple the Steelers, their signature win of the season."

It was thrilling. I truly believe the burn the boats analogy activated a switch inside our players to unlock another level of effort they did not know they possessed. The quote has stuck with me ever since, as I recognized that the philosophy had been guiding my decisions long before I was able to put it into words.

I've never been at war like Sun Tzu and Caesar, or literally under siege like Zelensky, defending democracy from evil, but the journey of my life has sometimes felt like a true battle. It's not just that I grew up in poverty. I grew up without hope. My mother—raising four boys on her own—was desperately ill, declining before my eyes until she finally succumbed when I was just twenty-six years old. It would have been easy to end up like so many kids in my neighborhood—on drugs, in jail, achieving nothing, or, in many cases, dead. My gift was that I saw another path. And then I took it.

I credit everything in my life to understanding as a struggling high school kid that the cavalry was never coming. The universe owed me nothing. I had one life to live and no one was going to show me the way.

I see this same pattern in every business I invest in, and in every successful person I know. They understand that it's all on them, and that it doesn't matter what other people do or even what they think. I'll talk in the chapters ahead about how important it is to trust your instincts and act. I've seen hesitation kill more dreams than speed ever will. And when you hesitate, or when you hedge, or when you divide your attention between your goal and the safety net you think you need to build, it all just begs the question: What are you waiting for?

◎   ◎   ◎

Science bears this out. Studies have convincingly shown that backup plans hobble us on the road toward success—that abundant choices end up rendering us paralyzed.

It's okay to be unsure if it's the right move or the right time, or to imagine that your good ideas should be obvious to everyone around you—but if you act on those doubts, I promise you're only sabotaging yourself. Breakout success means training your mind to pursue opportunity before the tipping point of evidence, in the interstitial space between intuition and data. By learning how to confidently burn the boats and set a match to whatever corrosive Plan B you're cradling, you will collapse the time delay between insight and action, and you will reap exponential returns.

◉ ◉ ◉

The Burn the Boats philosophy informs this book's three sections: Get in the Water (Part One), No Turning Back (Part Two), and Build More Boats (Part Three). Within each part are chapters that dive into a set of principles supported by stories from my own life, the companies I've worked with, and the research that backs up what trailblazers know instinctively.

By the end of this book, you'll be ready to tear down the barriers to living the life you're meant to live—indeed, you'll be ready to change the world. All that matters, wherever you're starting from, is that next big move. Get ready to burn the boats.

PART I

———————

GET IN THE WATER

CHAPTER 1

TRUST
YOUR
INSTINCTS

———————

For people who don't know my story, hearing that I dropped out of high school often comes as a shock. We have a stereotype surrounding high school dropouts—unmotivated failures, limiting their future possibilities to the extreme. My well-intentioned high school guidance counselor, Mr. Baker, told me I'd be throwing my life away. He insisted that the stigma of being a high school dropout would cling to me forever.

He didn't understand—no one did. Dropping out of high school wasn't just something that happened to me because I couldn't make it through. It was an architected plan that I was able to execute only because I saw a vision of a possible future, fully committed to it, and wouldn't be dissuaded. I trusted my instincts.

Let me explain: In the tiny rent-stabilized apartment in Queens where I grew up, my mom and I were really struggling. My biggest dream when I was a kid was simply having enough money so that we wouldn't need to worry about where dinner was coming from. I remember the near-empty fridge containing only Spam, leftover Steak-umm meat slices, and government cheese—quite literally, a five-pound block of mystery cheese product stamped with the words "American Cheese Donated by the US Department of Agriculture."

Our Thanksgiving ritual began with a knock at the door, the priest from our local parish on the other side. As far as I could tell we were not great Catholics. I could never remember the last time we had been to church, and I was never sure what I'd say if asked directly. But one of my earliest memories is of tugging on my mom's dress, peering through the gap in the door, and hearing her say, "Hello, Father." There were no questions asked, there was no judgment on the priest's face, there was no shame in that hallway. All I felt was love as he handed us a box of food for the holiday. The gesture has stuck with me all these years.

It was really rough. My father was out of the picture before I was nine. My three brothers, older than me, left the house as soon as they could scrounge together enough money to go. While my mom had a lightning-quick mind and could write like nothing I'd seen in the books at school, she too was a high school dropout—by circumstance in her case, not by design. She was depressed and physically struggling, increasingly confined to a chair by knees that couldn't support her frame, gaining weight by the day until she ultimately ballooned to 400 pounds. The one saving grace in her life was the classes she was taking at Queens College after getting her GED. She loved them. She would often have me tag along with her on Saturdays to her urban studies lectures, and I loved them, too.

Those classes inspired me. But inspiration didn't pay the bills. I got my first job at ten years old, trying to help my mom make ends meet. I sold flowers on street corners and hawked ten-dollar leather handbags from a van at local flea markets. I was eventually able to get a job at McDonald's, cleaning the gum from underneath the party-room tables. But as a minor, my earning potential maxed out at around five dollars an hour. That was never going to be enough. We needed so much more. I looked at ads in the local *PennySaver*—college students only, $9/hour—and I realized that maybe I didn't have to wait until I was eighteen to get there. What if I could pull forward all the trappings of adulthood two years early—college, a better-paying job, freedom?

I was fourteen when I realized that the traditional path wasn't going to work for me. I decided I would do it. I would drop out of high school—not because I couldn't hack it, not because I didn't want to be in school, but because I was desperate to escape the filth and depression and start my future now. I hatched a plan to leave school two years later, right at age sixteen, the first moment I was legally able to, and take advantage of a loophole in the system inspired by my mother's journey. If I could score well enough on the GED—the stigmatized, option-of-last-resort GED—I could jump right to college long before my high school class graduated, gain access to those higher-paying jobs, and fast-track the possibility of rescuing myself and my mother from the horror show we were living in.

I remember as a freshman in high school crashing the college preparation orientation night. I summoned the courage to approach the representatives from a few of the best colleges and ask for validation of my plan: "Excuse me, sir. If someone never actually graduated from high school but took the GED, and got a really, really good score, would you consider admitting them? Asking for a friend."

The answer was always rendered in the same diplomatic tone,

delivered with a self-congratulatory whiff of *noblesse oblige* and a condescending half-smirk: "I suppose so. We do believe in second chances, young man."

Did anyone understand what on Earth I was up to? No way. Not my friends, not my teachers, not my mother. But for two years, I clung to this road map. I intuited that I needed to fail all of my classes in order to make it work. If I was getting by, still earning some credits, there would be so much gravitational pull to stay the course and redeem myself, with pointless interventions by guidance counselors. It needed to be a total and complete annihilation.

I torpedoed ninth grade, twice in a row, and ended up held back for two years, sitting in the same homeroom, surrounded by high school drug dealers with beepers on their belts who were making very different life choices. Whatever our motivation, we all ended up dumped onto the same island of misfit toys. I would work overnight at the local deli sometimes, sleep in a bit, watch the Gulf War briefings from General Norman Schwarzkopf on CNN and saunter into school midday, evading the truancy police on the way in. I earned no credits except for typing class. (I figured it would be a useful skill to know—to this day, I can type more than ninety words per minute.)

I dug a hole too deep to climb out of except by executing on my vision. I created my own crisis. But it's one thing to have a plan, and quite another to go through with it. When the day came to actually drop out, I felt like a complete loser. I remember going to each of my classroom teachers to return my textbooks, head hanging low, the academic version of a walk of shame. I tiptoed into Mr. Rosenthal's science class, and handed him my never-opened book.

"Higgins, what a waste," he said, dripping with contempt, and looking straight ahead at the room full of students. "I'll see you at McDonald's."

I'm mostly Irish, so when I'm embarrassed, my red-tomato face broadcasts it to the world. I was so hot that I thought I was going to pass out as I slithered my way to the door in front of thirty-five laughing teenagers. But as I turned the knob, I got a burst of courage, and blurted out, "If you see me at McDonald's, it's because I own it."

The last words I heard in high school were "Ooooooooh, snap," and "Are you going to take that, Mr. Rosenthal?" I kicked open the metal prison doors to my supposed freedom. And then I sat on the steps of Cardozo High School for the last time, lit a Marlboro, and thought to myself, *Uh oh, he might be right.*

◉ ◉ ◉

My crazy chess move ended up working out. Two months later, I aced the GED, and before the summer was out, I was accepted to Queens College and began earning my nine dollars an hour working on the political campaign of Congressman Gary Ackerman. When my baby face showed up at the Congressman's makeshift campaign headquarters, they demanded to see proof that I was a college student. I showed them the promissory note for my student loans—and I was in. I ended up as president of the Queens College debate team, and ran for student body president, telling the school paper that I dropped out of high school because "I didn't feel challenged," my story to the world back then. From Congressman Ackerman's office, I jumped to a job as a researcher in the press office of New York City Mayor Giuliani—and onward from there.

As I sat down to write this book, I wrestled with how to tell my story, and whether burning the boats was actually a strategy that made sense for everyone, or just for people fortunate enough to be born with certain structural advantages. Yes, I grew up poor, with a sick mother confined to a wheelchair. But even so, society still endowed me with the undeniable privilege that comes from being white and male. That's why I've endeavored in these pages to share the stories of entrepreneurs who don't necessarily look like me, and don't share my background. In hearing those stories, similar and dissimilar to mine in a variety of ways, I realized that no matter where you begin, the answer really is the same. The journey may be longer or harder, depending on the hand you've been dealt, but to make the most of it and to reach your highest heights, you have to go all in, trust your instincts, and act.

Deep down, we all know what we are capable of. We all see visions of our future that no one else ratifies. Too often, conventional wisdom and external pressures sway us off course. From the time we are old enough to articulate our instincts, we are conditioned to dismiss them in favor of the institutions that govern us, and the people who are paid to know better. The advice of others may keep us safe from catastrophe—don't put foil in the microwave!—but it also keeps us from tapping into our own unique brilliance.

This entire book is about not becoming hesitant when your instincts don't match what the world is telling you to do. The key to unlocking potential is to embrace your highest competitive advantage: you are the only one who has the full story of your life. YOU are the one subject about which there will never be a greater expert in the world. And so of course you will see your path forward before anyone else will.

In other words, if you don't trust yourself, you will miss the chance to be extraordinary.

As Ralph Waldo Emerson wrote in his 1841 essay, "Self-Reliance" (a work that I return to again and again for inspiration), "A man should learn to detect and watch that gleam of light which flashes across his mind from within, more than the lustre of the firmament of bards and sages. Yet he dismisses without notice his thought, because it is his."[1]

Listening to yourself is how you begin to find your future. There are four principles to help you get there:

Destiny Starts with a Vision

For me, it was freedom. I needed to do everything I could to escape the limitations of being in high school. For you, it might be anything—but it needs to be something. You can't achieve a goal that you haven't defined. You need to know where you want to go; only then can you come up with a plan to get there. The best dreams are the ones that emerge from somewhere deep within you, where the ambition is inextricably linked to your unique take on the world, your gifts, your talents, and your soul.

Freddie Harrel envisioned a new reality for Black women like her, who wanted to express themselves through their hair without having to endure a costly, time-consuming, stigmatized experience. She wanted hair extensions—a $7 billion market for Black women globally—to be easy and fun, and yet fake hair was anything but. Freddie hated that women who wore wigs were made to feel ashamed. Even the word "wig" felt like it had a negative connotation. She and her friends were tired of their only option being beauty supply shops with questionable product quality and hair with texture that didn't match their own.

So Freddie raised more than $2 million to create RadSwan, a beauty startup changing the hair market for Black women, building a community around celebration and empowerment. "For Black women all around the world, hair can communicate so much about who we are, where we are, it's like a whole extra language," she told me. And the incumbent brands weren't seeing it. Only Freddie was.

Another example: my friend Brian Chesky dreamed of helping everyone with a guest room, an extra couch, or even just an air mattress earn some added income when he came up with the idea for Airbnb in 2007. When the website TechCrunch covered the company's launch a year later, the very first comment predicted instant failure: "If this ever becomes mainstream, the whole thing will come crashing down."[2] Cut to more than a dozen years later, and the company's initial public offering in December of 2020 valued Airbnb at $47 billion. My company RSE had a chance to be an early investor and we passed, focusing too much on potential regulatory challenges rather than trusting my instincts that Brian would overcome them. Huge mistake. And proof that inaction can cost you far more than failure.

My partner at RSE, Stephen Ross—real estate developer, owner of the Miami Dolphins, and number 267 on the Forbes Billionaires Index with a net worth of $11.6 billion[3]—had his own big dream that seemed impossible to onlookers. Hudson Yards had been the site of an old Manhattan railway, an open sore on the island's West Side for almost fifty years, a blight on the New York City landscape.[4] Redevelopment project after redevelopment project was proposed by a string of mayors and governors, and each failed, due to lack of budget and little support for investing in what was seen as a wasteland, too far from the subway lines for enough people to flock there. I had my own history with the area, as I was originally hired by the New York Jets to lead the effort to build a new football stadium on the very same Hudson Yards site. That effort had gone down in flames, a victim of NIMBYism ("not in my backyard"), just like the multiple attempts to turn the property into a new baseball stadium for the Yankees, a stadium for repeated failed bids by New York City to host the Olympic Games, and, finally, office towers, in a deal that fell apart during the financial crisis of 2008.

Stephen saw something no one else did—a chance to build an entirely new neighborhood from scratch, a mixed-use development with office buildings, performance spaces, condominiums, shops, restaurants, a public plaza, and a new soaring public art master-piece that would serve as a magnet to this unexplored area. It would become the largest development in New York City since the build-ing of Rockefeller Center in 1939, a $20 billion project when all was said and done, and it happened because he took on a nearly impos-sible combination of tough negotiations, the complex engineering challenges of building on top of active subway lines, and a financial crisis and a pandemic both threatening to derail the whole enter-prise.[5] His crystal-clear vision is what carried the effort through to success.

Throughout this book, we'll hear about inspirations of all kinds: Christina Tosi's dream to bake a cookie for everyone on the planet; Lauren Book's ability to see a way to use her own trauma from childhood sexual abuse to help improve life for millions; and Laurie Segall's mission to launch a media company built around bringing the metaverse to the masses (countering the "bro" culture that has dominated the tech space in the past), just to name a few. Intrinsic motivations borne of personal experience are the most valuable as-sets we possess. No visions are ever rendered to us in the dead of night that we are incapable of pursuing at the break of dawn. But we have to give ourselves permission to see them and then act on them.

Abhi Ramesh is the twenty-nine-year-old founder of Misfits Market, which sends discounted produce and pantry goods to peo-ple around the country, saving them money and helping to fight food waste. The company has raised over $300 million and has a multibillion-dollar valuation.[6] Abhi had an epiphany while picking apples at a farm with his girlfriend, seeing slightly damaged fruit on the ground and, after finding out from the farmer that supermarkets wouldn't accept them, wondering why those misbegotten yet perfectly edible apples were relegated to the trash. The genesis of that insight is worth reflecting on because it speaks to the importance of cumulative experience.

"The overarching theme of my life has been looking for value in places other people aren't looking," Abhi told me. In high school, he saw his friends tossing out their old textbooks, useless to them once the school year was done. Abhi bought them up (for thirty cents on the dollar) and resold them on Amazon (for sixty cents on the dollar), doubling his investment. After getting a degree from Wharton, he worked at a distressed-credit hedge fund, mining nuggets of hidden treasure in struggling businesses. "Finding hidden value is in my DNA," he says—and so when he saw the apples on the ground, he was ready to capitalize. The idea fit into the larger picture of his journey, his goal to unlock value wherever he could.

◉ ◉ ◉

Abhi understood what he was looking to achieve, and so embracing his vision did not require much of a leap of faith. Do you have that same clarity to recognize your own vision when it is revealed to you? When I talk to my Harvard Business School students, they seek advice on which private equity firm they should go to, or which consulting firm they should join, but I start by telling them to take a step back.

"I don't want to hear what you want to be. I want to know *who* you want to be."

That kind of existential question is what should really be driving our lives. Abhi says finding hidden value is what motivates him. My imperative is to further my ability to take action without interference by securing more freedom and autonomy, an impulse born at a time when I had neither. What's yours?

To surface those deep motivations, you can ask yourself some hard but critically important questions:

- ◉ What qualities make me someone I can respect and admire?

- ◉ Do I want to spend my days creating from scratch, or executing someone else's vision?

- ◉ Can I tolerate the risk of an uncertain future, or do I need predictability to thrive?

- ◉ Would I rather be thinking or doing?

- ◉ Do I feed off of human interaction, or does it drain me?

- ◉ When have I been happiest, and what would it take to feel that way again?

- ◉ What do I want my epitaph to read?

Having concrete answers is, to some extent, less important than thinking about the ideas. I find that most people who feel aimless got there because they bypassed introspection at the inception of their journeys. When they arrive, they feel lost because it turns out they embarked on the wrong voyage. We need to take the time to sit with ourselves, and see our own visions.

Next, we have to trust what we see.

Data Is Secondary; Make a "Gut Sandwich"

Stuart Landesberg had a vision of a consumer goods company that would let people actually live the values they espouse. He knew so many people who believed in protecting the environment, and yet when it came to the essentials that we all rely on every day, convenience dictated our choices. Most of us default to the most common, easiest-to-find brands, which aren't (in most cases) the best options for the planet. Stuart decided that there needed to be a company focused on creating consumer products that all of us use—such as hand soap, toilet paper, and laundry detergent—that were sustainable, healthier, and free from single-use plastic. He left his job in private equity and committed to making that mission a reality, but 175 investor pitches were met with 175 rejections over the course of more than a year and a half. Not a single investor saw what he was seeing.

After all of that rejection, most people would have concluded that the marketplace had spoken through its designated proxy—the returns-driven world of venture capital—and the message seemed to be loud and clear. No one wanted Grove Collaborative, the name he'd chosen for his business. But Stuart decided that he just hadn't yet found the right enlightened investor. He understood that not everyone would see it until he'd already made it a reality that couldn't be ignored. But he needed *one*. One investor to see it, or at least to trust that Stuart was seeing it and let him prove his vision right.

Stuart followed Jacob Riis's timeless advice:

> *When nothing seems to help, I go and look at a stonecutter hammering away at his rock, perhaps a hundred times without as much as a crack showing in it. Yet at the hundred and first blow it will split in two, and I know it was not that last blow that did it, but all that had gone before.*[7]

Stuart did something most entrepreneurs are too embarrassed to do. He reached back out to one of the investors who had rejected him, Paul Martino at Bullpen Capital, and tried for a second bite at the apple. "I knew he was close," Stuart told me. "He wanted to do it, but his teammates were blocking him, or something like that. I told Paul, 'I want to work with you. I know the answer has been no, but there's gotta be a price.'"

Stuart sensed that this was going to be the right match, and was willing to do whatever it took to get it done. "Bullpen's whole story was about good businesses that are ugly in some way," Stuart remembers. "In our case, it was that e-commerce was very out of fashion. We did not pattern match to any big successes. Bullpen's whole mandate was to do uncool deals . . . and selling soap only recently got sorta, kinda, a little bit cool."

Paul came back with a price, and it was one that Stuart could live with. "It was fair to both Bullpen and the company," he says. And so, after 175 rejections, he made a deal. Now, five years later, Stuart has become a hero of the sustainable movement, Bullpen is thrilled that Stuart never relented, and Grove Collaborative is making headlines. The company will collect $400 million in top-line revenue as of 2023, and recently announced its intention to go public backed by British billionaire Richard Branson, at a $1.5 billion valuation.

◉ ◉ ◉

The data was telling Stuart to quit. Stuart didn't agree. The best leaders make decisions that masquerade as data-driven choices when they are actually what I call gut sandwiches: data sandwiched between insights and intuition that we can't justify with numbers alone. Game-changing ideas have too many ingredients to be reduced to a formula. Steve Jobs knew we wanted to carry ten thousand songs in our pocket before we ever knew it was a possibility. Katrina Lake, the founder of Stitch Fix, understood the possibility of a fashion subscription service before anyone else—and became the youngest woman ever to take a company public. Jeff Bezos launched an online bookstore and, with few seeing it coming, turned it into a cloud company, a grocery store, self-driving cars (with Amazon buying self-driving startup Zoox in 2020), and on and on.

These moves weren't driven by numbers and statistics. We can marshal those supporting elements later, but leaders rely on hunches purported to be backed by proof. Steve Jobs could have taken an incremental approach to music, and added more CD capacity to his version of a Sony Walkman. But as a music fan, he started with the problem and worked backward to find the solution: How do I take my Beatles collection, made up of hundreds of songs, with me wherever I go? He walked onstage in 2001, reached into the front pocket of his jeans, and showed the world an iPod for the very first time.

My fellow Shark Katrina Lake had an instinct that shopping for clothes didn't work for so many consumers, having to sort through an unending pile of options to find something they liked. With

Stitch Fix, she reimagined the personal shopper as a possibility for everyone, not just the wealthy, and grew that idea into a curated online clothing business that now brings in almost $2 billion in revenue every year—and which has launched countless products-in-a-box imitators.

Conventional wisdom would have insisted that Jeff Bezos be content with Amazon becoming the largest book retailer in the world. *Stay in your lane and keep your eye on the ball. Lack of focus and clarity will chip away at your success.* But Bezos had a bigger insight, which he called Day One: What if he built a company on which the sun never set, where each day brought another opportunity to expand into a new facet of your life? He ran with it, and two decades later he's the wealthiest person on the planet, or at least in the top five.

At RSE, we invested in Jordana Kier and Alex Friedman, who had the instinct that if women knew more about what they were putting into their bodies, they would flock to a feminine hygiene company committed to 100 percent organic ingredients and a culture of openness and stigma-busting. Their revelation came when they happened to notice the long ingredient list on the back of a box of tampons, and the words "may contain" followed by a laundry list of things they'd never willingly let touch their bodies—including bleach. There was no data to confirm their insight—in fact, skeptical venture capitalists insisted that there was no market opening, the space dominated by three corporate giants, including Procter & Gamble, with research showing women's preferences to be firmly entrenched. But the research turned out to be wrong, or at least incomplete. No one had actually asked women the right questions.

"Most venture investors and leaders of feminine care brands are—and have always been—men," Alex explained to me. "I knew the problem was real because I experienced it! I couldn't figure out what was in conventional tampons, which made me feel disrespected. I used the same brand over and over because of inertia and lack of options—not because I was loyal. I had a hunch that other women felt like me and behaved like me. I knew that if there were a period product out there with transparent ingredients and convenience, from a brand that resonated with me, I would switch immediately. Talking to other women validated that they would, too. We spoke with hundreds of women who were quietly dissatisfied with their feminine care brands. Their responses reinforced our instincts, and we built LOLA to solve a very real problem for them and for us."

Four years later, LOLA's products are displayed in every Walmart right next to the market leaders, growing their share every single day. Alex and Jordana's instincts weren't going to move the legacy players, as the data insisted that the existing products were perfectly fine for most women. But the two founders knew the data didn't tell the full story, and the women they talked to backed up those convictions and gave Alex and Jordana the strength to push forward. So often, data is merely insurance against self-delusion. It won't (and it shouldn't) provide the green light. In fact, research too often ends up serving as a reason people give up before they start. Don't let numbers hold you back when you know in your gut that you're onto something, and don't be afraid to go digging for the support you know in your heart must be out there somewhere.

There's a larger point to be made here, too, and it came out in a conversation I had with Sean Harper, the cofounder and CEO of Kin Insurance, the company I sought to take public until our deal fell apart. When you rely solely on data, there's so much opportunity to second-guess yourself. The data might be wrong, or your analysis of it might be flawed, and lead you in the wrong direction. "But if you just do what you feel like—what your instincts are telling you—then you can't second-guess," Sean insists. "You can't argue with your feelings. And that can ultimately give you a great sense of peace about whatever the decision is."

Jordana and Alex didn't dismiss their gut. They resented the feminine care products they had been using. They knew other women must feel the same way—and they were absolutely right. Most of us talk ourselves out of sticking with our instincts. Winners like Sean Harper and the founders of LOLA don't.

Trusting Your Instincts Is like a Muscle— You Get Stronger over Time

A life spent going all in and burning the boats isn't easy, largely because it's not about just one right decision. Achieving sustained success is about continued motion and successive choices. Kevin O'Leary of *Shark Tank*—aka Mr. Wonderful—began his career by co-founding an educational software company. From there, he could have grown in that same industry and become a giant. Instead, he used his experience to jump to private equity and venture capital, and then got himself on television, first in Canada (on *Dragon's Den*, their version of *Shark Tank*), and then in the US. Kevin has since launched an empire across industries, and even used his fame to catapult himself into Canadian politics.

Lori Greiner is another great example. She began as an inventor, creating and patenting an earring organizer that was ultimately picked up by JCPenney—and she leaped from there to television stardom. She now holds 120 patents for some of the most popular household inventions in the world, has created and marketed more than 800 products, and—building on her television bona fides—has started a TV production company of her own. Neither Shark has stood still, even on the heels of massive success.

◉   ◉   ◉

I was a high school dropout working in the New York City Mayor's Office and could have decided that the job was enough for me to relax and trust that my life was back on track. But I didn't want to stop there. My instincts told me that there was so much more to do. First, I knew I had to cleanse the stigma of being a high-school dropout. Looking ten steps ahead, I didn't want that blight to ever stand in my way—so after getting my degree from Queens College, I decided to go to law school part-time at night. A degree from Fordham Law would take my résumé up a notch. I figured no one could hold it against me for leaving high school if I not only graduated from college, but I was a lawyer as well, with a degree from a top school, and on *Law Review* for good measure.

At the same time, I asked for a promotion at the mayor's office. I wanted to be a deputy press secretary, even at age twenty-three. I knew my work showed I deserved it, and it would mean a substantial raise, inching me closer to getting me and my mother out of poverty. Given my relative youth, they said I should wait my turn, and that others who were older and had served longer were ahead of me in line. That's when my instincts told me to make another bold choice: to quit.

You have to be in the driver's seat of your life. Justice won't be meted out on your behalf. If you sense that you are being exploited, or being held back from your time to shine, you can't stew in your own resentment and wait around to be recognized—or, even worse, indulge in self-pity. The law of compound interest applies as much to ideas and achievements as it does to money. The faster you secure new accomplishments, the more time you have over the course of your life to reap the fruits of exponential growth. It's why in the musical *Hamilton*, Eliza pleads with her husband, "Why do you write like you're running out of time?" Alexander Hamilton writes furiously because he recognizes that we're all running out of time.

I was not going to wait in the mayor's office forever. I had to achieve escape velocity to rise out of poverty securely and permanently. So I got a job at New York Life, a massive insurance company, in their government affairs department. They offered me a higher base salary in addition to paying for law school. My colleagues in the mayor's press office said I was making a mistake, but I did it anyway. Of course I did. They didn't have a stake in my future; only I would be held to account for my choices.

The job was soul-crushing and terribly dull—the first and last nine-to-five job I've ever held—but then, four months later, City Hall called me up and invited me to come right back as deputy press secretary. The move paid off. I sprung to the front of the line based on merit, not age, just as I'd wanted—with a raise that didn't give me enough to pay for law school (I ended up with a pile of student loans), but at least I would have enough to take care of my mother.

I didn't know back then that I was following a pattern I'd see in the paths of so many others throughout my career. I didn't know that being unafraid to make leaps and take risks was anything more than my own idiosyncratic approach to the universe. But as it turns out, it really does work. I see those very same instincts at play in the career of Jason Feldman, cofounder and CEO of Vault Health, the leader in saliva tests to detect COVID-19, who partnered with governments and corporations around the world to save lives.

Jason's career path prior to making a difference in the health care space hopscotches all over the place. He started his career at the

US State Department, but pretty quickly jumped to the retail world, moving up the ranks as he went from The Home Depot to The Body Shop to Hanes and then to Amazon, running Prime Video Direct, helping content creators make their videos available on Prime around the world.

From there, Jason was about to become the CEO of Jenny Craig, the weight-loss giant, when a meeting with the people who would become his cofounders at Vault Health changed Jason's entire trajectory. The company was about to become a startup in the men's health care space, driven by the idea that men needed to pay more attention to their cardiovascular wellness, and planning to use telehealth to achieve that goal. Jason was inspired by their mission. He signed on to cofound and run the company. A year later, COVID struck.

"The day we were to officially launch the company's core product and spend the majority of our marketing budget, the stock market crashed," Jason remembers. They had to pivot—and Jason, who'd spent his career pivoting, was exactly the right person for the job. Jason came across a saliva test that was sitting on a shelf at Rutgers University, and decided there must be an opening to bring the test to market and serve people who were scared off by the kinds of COVID tests that required swabbing the back of the nostrils, practically all the way up into people's brains.

He hustled to get that saliva test into the hands of millions, forging relationships and partnerships with entire states and sports leagues to run their testing programs. Who would have the confidence to jump in and figure it out except someone who'd been jumping in for years? "Pursuing each opportunity in my career helped me build my tool kit with a unique set of skills that I earned from succeeding and failing," Jason told me. "I remember being frustrated when an early manager labeled me a 'generalist' in a performance review. That manager had spent years slowly climbing the corporate ladder, and said I would never get anywhere if I didn't focus and become an expert at something specific. I had a very different path in mind."

In the setting of a pandemic, that path paid off.

◉ ◉ ◉

Jason's leaps from industry to industry remind me of my own story. After returning to the mayor's office as deputy press secretary, I ended up leaving again—but when the startup I joined ended up failing, City Hall asked me to come back, this time as press secretary. I was only twenty-six years old. The mayor's term had less than a year left. His team was abandoning ship, lining up their next gigs. I didn't know quite how I would do the job—the hardest press gig in America, right up there with White House press secretary, running the largest municipal press operation in the world, tethered to the phone twenty-four hours a day, racing from one catastrophe to another—while still living a secret life of shame in squalor, bathing my own mother, *and* going to law school at night. But I knew I had to try.

Opportunity is not an inexhaustible resource, and when you see an opening you have to take advantage. As the youngest press secretary in New York City history, I felt like I was writing my ticket to professional security, then and forever. This was going to be an impossible undertaking—but I truly thought that accepting the job was going to be the last hard decision I'd ever have to make. My story was no longer going to be that I was a high school dropout; "youngest press secretary" was going to be the first line in any introduction, at least until I did something better. I could see my desired future as clear as day: I'd burned the boats and, in just a decade, transmuted myself and my mother out of poverty.

It didn't quite turn out that way.

Your Instincts Are What Will Save You— Even When Things Fall Apart

It was April 2, 2001, my first day on the job. I was so excited to finally be earning enough money that I could hire some help for my mother, and even get a small place of my own, maybe have a date over for once in my life. My mom had been struggling more and more, but when you live in a never-ending nightmare, you become somewhat immune to signs that things are deteriorating. In retrospect, my mom's face was practically purple that morning—but I just couldn't see past her oxygen mask or our empty bank account. I'd been earning money, but the cost of taking care of her was outstripping my salary. I could no longer pay for a home health aide to come in and bathe her. We had nothing. I was twenty-six and felt like I was drowning from the pressure. This new appointment as press secretary was supposed to be my lifeboat. Mom told me that morning that she didn't feel well, and pleaded with me to stay home—but she never felt well, and I had to be on time for my first day back at City Hall.

When I sprinted up the marble steps to the front entrance in downtown Manhattan, Chris, a young cop with a Brooklyn accent straight out of central casting, buzzed me in and greeted me with a high five.

"Matty Boy, you're back!"

I settled into my desk in the corner. And then at ten a.m., Angela Banks, who ran the office, called out, "Matt, your mom's on the line."

She had called an ambulance. She was having trouble breathing.

My first reaction was relief. Finally, someone else might take the reins and do something—anything. I told her I'd meet her at the hospital in Queens.

I stopped by our sad little apartment to pick up some clothes for what I hoped would be my mother's extended stay in the hospital—wishful thinking, since every previous ER visit seemed to end with no answers and me pushing her wheelchair back to the car. When I arrived, there was an abandoned ambulance in the middle of the road with its doors swung open, the first ominous sign that something was very wrong.

I'll always regret those few precious minutes I wasted stopping by the apartment.

"I'm so sorry," the front desk receptionist told me when I got to the hospital. "She passed away five minutes ago."

◎   ◎   ◎

The greatest professional success I'd ever experienced happened on the worst day of my life. As a little boy, I desperately wanted to rescue my mother. To this day, it is my greatest personal failure, and a festering wound that never heals. Some things you just don't get over.

My mother's pain ended that morning, but her legacy lives on in what I learned from her journey—first, the enormous empathy I feel for those who are trying to better their lives under the crushing weight of poverty or disability, and second, a lesson that has driven me ever since—we're not guaranteed a happy ending.

Things fall apart—they will, to some degree, for just about all of us, in one way or another, especially if we aspire to achieve something great and meaningful. When they do, all you're left with is yourself and the decisions you've made along the way. Just like Sean Harper of Kin said, you can't second-guess feelings. Trusting your instincts is the only way to live without regrets. For me, no matter what happened to my mother, I was still going to be faced with my own life going forward. I look at where I would have been if I hadn't dropped out of high school when I did. My mother was still going to die, maybe even sooner without my growing salary to help get her the care she needed. And where would I have been? I wouldn't have made it to the mayor's office. I probably wouldn't have even gotten into college. My childhood trauma might have set the ceiling on my adult life, and I'd resent my mother for squandering my potential.

Instead, despite being emotionally devastated, I had a professional future.

⦿ ⦿ ⦿

What do you do when it would be so easy to fall apart? You keep on going. There's no better example to prove that lesson than Kaley Young. She was dealing with so much when she and her two siblings, Keira and Christian, charged through the famous wooden doors on *Shark Tank*. She had dropped out of college at nineteen years old, as her mom was dying of breast cancer. She helped her dad, a firefighter named Keith, raise her two younger siblings—and then he got cancer, too, linked to his service at Ground Zero, where I quite possibly crossed paths with him as I ran press during the aftermath of 9/11.

Keith, in his time away from the firehouse, was a passionate cook—he'd been on Food Network and beaten Bobby Flay in a chicken cacciatore throwdown—and an innovative entrepreneur. He had invented a new cutting board, one with a tray that hung over the counter's edge to catch scraps and juices. After multiple rejections, his ticket to *Shark Tank* finally arrived . . . three months after he lost his life.

Kaley, still grieving terribly, could have tossed the letter in the trash. But she made the decision to carry on her father's legacy—and use what he'd left behind to better her family's circumstances. Along with the two siblings she was now raising, she flew to Los Angeles to be on the show. It was such an emotional moment. I wanted to jump up and protect Kaley, tell her she would get through this, and that everything would be okay.

The cutting board was brilliant, but the family needed help. The tooling that Keith invested in to make more cutting boards had rusted while he was sick. The kids needed $30,000 just to make new tools and get the product to market. We asked them to step out for a few minutes so we could all talk. I huddled with Mark Cuban, and all five of us Sharks hatched a plan to back this family, putting up $100,000 for 20 percent of the business, donating all proceeds to the families of firefighters dealing with 9/11-related illnesses. We all went in together to make the family's dreams come true.

Within three months, Daymond John's team got them an audience with Williams-Sonoma, and it's now the top-selling cutting board in the entire chain. Kaley and her family are now financially set, an unbelievable story—and it happened because she refused to stop pushing, even in the face of such overwhelming tragedy. She went all in, and she reaped the reward.

◉ ◉ ◉

The circumstances of your life do not make your journey inevitable. I was all set up to fail; trusting my instincts gave me a way out. Same goes for Kaley. We all have it in us, we really do. We just have to listen to the voice inside—even when it strains to be heard.

CHAPTER 2

OVERCOME YOUR DEMONS AND ENEMIES

If you're anything like me, when you were a kid, perhaps you imagined that once you were really old—like maybe thirty—vast stores of knowledge would finally be revealed to you, helping you navigate this crazy world. By then, you would have overcome your childhood traumas, tamed all the demons holding you back or pushing you toward bad choices, and you'd have all the answers. You'd be calm, steady, and completely self-possessed.

Alas, I keep waiting for that magic moment.

Don't get me wrong, I can handle crisis just fine. After running the media response to the 9/11 attacks, and spending two years living at Ground Zero in a 24/7 effort to help New York City rebuild, how could someone not feel like they have the tools to get through anything? I ended up helping to lead the effort to build the 9/11 Memorial—while also finishing up law school—and then, unexpectedly, I got a call from the New York Jets to manage their improbable effort to build a new football stadium on the west side of Manhattan. They hoped it would be the linchpin of New York's ultimately unsuccessful bid to host the 2012 Olympics, and my experience navigating NYC bureaucracy made me the perfect fit. And yet even as I was thriving professionally, I was still personally struggling, in more ways than I realized at the time.

I became an executive at the Jets, eventually in charge of the team's entire business. I had a new deal in hand, a three-month-old baby boy, and a beautiful apartment in Brooklyn Heights. I finally felt secure, happy, even a bit healed. I thought I'd conquered the tragedies of my childhood.

Then I got cancer—testicular cancer, on the list of cancers that could have been related to exposure to Ground Zero after 9/11. I was growing a massive tumor, diagnosed after weeks of pain and denial. Even though my life was potentially on the line, all I could think about was how to hide the diagnosis. I had so much lingering shame, so much insecurity over my rocky beginnings, that I was afraid to ever show weakness. I thought for sure that if anyone knew I had cancer, my draft employment contract for my latest job title—which would give me the kind of security I'd always craved—would be scrapped. Even though I knew I'd proven my worth to the Jets, I worried I could lose it all in an instant, and be right back in that filthy Queens apartment eating government cheese.

I went back to work a day after having surgery to remove the testicle, a three-inch scar across my abdomen still caked in blood. There was a Jets dinner with a group of coaches. I forced myself out of bed, threw away the painkillers for good, and decided I would prove that I was still undefeated. I walked into the private dining room where Jets head coach Eric Mangini was holding court at a table full of his staff. I nonchalantly grabbed a chair as if nothing had happened. It was impossible not to notice that I had a big bag of ice lodged between my legs. With a toast of wine, I rolled out my new motto, soon to be brandished on dog tags around my neck: HALF THE BALLS. TWICE THE MAN.

I thought I was being a hero, showing toughness and grit—but now I just cringe at the memory of that night. All I was demonstrating was my own weakness. And I was sending a message to everyone who worked under me that if I was coming back to work a day after surgery, you had better set aside your own struggles and suck it up. I know now that I was such a flawed leader back then, demanding, uncompromising, rigid—because that's exactly how I was with myself. You can't empathize with others if you don't extend to yourself the same fundamental kindness. I didn't trust anyone to give me the benefit of the doubt, to cut me any slack, to accept that I was not superhuman. I was wrong.

◉　◉　◉

No matter what you achieve, it's so easy to convince yourself that it's not enough, that *you're* not enough, and that the vultures are waiting to take you down at the first sign of weakness. But whether the vultures are real, or just the voices in our own heads, we can't let them peck apart our self-esteem. Before we can burn the boats, we have to be confident in who we are, unafraid of being felled by the forces gunning for our demise. We have to take back the power from those who seek to tear us down, from our past shames and failures, and from deep within, destroying all doubts, and steeling ourselves for the hard work of success. This chapter will cover the principles I believe are so critical to overcoming the past and readying ourselves for an unlimited future.

Vanquish the Haters—and Cradle Your Ideas with Loving Support

When Dave Chang first decided to serve an Impossible Burger at one of his Momofuku restaurants in New York back in 2016, he was met with deep skepticism. "No one will want vegan burgers," he was told by everyone, including the *New York Post*. "It's taken [creator Patrick O.] Brown's Impossible Foods lab five years and $80 million—$80 million—to turn out a burger I wouldn't pay 80 cents for," wrote Steve Cuozzo, a *Post* columnist and food critic. "And I definitely wouldn't pay $12 for it, which is how much it will go for at Momofuku Nishi."

I was standing in the back of the room, next to Steve Cuozzo at our press unveiling, watching Dave introduce the burger, dutifully eating one myself—and secretly thinking the very same thoughts. As someone who has spent my entire adult life struggling with my weight, as soon as I saw that the Impossible Burger's calorie count approximated the real thing, I didn't understand why anyone would ever bother to choose it. Go big or go home, right? Nevertheless, I was Dave's loyal partner and smiled in agreement when he predicted that this was going to lead the way in a seismic societal shift.

What I and others didn't fully appreciate was the escalating climate crisis and the ethical trends toward vegan food that were about to take off. Dave sensed the threat way before most of the world. He understood that meat was contributing to planetary disaster, and that this was going to move people to explore alternatives. Momofuku Nishi became the first restaurant to sign a deal with Impossible Foods—and Dave's instincts proved to be absolutely right. We took a small share of equity in return for being an early adopter. Four years after the *Post* declared they wouldn't pay eighty cents for it, the Impossible Burger was valued at $4 billion by investors who begged to differ—and as I write this, the company just raised its latest $500 million round of funding.[1] Dave saw the future so much more clearly than the rest of us—but if he had listened to me, or to the *New York Post*, he would have waited and watched an opportunity pass by.

"You see it by being in it," Dave explains. "When you're in an industry every day, you have insights, you know more than an outsider, you see where things are going. No guarantees, but of course I would know more than the average person about where the food industry is heading. With the Impossible Burger, I felt like an artist that didn't want to make the same album again and again. I knew we needed to change, to do something different. It's funny, when I was younger, people criticized me for not wanting to accommodate vegans and vegetarians—but over time I saw where the world was heading. People want to eat healthier and be conscious of the planet, not to mention we're heading toward a protein shortage by 2050. It's inevitable that change is coming. And I wanted to act on it way before the tipping point, especially knowing that by acting—by making the choice to get involved—I would be helping to accelerate progress."

◎　◎　◎

When I first invested in drone racing, I was ridiculed just like Dave. No one saw this as a sport. No one could imagine people caring about viewing the world from the perspective of a drone, watching these expensive "toys" crash into each other at a hundred miles an hour and race around a track of pipes and broken windows in an abandoned warehouse. But I had something the skeptics didn't have—faith in a founder whose vision I completely understood.

A prescient twentysomething on my team first brought Nicholas Horbaczewski into my office, and the founder laid out his picture of the future: What kid doesn't dream of being able to fly? Drones give people the opportunity to have an out-of-body experience, seeing the world from a new vantage point for the first time. Not only was this sensation highly addictive, but it was about to be accessible to the masses thanks to the high-performance drones this new sport would launch into the world. It sounded great, but the vision wouldn't matter if the founder didn't have what it took to bring it to life, monetize it, and scale it. Nicholas had the perfect credentials for the mission: an MBA from Harvard, experience as chief revenue officer of Tough Mudder (a once-fringe obstacle course for weekend warriors that had gone mainstream), and a producer of short films, with the skills to make drone racing look as polished as anything else out there.

I wasn't plugged into the same world as Nicholas was, but my team and I did the research to find early indicators of traction that were supporting Nicholas's vision. Searching YouTube unearthed a subculture I'd never known about: kids in parks and garages were already racing drones, all around the world, and I realized that with the rise of e-sports, drones could fit right into that trend.

These weren't fully realized races, but early adopters were already organizing themselves and holding makeshift competitions. And while the content was grainy and user-generated, it looked great anyway. It wasn't a big leap to imagine how—with some investment in tech to extend battery life, logistical support for operating races, and production to create a compelling finished product—this could be a legitimate sport. Just like people were watching one another play video games, they would watch people racing drones. And the ability to sell sponsorships—critical in making the leap from hobby to viable league sport—seemed entirely possible given the existing presence of drones on YouTube coupled with Nicholas's background.

But most people didn't see it. They wanted revenue numbers, and there weren't any. When you're investing pre-revenue, you can't worry about looking right. You just have to *be* right.

"It was a huge project," Nicholas remembers. "I was trying to figure out how to build a global sport that relied on untested and incomplete technology. It was the coolest thing I had ever seen, but I knew it was complex, risky, and capital intensive. When I came across a naysayer telling me I would fail, in a way they were telling me something I already knew: that this would not be easy and that there were obstacles between me and my vision of a new global sports franchise. What I tried to do was listen. Were they thinking about a risk I was already considering? What would I have to achieve for them to start to believe?"

Nicholas had exactly the right attitude. "Like most entrepreneurs," he continued, "I was looking at a complex problem with imperfect information, so I had to take every opportunity to challenge my assumptions and refine my thinking, even if the criticism was coming from a naysayer. That said, I was also seeing major cultural shifts around me. It was clear to me that the integration of gaming and innovative technology in sports were not part of a temporary trend but rather the foundation of the future of sports business."

I didn't have to be a genius to put the pieces together and understand Nicholas's case—but I had to do enough thinking and enough exploration to understand what most didn't. This wasn't a hobby, it was a sport, or at least it had the potential to be one. Of course, there are lots of people who've tried and failed to take a niche activity and make it a sport. So I honestly don't know how the story will end when it comes to the Drone Racing League, and how mainstream it will become. What I do know is that Nicholas will iterate through any and all challenges and figure it out. Already, we've spun off a new company to take advantage of Nicholas's cutting-edge technology. Performance Drone Works develops small, unmanned robotics that can be eyes and ears where people can't reach, delivering tactical advantages to the military and law enforcement, and preserving human life in dangerous situations.

◉ ◉ ◉

We can't let detractors win. To make progress in our lives, we have to ignore the negativity and pursue our ambitions no matter what anyone else is saying. Life is a constant tug-of-war between creators and destroyers. Creators are destined to win in the end—that much has been preordained, borne out over history—but that doesn't make vanquishing the destroyers any simpler. Lamenting that there are naysayers trying to tear you down is like wishing there was no gravity. The higher you rise, the more people will try to put you in your place.

But you don't have to let yourself be attacked. Instead, look upon the critics as a source of useful data, a proxy for some inevitable percentage of the population that will reflexively reject your idea. They test and strengthen your resolve. If you can't defend the merits of your business to someone questioning its need to exist, then maybe it doesn't need to exist at all. And the naysayers prove that there is alpha—the possibility of increased reward—in risk-taking. If everyone saw the wisdom of an idea or had the courage to pursue it, there would be no opportunity to move first, to break out before others see the potential.

Haters hate because they are themselves broken. I don't begrudge them; I have empathy for them because I know the hate comes from a place of darkness. And yet when it happens to you, it can still sting.

To prevent the hate from sticking, it helps to first understand some common motivations of people who try to derail us and think about how those can play out:

Missing Information

People can be blind to the opportunities you see because they don't have the context, understand the vision, or possess an ability to predict the future. The Impossible Burger and drone racing are great examples. Another is in my work as COO of the 9/11 Memorial project. When we started developing the plans, the city was so divided over the actual mandate. There was a faction that wanted to regard the entire sixteen-acre site as a cemetery, and not rebuild at all. But to countless others, to do anything short of restoring everyday life to the site was seen as a capitulation. Still others wanted to simply erect a carbon copy of the Twin Towers (the original design of which was actually reviled by much of the architectural community for being out of proportion with the rest of the Manhattan skyline—of "inhuman scale and size," said some[2]), and couldn't understand why we would think about doing anything else.

We were in a unique situation. Usually memorials aren't built when people are still grieving, but rather years after an event, when there's been time to process what it all means from a historical perspective. Usually memorials aren't built on acres of land in the financial heart of a city, with the dual need to commemorate what happened but also revitalize a suffering economy. Usually memorials aren't built on ground that also serves as a final resting place, especially when some remains haven't yet been recovered. We were tasked with reconciling conflicting impulses and destined to make no one happy.

Along with my colleagues from the Lower Manhattan Development Corporation, I visited a number of other sites—the Pentagon soon after the attacks, the crash site of Flight 93 in a field in Shanksville, Pennsylvania, the Civil Rights Memorial in Montgomery, Alabama, and the Oklahoma City National Memorial. Seeing how those memorials approached their own challenges gave us fresh perspective. We realized that literal efforts focusing solely on memorializing the dead are less likely to remain relevant over the long arc of history. Once one generation is gone, these types of memorials lose their emotional resonance—which ends up doing a disservice to those they are trying to commemorate by failing to impart what happened, and why it happened within its historical context. We saw that the biggest challenge was going to be to simultaneously create a commemoration for those who died and a site that would transcend the literal and be something that would allow future generations to immediately grasp the magnitude of violence done to our nation.

Maya Lin first gained notoriety in 1981 as a twenty-one-year-old student at Yale who won a public competition to design the Vietnam Veterans Memorial. Maya was condemned in the press for advocating a vision more abstract than literal, accused of failing to honor the dead. The finished product was referred to by some as "The Black Gash of Shame" before eventually earning acceptance and becoming the prototype for memorials of its kind.[3] We knew that she, more than anyone, understood the competing priorities at stake, and so we placed her on the jury for the World Trade Center Memorial.

There were 5,201 submissions in our competition, from forty-nine states and sixty-three countries.[4] Maya and the rest of the jury reviewed them all under extreme pressure. In the end, after developing an overarching plan for the memorial site, encompassing the footprint of the towers, we set aside four and a half acres for the winning memorial design (called Reflecting Absence) with a tomb for unidentified remains underneath the site, which families of the victims could visit, along with a museum to explain the losses and tell the story of the tragedy. Adjacent to it, we built the tallest building in the northern hemisphere, One World Trade Center, also known as the Freedom Tower—1,776 feet tall. Judged as two separate projects, the result initially left each constituency unsatisfied, but taking a step back, the entire site ended up reading effectively as a complete composition. Both impulses—reflection and rebirth—were met. It has become arguably the most celebrated memorial site in the world.

The context we understood, through the time we spent researching and developing, enabled us to confidently move past the detractors and create something truly special. But there was no way to communicate that context to the entire planet. We had to be at peace with being misunderstood and let history be the ultimate judge.

Envy

People sometimes lash out because you remind them of the success they wish they had in their own lives. One research study has looked at the ripple effects of awards given by the business media to corporate executives for their vision and performance.[5] It is a surprising example of the crazy things that envy can drive people to do. When an executive wins a high-profile award and becomes what the study called a "superstar CEO," the data shows that his or her rivals are more likely in the post-award period to go on spending sprees and pursue new acquisitions. Those deals, more often than statistics would forecast, fail. Jealousy drives those rivals to deviate from their plans and make bad moves—just because their competitors have been lauded by the media—and the effect is even more pronounced for the CEOs who were closest to winning the awards. The runners-up are the most likely to do stupid things after they lose.

Envy is such a powerful emotion. The naysayers around us, consumed with our success, are driven to make worse judgments. In this sense, we shouldn't place any credence on their compromised opinions.

Discomfort

A third set of critics want the world to stay as it is, simply because change is uncomfortable. They need you to fail in order to justify their own inaction, and ratify their belief that venturing outside of your comfort zone is dangerous. They stay where they are, keep doing what they're doing, and find happiness when momentary failure forces you to regress.

This was very clear to me during my time with the Jets. I was convinced that fans wanted to get as close to the players as possible, and this drove me to push the boundaries of social media in the Wild West days of the Internet, trying to drag the NFL into the modern era. I believed that it was critical for teams to go where the fans were, and not expect the public to always want to engage through our official team channels—which back then just meant a website. My mantra was to engage with our fans everywhere and anywhere, and worry about monetizing those impressions later, once we built up an audience. We garnered a large following on MySpace, a precursor to Facebook—and then the league sent us a letter saying we couldn't be on the platform. I moved to Twitter, and was turning our players into pop culture superstars, but again the league pushed back. They wanted to restrict our ability to put out content by any means other than the official channels, to keep fan communications within the walls that the league could control. It was a fundamental disagreement about the right approach to reach our audience. One year, we used Twitter to broadcast our draft picks before the NFL commissioner announced them from the podium (in hindsight, not exactly a classy move), purportedly because we knew our fans on Twitter were anxious for the news and didn't want to wait. Truthfully, we did it to build up our following. We knew the picks would be retweeted thousands of times. It's easier to ask for forgiveness than permission.

The league was understandably furious, but instead of embracing our strategy as innovative and following our lead to grow fan engagement, they passed a rule banning what we were doing. It was incredibly frustrating, and incredibly misguided. Instead, they should have borrowed a page from Wayne Gretzky—"skate to where the puck is going"—and joined us, getting as close as they could to the fans. This problem continues in professional sports even now. With a couple of exceptions, most sports teams and leagues are in the business of preserving the status quo and have to be pulled kicking and screaming to embrace new communications tools. North Korea was on TikTok before many major sports teams.

Exposure

Finally, some people fear that our boldness—our big moves—will expose them as weak and inferior in comparison. This makes them feel a need to preemptively destroy us. People who believe they are inadequate are often tempted to bring someone down to their level or shame them for shining too brightly. Tall Poppy Syndrome is a term that took hold in Australia and New Zealand. It refers to the idea that all flowers should be the same size, and that if one grows too tall, it needs to be cut down. One study from Canada, "The Tallest Poppy: Successful Women Pay a High Price for Success," looked at more than 1,500 high-achieving women in the workplace, and found that 87 percent had seen their efforts undermined by co-workers.[6]

The anecdotes in the study range from annoying to terrifying:

"In my first few weeks at a new job," one respondent said, "I received praise for something I had done in a weekly e-mail from the boss. . . . Coworkers openly stated their jealousy and talked about it all week."

"Three executives, the former owners of the company, surrounded me and herded me over to the handrail overlooking the floor below," another respondent reported. "They were hostile, scathing, physically threatening. Then they herded me into my office, blocking the door and cutting off my exit."[7]

Rather than creating an environment for stars to soar, naysayers prefer to beat everyone into submission, down to the lowest common denominator.

The "poppies" term has even inspired a Facebook community where tens of thousands of parents of gifted or otherwise exceptional children share stories about educational systems around the world making it hard for students to get the support they need to shine, in order to avoid exposing the rest of the students as typical or average. This creates a culture of mediocrity—exactly the opposite of what we should all be striving for.

◉ ◉ ◉

These are all powerful motivations for why people try to tear you down—but, in the end, the motivation doesn't really matter. It's how we handle the criticism that makes all the difference.

Thankfully, there's one key secret to handling it well.

The Power of Self-Talk

When I sat on the *Shark Tank* stage the very first time, I completely froze. I panicked, my anxiety took over, and I almost blew my shot. Ten seconds into the taping, as I was already drowning, unable to get a word in, Mark Cuban shot me a quizzical look, probably wondering, "Who invited this guy?" But I remember the instant that I turned it all around. I grabbed hold of the voice in my head, and insisted that it was not going to take me down the path to failure. "Listen, Matt," I said to myself. "You belong here, and the proof that you belong here is that you are actually here."

It worked, and any practitioner of daily affirmations knows why. Self-talk has been proven to lift us up—but it depends on how you do it. Notice I referred to myself in the third person: "Matt, you belong." Using your own name, rather than "I," lets you self-distance in a way that makes the pep talk far more likely to resonate. This has been proven out in a series of experiments about how we can minimize stress and social anxiety.[8] You create this superego authority figure with your best interests in mind, whom you don't end up questioning. It's a wild finding and something we can all easily train ourselves to do.

The written word is even more powerful. In one study, students from marginalized groups who wrote about the values that are most important to them—like confidence, creativity, empathy, and independence—received higher grades than a control group.[9] In another study, dieters who wrote about what they valued the most in life—relationships, religion, and health—lost more weight than those who didn't.[10] Strengthening your identity—reaffirming what you stand for and what you believe in—makes it easier to hold your ground when confronted by challenges from outside—and even from within.

We all have to train the voice in our head to be our biggest ally, because the most impactful conversations you'll ever have in life will be with yourself. Too often, we let our self-talk tear us down before the world even gets a shot in. Who gives you a harder time, your boss, or you yourself, anticipating what your boss is going to say to you over some perceived shortcoming? We short-circuit our efforts and become even worse than the haters we fear. You can't do that and expect to succeed. Instead, you need to treat yourself with the same kindness you'd extend to a friend. When we come to understand that the only approval that matters in life is our own, we realize we have the power to inoculate ourselves from all external scorn and ridicule.

⊚　⊚　⊚

Still, we need to try our best not to expose ourselves to people who will pick us apart and criticize the goals we've decided to chase. We need to harness every ounce of positive energy we can in order to pull off big ideas. Be careful who you consult with, who you let into your circles, and who you trust with the things you value most. I warn people who are incubating brand-new companies or ideas that these new ventures are very fragile in the beginning. Cradle your dreams with the utmost care. You need to create the right environment to stick with your nascent plans and keep your instincts from getting drowned out. Many of us have a predisposition for self-loathing, a secret feeling so shameful that we often conceal it even from our closest loved ones. So the last thing we need are even more negative voices to lend credence to the skeptics in our own heads—especially in the early, more tenuous days of a new venture.

The television show *Brain Games* ran a fascinating experiment where they took a great free-throw shooter who had made nine shots in a row in front of a cheering crowd, and then blindfolded him.[11] Instead of cheering, the crowd now booed with each shot, regardless of whether or not it went in the basket. When they took the blindfold off, his vision restored, suddenly the gifted free thrower was missing shot after shot. In front of a crowd of haters, he completely lost his game.

We all need gentle support and tender loving care. If you surround yourself with the wrong people, it can really zap your energy and momentum. We should shield ourselves from unnecessary criticism until we've gotten off the ground, and gain momentum from early, agendaless supporters—or what I call pragmatic optimists. These should be people with enough context to see a glimmer of what we do, inclined to cheer us on instead of striking us down. There is plenty of time to pressure test your ideas with critics—but not at the critical early stages of incubation.

The *Brain Games* experiment went on to show that even a small dose of external support can disproportionately lift you up. One woman missed ten out of ten shots. Then the producer put the blindfold on her and had the crowd go wild as she missed two baskets—leading her to think she had sunk the shots. Their cheers triggered a flood of endorphins and endowed her with newfound confidence. Blindfold off, she took ten more shots—and made four, an almost inconceivable improvement from the first round.

◎　◎　◎

That all sounds great, but what if you feel held back not by the voices in the crowd, or the voices in your head, but by the story of your life? That shame I carried around for so long hampered my growth until I figured out how to reframe it, and how to see my challenges as my superpowers. My struggles gave me the grit, the fortitude, and the insight to see the path ahead.

In a particularly dark time, I once met with Father Leonir Chiarello, a global champion of the poor and the persecuted. He's a longtime colleague of Pope Francis who oversees all the migrant and refugee programs throughout the world as head of the Scalabrini order of the Catholic Church. This ancient order has a deep history of serving on the front lines of war and poverty. Father Leonir and I spoke about the iron grip of shame, and how hard it is to shed the accumulated taint of our lives. He told me to close my eyes and imagine a diamond ring slipping off a hand and landing in a sewer, the most repugnant environment I could conjure. "My son," he told me, "when that ring is found years later, and all the filth is washed away, it is only then we realize it was a diamond all along."

Turn Your Deepest Flaws into Your Most Astonishing Triumphs

Rex Ryan was the coach of the New York Jets from 2009 to 2014. He had tremendous positive qualities—unrelenting perseverance and a big heart to match—but his career threatened to be derailed by a source of personal shame he had kept hidden throughout his years as coach. In the midst of the Jets' 2010 playoff run, a video was discovered showing Rex pretending to be a police officer, pulling over his wife, and worshipping and massaging her feet in a sexually suggestive way. Even more videos like this surfaced, and media coverage ran wild. Rex was embarrassed, and thought it was going to be the end of both his marriage and his career. Justified or not, Rex saw the reveal of these videos as the unmasking of a deep character flaw inside of him. He worried that it would invalidate everything he had accomplished, and that for the rest of his life it would be something he needed to run from. I remember walking into Rex's office. He had just finished praying with Bruce Speight, our VP of communications and a devout member of the organization.

"Rex, I didn't know you prayed," I said.

"I do now."

More than a religious conversion, what Rex needed was to reframe his thinking. How many men are so in love with their wives after twenty years that they still feel this level of sexual devotion to them—and their feet? "You shouldn't be ashamed—you should be on *Oprah*! You're going to have a five-book deal on how to spice up your marriage!" I told him.

He made it through the scandal, and the Jets made it to the AFC championship game. To this day, whenever Rex sees me, he blurts out, "Oh, here's Oprah!"

"I needed you," Rex told me recently, "and you were there for me. I'll always remember that."

Rex's humanity made so many people rally behind him. "I love my wife," Rex explains, "and you wouldn't believe how many people came up to me after the whole thing happened and said they supported me. In a way, it proved what I had said to them from day one: I'm not perfect. I told them I would make mistakes, and then I did. We all make mistakes. And once people see that you understand that very human truth, they're willing to trust you. They know you're real, and—in an NFL locker room more than anywhere—players will see through a phony in an instant. My shame became my strength."

Your shame can become your strength, too. Whatever you worry is holding you back is just a part of your story. Everyone has parts of their story that they ruminate about, hide from the world, or feel embarrassed to discuss. But once you realize that we all hold those kinds of secrets inside, their power over you diminishes. No, you can't mistreat people, and (fortunately) we've seen especially over these past few years that actual bad behavior—bigotry, discrimination, harassment, and worse—can in fact be justifiably punished. But simply being human, and sometimes letting that humanity show? That's a triumph, not a problem.

"I put it all out there," Rex says. "Great leaders have to have humanity."

They also need a sense of humor. Even now, more than a decade later, the incident still sometimes follows Rex. In December 2021, he found himself on ESPN, discussing quarterback Aaron Rodgers's toe injury. "I'm a toe expert," Ryan quipped, sending his co-hosts erupting into laughter.[12] You have to be human, as Rex says. You have to own it.

◉ ◉ ◉

My partner Dave Chang's story illustrates the same principle in a different way. Far beyond the Impossible Burger, Dave had experienced what looked to outsiders like a storied rise—from his first restaurant, Momofuku Noodle Bar, which he opened in New York City's East Village in 2004, to a restaurant empire, his own magazine (*Lucky Peach*), television series, and more. Only those of us close to him knew that behind the scenes he was struggling with bipolar disorder. In 2018, he started to open up about his demons, and how he'd spent his life concealing them and often succumbing to long periods of depression. He went public with his struggles, even writing a book about them, and has endeared himself to the world for having the courage to share what was once considered a taboo topic. "I get a lot of response from people not even in the food industry," Dave says. "I think it's important for anyone to talk about these things, and I have found that my struggles really resonate with people."

People not only accept our flaws, they love us for them—because they prove we're real, and show others that a path to success, no matter your background, and no matter your struggles, is absolutely possible. Bryan Stevenson, a lawyer, law professor, and founder of the Equal Justice Initiative (which, through its representation of people who have been sentenced to death, has stopped more than 130 executions), wrote in his widely acclaimed memoir, *Just Mercy: A Story of Justice and Redemption*, "Each one of us is better than the worst thing we've ever done."

Everyone stumbles. We should never sit in judgment, lest we be judged.

◉　◉　◉

Then there's the astonishing story of Isaac Wright, aka Drift—a photographer and urban explorer who started taking pictures while he was serving as a paratrooper in the army in 2018. Isaac realized that the perspective he could get from great heights could produce both stunning pictures and an incredible sense of limitless possibility.

Isaac went all in on his passion, selling his car for money to invest in camera equipment, and scaling any structure—bridge, building, or otherwise—high enough to give him the views he craved. Of course, he didn't own those structures, and after being caught trespassing he was charged with burglary (entering illegally to take pictures) and served a hundred days in jail.

That could have been the end of Isaac's story: another young Black man whose potential was tragically cut short by incarceration. Instead, it was just the beginning. The art couldn't be ignored—and even throughout his time in jail, he was convinced that better days were ahead. "When I was locked up, I had the same faith in myself as I do now," Isaac told me. "I was telling guards and my fellow inmates that my art will change the world, and that this was just a stepping-stone. I felt like I was being tested to see if I could handle what was coming, and I just had to keep on grinding away."

Isaac was released from jail on April 9, 2021. Exactly one year later, he dropped an NFT titled "First Day Out," with a photograph capturing his return to his art. It became the highest-selling photograph of all time, with 10,351 NFTs of the same image earning him $6.8 million. He pledged more than a million dollars of the money to help free inmates through the Bail Project in Hamilton County, Ohio, where Isaac was incarcerated.

The lesson couldn't be clearer as far as using your toughest circumstances as the fuel for your success. As soon as he started shooting photographs, Isaac knew he and his work were destined for greatness. "My goal and vision for my art is to expand human consciousness as to what is actually possible," he explains. "When people look at my work, they see a big, expansive world—the same big world that I see when I'm climbing, and that opens my mind to what else could be expanded, and to what else is possible in everyday life. My mindset—To the Moon and Never Back—is about finding the edge and diving off it. For a lot of people, that's scary, but just past that thin line of vulnerability is where we find human growth. I want to get people to see the vastness of what is possible."

◉   ◉   ◉

I give talks to GED students, some of them homeless, who barely see possibility in anything they do. I show up no longer looking much like that kid from Queens, the remnants of my past cloaked in custom suits. So naturally they assume I was born on third base. It's always at these moments that I most understand why I struggled so much as a kid. To share your vulnerabilities with someone in need is to make a gift of your grief. As you might imagine, these are hardened kids, many of them running with a gang, or having fled an abusive parent. When I unpack my story in more gut-wrenching detail than I feel comfortable putting in print, it sucks the cynicism right out of the room. The tears flow. Suddenly, instead of seeing me as a successful stranger, they see a glimmer of their future selves. They start out believing their backgrounds will impede their success forever—the stigma of being a high school dropout, or homeless, or a victim of abuse. But I tell them I'm living proof that their rise from miserable circumstances will not only make them stronger, it makes them special.

"Imagine what an employer is going to think when they learn you had to dig yourself out of a homeless shelter, or earn your GED without a roof over your head?" I tell them. "They will know what you're capable of, and that you can accomplish anything you set your mind to."

The lower you start out in life, the more striking the juxtaposition of your subsequent success. In the hierarchy of people I admire in the world, the ones at the top of the list are the people I meet who are simultaneously surviving and aspiring. I'm talking about the type of kid behind the counter at 7-Eleven who drives an Uber after his shift so he can save up enough money to buy a franchise. It is hard enough just to survive. But to reach for more at the same time is extraordinary.

It's more than just our pasts that keep many of us down. It's also the inevitable bumps and bruises along the way—the very public failures, the projects that never really took off, the wrong decisions, the setbacks that every successful person suffers on any road to victory. We all have wins and losses, and as I've studied the successful people around me, there's one trick I've seen virtually all of them employ.

Absorb Your Wins and Reflect Your Losses

Michael Rubin is not yet a household name, but he will be. A born entrepreneur, as a high school student, he opened a ski shop—and, despite pulling in $125,000 in revenue, he was soon broke. He was $100,000 in debt, and his biggest asset was a Porsche he bought as a sixteen-year-old. Rubin hired a bankruptcy attorney, and while he was too young to file for bankruptcy himself, he ended up settling his debts and closing the shop. From there, he went to college—but dropped out after six weeks and started another retail business, which became a wild success. He pivoted to launch an e-commerce business, which he eventually sold to eBay for $2.4 billion. Michael bought back a small part of the business that eBay didn't care about, Fanatics, a provider of licensed sports merchandise. He's built that into a gigantic enterprise, the largest licensed sports merchandise business in the world. The company has trading card rights with Major League Baseball, the National Football League, and the National Basketball Association, upending decades-long relationships, such as the one the MLB had with Topps. Fanatics is now valued at $18 billion.

I know from experience: The NFL is like the United Nations—it's almost impossible to get all the owners to want to coordinate and do business together with one individual. Some place great value on pedigree—and Michael doesn't have one. Yet he has not only dealt successfully with some of the richest people in the world, he has also become one himself. What's his secret? Rejection after rejection after rejection, and he just goes back for more. "I like my losses," he told me. "To me, a loss is a precursor to a win. I learn from them. I grow from them."

In other words, he doesn't let his losses define him. He may fail, but that doesn't make him a failure. This is the single most important attribute I see in people who have had unexplainable breakout success. The highest achievers let their wins become part of their identity, to bolster their belief in themselves—just like the terrible free-throw shooter from *Brain Games*, building on the illusion that she made her two shots while blindfolded. The difference between victory and defeat is leaving the losses behind. Extract lessons, absolutely, but once you pick over the carcass of failure, bury it in the desert and never return to pay your respects. It's gone for good. Every time these achievers fail, they simply expand their definition of success to accommodate the failure as a stepping-stone along the way.

Dave Chang says that failure "is the price to pay for leveling up. We want to hit home runs, and we want to be so good at what we do that we destroy everything around us—but to do that, we have to accept that failure is possible, and even encourage it, because it means we're taking big swings."

I process failure in four stages:

---

1.   I have failed.

2.   But I am not a failure.

3.   I will unearth what failure was trying to teach me.

4.   And next time, I will win.

It's not that we ignore failure or avoid responsibility. That's delusion, and I'm not arguing that anyone should be delusional. You have to be intellectually curious about your failures, figure out what went wrong, and reflect on how to do better next time. You can't let failure co-opt your identity.

◉ ◉ ◉

This lesson ties back to the evolutionary concept known as *loss aversion*. Loss aversion is simply the very human tendency to prefer avoiding losses to acquiring gains. Most of us will feel worse losing a hundred dollars than we would feel bolstered by a hundred-dollar windfall.

In the wilds of human history, this bias made sense. Losing a day's food might kill you, but finding extra food wouldn't necessarily help you live any longer. Our hunter-gatherer ancestors had to safeguard their gains even if it meant failing to generate new ones. Not quite as important in an age of abundant food and widely available Wi-Fi. And, frankly, being okay with a potential loss is a huge point of information arbitrage, because it's an asymmetrical game.

Sean Harper of Kin is an expert on calibrating risk—his entire insurance business depends on it. "There's a limit to what you can lose," he says. "You can only lose what you have. But on the flip side, you can gain so much. There's no end to what you can gain. You can gain the world." You just have to rewire your brain to care less about the losses, and focus on the wins. It pays off—and ultimately it's how high achievers make leaps, even in the face of past failures.

None of this is meant to convey that I think failure is a good thing. Quite the opposite. There's a fetishization of failure in our society, like we all have to fail in our rise to the top. We may fail, but it's not a prerequisite, and we shouldn't act like it is. I don't believe in celebrating failure. Instead, I celebrate the underlying act of calculated risk-taking, regardless of the outcome. As far as the failure itself, I believe in avoiding it at all costs. Failure sucks, and people who say otherwise are perpetuating a lie. But when it does (almost inevitably) happen, make the best of it, and then do your best to make sure it doesn't happen again.

One final lesson, as we build the confidence we need to embark on any journey.

It's All about Empathy—for Yourself and for Others

I was such a disaster in the wake of my cancer diagnosis. I refused to give myself time to heal, or any permission to cut myself some slack. This didn't just hurt me, it hurt the whole organization. I've seen it happen time and time again: the least empathetic managers are also the ones who are most unforgiving to themselves. When you treat yourself poorly, you treat others poorly, too—and, eventually, the mission suffers.

On the other hand, if you love yourself, and you own your story, you can turn your pain into the asset that drives you, not the anchor that drags you down. I wish I could say that my illness changed me, but the truth is that my epiphany didn't come until a few years later, during my divorce.

Up until that point, I thought I could will my way to success—but the divorce was something I couldn't hide, and it felt unambiguously like the biggest failure of my adult life. There is a real shunning that can happen after a divorce. Many of your alleged friends abandon you, people look at you differently, and your personal life becomes a matter of discussion in a way it never was before. My identity, in my own head, was that I was someone who could always intellectualize or engineer my way out of any bad situation, but this time I couldn't.

The problem with a self-worth contingent on success is that when bad things happen, your identity crumbles to the ground. My nickname growing up was Doogie Howser, after Neil Patrick Harris's television character from the early '90s who became a doctor at age fourteen. Without realizing it, my self-esteem was dependent on being perceived as achieving milestones before my time. And then, in my thirties, I was getting divorced—certainly not a milestone I had any interest in being associated with.

For such a long time, I felt worthless, like I was in a dark hole it would be impossible to ever climb out of. And then one night, it hit me. I was so depressed and desperate, alone in a hotel room, awake for three days straight, staring at my phone, tears streaming down my cheeks. I lay in bed that night pleading with my brain to please let me get some sleep, and suddenly I heard the most soothing voice whisper in my head with undeniable authority, "Matthew, you are okay." I'm not one to believe in apparitions but this is the closest thing I have ever experienced to a divine intervention. It spoke to me like unquestionable truth. I repeated those words to myself— that third-person self-talk again—and came to the realization that we are born whole, and from the day we take our first fledgling steps until our very last breath, we are equipped to stand on our own two feet. I was okay. And you are okay, too.

I realized what a disaster I was becoming at work. I was making bad decisions. I was so consumed with my own fears of being "discovered" for being human that I didn't have the space in my head to think about anyone else and their needs. I was telegraphing to everyone in the organization: hide your problems, suffer through them, and put on a brave face no matter how you're really feeling.

Leaders who foster that kind of atmosphere don't grow loyalty. They end up with higher turnover and can't withstand organizational crises. Their repressed employees conceal struggles and make bad decisions. Before my divorce, I used to subconsciously judge anyone who admitted to a personal problem. I'd gotten over my childhood (or so I thought), and I figured everyone else should have gotten over their messes, too. I imagined other people just had lower breaking points, less inner strength to protect them.

Garbage, all of it. The divorce was my breaking point, and it broke me. But it left me with a much better understanding of how to support people, and how to foster an environment where you can bring your whole self to the job without feeling shame or embarrassment to admit when you have a problem. We need to give people the mental space to be smart.

What do I mean by that? We spend as much as 70 percent of our waking hours at work. If you have room to breathe in your professional life, the healing process is accelerated, and you can return to your normal self so much faster. We need to be seen, and we need people to care. We need empathy—even at work. Or perhaps especially at work. Offering that empathy will get people to run through walls for you.

I should say that fostering empathy at work is different from what people talk about as "work-life balance." I think the search for an ideal work-life balance is a lie. Successful people will always seesaw between times of extreme effort interspersed with periods of recovery. Extraordinary things can only be achieved through extraordinary effort. We need to be intentional about our choices, absolutely, and prioritize the things that are important to us. I spent years flying back and forth to and from Miami so that I wouldn't miss a moment of seeing my kids in New Jersey. But to think that you can have it all—outsize professional success and a predictable forty-hour workweek that never infringes on your personal time—is not the way the world works. That's why it's so important to be pursuing something that matters to you. That's what will fuel your willingness to put in the work it will inevitably take.

◉　◉　◉

In a 2018 documentary, *Pope Francis: A Man of His Word*, the Pope talks about how so many of us live our lives like we are not going to die, but this ignores the reality that death is inevitable, and we need to reconcile with that truth. Ultimately, this is how we overcome our critics: we realize that we have one life, it's going to end, and all that will matter is what we did with our time here. No one will reward us for how much we cowered in the face of fear or buried ourselves in the traumas of our past.

I have an app on my phone, WeCroak, that reminds me five times a day that I'm going to die. It's built off ancient Bhutanese wisdom, which is especially meaningful because studies show that the happiest people on Earth live in the tiny kingdom of Bhutan. In their culture, lives are anchored by the practice of regularly contemplating the end of life. Continuous awareness of mortality does the opposite of what you might think. Instead of fostering anxiety about the unknown, thinking about death reminds us that our stresses are transient, and our days are precious. Most things simply don't matter—not the nice cars, the money, or the fame. Those can be tossed away, leaving you more nimble, more fearless, and ready to take the leap. The present is the only promise in life we are guaranteed.

"We all die a little every day," Pope Francis has said.[13] "It is death that allows life to remain alive!"[14]

It's that knowledge and acceptance of death that helps us summon the courage to live big, and to dream big. We can't waste the one life we've been given.

CHAPTER 3

TAKE THE LEAP

———

There you are, at the precipice, ready to change your future with a big move. But something is still holding you back. I've jumped so many times—but each time, I've been petrified. I know things don't always work out. My instincts aren't perfect. But I also know that great things don't happen when you stand still, or, even worse, when you leap half-heartedly. We all have thoughts that stop us from acting on our instincts, but the secret to success is not letting those thoughts prevail. This chapter is all about the beliefs that hold us back, and how to fight your way past them.

"It's Too Risky."

Jesse Derris was the best public relations professional I had ever worked with, the rare genius who had no problem speaking the raw, unvarnished truth to CEOs and politicians twice his age. I'd first hired Jesse's firm to help the Jets when he was twenty-six, a young publicist at an old-school shop run by Ken Sunshine, a legend in the field and a fixture of the New York political and media worlds. I recognized something unbelievably special in Jesse. He could forecast human behavior in a way that made you feel just a little bit violated, challenging the very notion that we are free-thinking human beings.

To Jesse, everything in the world unfolded according to a preordained playbook, and he had memorized it cover to cover. I would chide him as a practitioner of the dark arts, since his pattern-recognition skills bordered on the mystical. But as much as Jesse seemed to be able to see everyone's else's future, his own destiny left him hobbled with fear.

Jesse never saw himself as an entrepreneur growing up. He thought he'd have a traditional career, and in fact in just a few years at Ken Sunshine's agency, he had risen to become a partner and was in talks about getting his name on the door. He was succeeding, no question. And yet, even if he reached that point, his fate would still be intertwined with the man whose name took top billing. The firm was going to rise and fall largely based on Ken's success or failure, out of Jesse's control, and he'd have to navigate the politics of partnership for the rest of his career. I knew that Jesse's destiny was to run his own firm. Anything less would mean that he had sold himself short.

I asked Jesse to take a walk with me to consider a proposal. I painted a picture of how his life might play out in one of two ways:

"First, you can stay with the firm, grind it out until you're forty, and if your name is not emblazoned on the door by then, you can hope that you will have the intestinal fortitude to make the leap. Of course, by then your set of excuses will have grown exponentially, perhaps with little mouths to feed, and college savings accounts to fill. And if you can't summon the courage to make the move, you'll spend the rest of eternity wondering what could have been if only this walk ended differently.

"The alternative: quit. Pack your things. Tomorrow. We will put two million dollars in a bank account, and, next week, Derris and Company will be born from my offices at RSE. If we fail, we will grab a beer and know we gave it our best shot."

Looping Madison Square Park in Manhattan over and over that afternoon, grabbing some Shake Shack burgers along the way, I had no doubt that RSE's $2 million would never be in jeopardy. I was sure Jesse could build one of the best PR firms in New York, provide tons of good jobs for great people, and be financially set for life.

Jesse was still petrified—and this becomes a great example of why it's critical to have great partners not only in business but back at home, too. He had the confidence to make the leap because his then-girlfriend Jordana (a name that may sound familiar, as it's the same Jordana who launched the feminine care company LOLA) convinced him it was the right move. Jesse's gut, his mentors, and now his partner were all telling him it was the way to go. Jesse knew that even if this venture failed, the people who believed in him now would still believe in him. He could always go and get a "regular" job again anyway.

In the end, it doesn't matter that he took those first steps tentatively—all that matters is he took them. (As for the $2 million, Jesse did so well, he never even needed to touch it after the first year.)

There are two lessons I want to pull from Jesse's story. The first is that sometimes people will spot the greatness in you before you see it in yourself. They will see your strengths much more clearly than you do because they're not weighed down by whatever you might be struggling with. Instead, they're bolstered by the experience of seeing the path in front of you. People who are further along in their careers have done it themselves and so they understand the trajectory. Don't dismiss the people who see a future version of you that exceeds even your own expectations—ask instead if you might just be aiming too low.

The second lesson is that what seems like the riskier path isn't always. In fact, the path you see as safe may be the one laden with far more uncertainty. Jesse was putting his faith in others—his partners at the firm—to shape his fate. Sure, maybe it would work out. Maybe it would all play out perfectly and he'd end up leading his firm to lasting success. But in the world of football, I'd seen even the seniormost executives fall out of favor with their colleagues and eventually be pushed out. Unfortunately, when you're an at-will employee, you have to assume loyalty to be a one-way street—and there was always a chance that would happen to Jesse.

Maybe an older partner would fail to keep up with the shifting media landscape, dragging Jesse down with him. Some people grow complacent as they reach retirement age, and the business atrophies. Even a "safe" path contains endless possibilities for failure. So much was out of Jesse's control. That's what I hoped to illuminate on our walk.

Anytime you are depending on someone else's behavior for your prosperity, there is risk. You should want as much control over your fate as possible, as much power to plot your own future. The safest bet is the one you place on yourself. You have the best odds in the house because you know exactly what makes you tick. That inside information is gold.

Fast-forward seven years. As it turned out, Jesse likely would've flourished if he'd stayed put at his old job. But that didn't matter, because he'd taken the leap. Jesse became our partner at RSE, and together we've built a world-class public relations firm with eighty employees, the number-one agency in the direct-to-consumer space, with equity stakes in more than one hundred of the top brands in the country. By trusting his abilities and his mentors, Jesse now has a degree of wealth and freedom he never would have been able to achieve tied to an existing firm. We've been along for the ride as fifteen of Jesse's clients have morphed into unicorns—those mythical-seeming startups that end up worth more than a billion dollars. Jesse turned out to be every bit as prescient as I knew he was, and an even better administrator and manager of people than I had imagined. The extraordinary end to this story is that in the summer of 2022, the public relations giant BerlinRosen acquired Derris. Jesse, a middle-class kid from Syosset, Long Island, is now a self-made millionaire many times over—all because he agreed to go for a walk around the park, and was brave enough to take the plunge.

Of course, there are never guarantees. Certainly, a big part of Jesse's story is specific to him and his amazingly rare talents. I was ready, with RSE behind me, to put Jesse in charge and jump-start his firm. But the point is that even without me or RSE's money, Jesse was going to be a star—because he had the courage to conquer his trepidations. Deep down, you do, too.

◉　◉　◉

We all imagine that the perfect moment will eventually come—if only we were more senior, or a little more financially secure. We delude ourselves into thinking we'll be able to handle more risk with more experience and more seasoning. But it's never going to be easier to take a gamble than it is today. Our risk tolerance doesn't increase as we get older. Obligations accumulate, and rising seniority makes it that much harder to walk away from the trappings of corporate success and launch something without the phalanx of staff you've grown dependent on.

There are ways to minimize these kinds of issues. You can define your requirements narrowly and maintain the distinction between "wants" and "needs." But at the end of the day, letting others hold your fate in their hands puts you in peril. You think it's too risky to pursue your wildest dreams? The real answer is that it's too risky not to.

The next belief holding people back:

"It Goes against the Grain of All Conventional Wisdom."

Burning the boats is meant to be a metaphor, of course, but the way my friend Emmett Shine jettisoned his hugely successful business is worthy of full-length magazine profiles. Emmett and his partners Nick Ling and Suze Dowling are the masterminds behind Gin Lane, the marketing powerhouse that helped launch and grow giants like Harry's, Sweetgreen, Smile Direct Club, Hims, Quip, Warby Parker, Bonobos, Everlane, and more. Every hot new Silicon Alley consumer startup lobbied Emmett to take their business. But as successful as the company became, and as much money as Emmett started to earn, over time he felt like marketing other people's brands wasn't what he was meant to do. The whole endeavor began to feel a little empty to him, and he longed to engage in more meaningful work.

"We climbed the mountain," Emmett told me. "We had a huge sense of accomplishment building a respected, independent creative agency that made our customers really happy, but we wanted the next challenge. We kind of felt like ten years of hard work had come together, and we wanted to end on a good note and do something else."

Emmett, Nick, and Suze pulled the ultimate burn the boats move: they transitioned their entire business to do something new. Rather than using the marketing formula they'd mastered to sell brands and turn their founders into billionaires, why not use it to pursue something they cared about and build companies right alongside their former clients?

Instead of developing marketing campaigns, they decided to create brands of their own, conceiving and operating companies building on the skills they'd developed at Gin Lane. "We were kind of tired of telling other people what to do for their businesses," Emmett continues. "We wanted to create and run our own brands and own the commerce journey from end to end."

Together, with their team on board, they decided to start Pattern, a family of brands for the home that are dedicated to helping people cope with the pressures of the world. "My cofounders and I felt like everyone around us was paying so much attention to work and to social media, and we craved the time we had at home. Pattern became about turning everyday routines into rituals, finding pleasure in things like cooking and organizing."

Their first brand, Equal Parts cookware, was designed to help home cooks savor their time in the kitchen, and find balance in their lives. Since then, they've launched Open Spaces—a home storage company—and purchased GIR, which makes spatulas and other kitchen tools, and Letterfolk, which offers creative, modern home decor for people to personalize their spaces.

In the Hollywood version of the story, I would focus on the fact that twelve months after launch, Pattern was worth tens of millions of dollars—a much higher valuation than Gin Lane ever could have hoped for as an agency business—and, even better, it was a venture Emmett and his team felt great about. They burned down something that had brought them success, and used what they learned to chase the next dream and embark on an even bolder journey.

But the truth is always more complicated. Launching Pattern

wasn't as easy as Emmett, Nick, and Suze had expected it would be. It was hard to build a brand from scratch. Despite the critical roles they played in launching brands at Gin Lane, they realized they weren't good at everything. Developing top-notch products and handling supply chain issues were complicated. They realized they were in some ways better at taking existing brands and unlocking hidden value than they were at starting from scratch. So, armed with self-awareness of their limitations, and the confidence to acknowledge their own shortcomings, they very quickly iterated from the initial plan and ended up raising $6 million (from RSE among others) to buy nascent brands (like GIR and Letterfolk) doing between $2 million and $10 million in sales and boost the growth of these companies with their time-tested brand, marketing, and operating alchemy.

"Some of our initial hypotheses were right, and some were wrong," Emmett explains. "Supply chains and lines of credit were new issues for us, but we learned. The model is different from what we architected in 2019, but I am proud of that. We're not fighting the current, but we're listening to the wind."

At the time they walked away from Gin Lane, colleagues publicly heaped praise on the bold decision and privately scratched their heads. Why mess with a good thing? Well, you mess with it to do even better. Conventional wisdom keeps you in place—burning the boats gets you to the next level.

"I've Already Put in so Much Time/Energy/Money."

We all struggle with this one. It's human nature. I spent four years killing myself to get through night school at Fordham Law, and absolutely thought all the way through that the only way this made any sense was for me to become a lawyer. In the weeks after 9/11, while somehow keeping it together enough to manage the city's response to the crisis and leave a small part of my brain focused on finishing law school—not to mention still grieving the loss of my mother—I interviewed at law firms for jobs that would start the following fall. I got an offer from Skadden, Arps, one of the largest law firms in the world, and perhaps the most prestigious. I was fully prepared to take this offer. I signed a contract, accepted the signing bonus, and was all set to go.

Except by the spring, I'd moved from the mayor's office to helping lead the redevelopment of Lower Manhattan. I had lived with a very clear vision of my redemption for a long time: I was going to be a lawyer. But I had now spent some time in the world, and knew the track to becoming a partner at a law firm like Skadden was a long and unlikely one. Most associates never make it to partnership, but even the ones that do can't get there quickly. You move in lockstep with your entering class. For the ones who make partner, the firm told me that it would likely take eleven years. A true rock star might be able to pull it off in eight or nine. "How do you become a rock star?" I asked. Well, you work more hours than anyone else, that's the measure. And those hours—that I'd be diligently tracking, by the way, like I hadn't needed to do since I worked at McDonald's, years spent making my own future only to go right back to being judged by the clock—would be spent in a basement somewhere, cracking open old boxes of documents, going line by line hunched over with a yellow highlighter in a process called "discovery" that seemed more akin to purgatory.

I was very fortunate to have the offer from Skadden, but I recognized that working there wasn't going to let me keep accelerating my path upward the way I'd been doing since I was sixteen. And yet—the prestige, the push to minimize risk, and, most critically, the sunk costs, the time and energy and money I'd spent on pursuing the law degree, made it so hard to say no. I didn't know what would come next at the Lower Manhattan Development Corporation once the 9/11 Memorial was finished. But I knew the right decision wasn't going to involve taking a salary cut to become a first-year law firm associate.

I gave the signing bonus back to Skadden. And to this day I haven't taken the bar exam. Not because I can't pass it, and not because I have anything against the idea that I could practice law someday—but because I knew that if I took the exam, and left that door open even just a crack, it might have been too tempting. It would be too easy to make a career choice that I feared I'd regret. So I burned my boat.

◎　◎　◎

Two lessons from this story: The first is that you're actually allowed to collect choices and then see how they feel. I imagine life unfolding as a kind of choose-your-own-adventure story, like the ones I loved to read as a kid. How empowering it felt to change up the ending!

Never let pressure or convention keep you from indulging alternate realities. It's far easier to know how you'll feel about a choice when you actually have the choice to make. I definitely wanted to be a lawyer, until I was faced with choosing my start date at Skadden, and had to come to terms with all that I'd be giving up to go there.

The second lesson is about those sunk costs. It's difficult to wrap our heads around the concept. We don't like to feel like we've wasted money, time, or effort. We think that just because we bought the nonrefundable ticket, we have to go to the concert, no matter how much we'd rather stay home when that night finally comes. Guess what? You already spent the money. What you do now ought to be what's best for you going forward, not to justify what happened in the past.

I see this come up in business all the time. My friends at Magic Spoon spent five long years trying to sell cricket flour. They were deep into the world of insect protein, and convinced that cricket snacks were going to be a monumental success. They sunk money, time, and effort into it. They could have kept going, thinking they had to justify that initial belief, play it out until they could bear it no longer. Except one day they had a better idea—protein-based breakfast cereal for a new generation, but without the crickets—and they went all in, and built a delicious product. The right time to jump ship isn't when all hope is lost. It's often much, much earlier than that. The right time to take a leap is as soon as you see something better. Whenever you find yourself holding back because of the effort (and money) you've already invested, think instead about the opportunity cost of maintaining the status quo. Sunk costs can feel debilitating, but the chance to capture a new opportunity is what ought to get you unstuck. The past is the past. You cannot change it. Let the sunk costs sink.

"I Have to Keep Doing the Thing I'm Already the Best At."

You may have heard of Sarah Cooper. If her name doesn't ring a bell, you've probably at least seen her videos online. For fifteen years she worked in the tech industry, as a visual designer at Yahoo! and then at Google, where she helped design a product that millions use each day: Google Docs. And yet she dreamed of being a comedy writer and comedian. Sarah started writing online blog posts poking fun at the tech world. A few went viral, and she even ended up publishing a book, but what made her famous is when she started lip-syncing to President Trump's press conferences, posting short videos on TikTok and Twitter that rocketed her to instant fame, eventually earning a Netflix special and a guest-hosting stint substituting for Jimmy Kimmel. Recent articles about Sarah don't even mention the years she spent in Silicon Valley, not a word about the comedy brand she'd worked for years to build as someone who satirized the tech world, no indication that she's anything but a Donald Trump lip-syncer launched to stardom.

If Sarah Cooper had felt beholden to stay in her lane—a comedian working to wring material from her time in corporate America— she never would have broken out. If she had been concerned about wasting her tech skills, she never would have left Google to begin with.

"Leaving Google was really hard," she has said.[1] "It took six months of going back and forth and 'Should I leave? I'm not really sure . . .' The fear you have is that nothing will be better than working at Google.

"It was kind of ironic that I felt like I was giving up on my dream. A lot of other people's dreams [are] to work at Google, so my fallback career is other people's idea of a great career."[2] (I felt exactly the same way about my job at the Jets.)

Sarah had the courage to leave and try something completely new. It paid off, but even if it hadn't, one thing we sometimes forget when it comes to making bold moves is that we never lose the skills we've gained, even if we don't see right now how we might deploy them later. I can imagine Sarah Cooper one day starring in a hit television show all her own, combining her pitch-perfect ability to mock leaders in power with a satire about the tech world she left behind. At that point, her journey will have made perfect sense, even if only in retrospect.

◎ ◎ ◎

Gifts don't evaporate. I use my old skills as a journalist—my day job during college, before getting to the mayor's office—every day, asking questions to entrepreneurs, drilling down to get them to reveal who they really are and what's behind the slide decks they're trying to impress me with. I've overseen the work of dozens of lawyers—and going to law school made me so much better at understanding their work, protecting myself and my companies, and advocating for every deal point. Being a reporter taught me pattern recognition, invaluable in the work I do each day. Being a political operative taught me how to survive cutthroat environments, how to navigate government regulations, and how to advocate within the halls of power. Everything I've done has given me new abilities that add value no matter where my career takes me. Do not let the fear of wasted skill acquisition ever hold you back from moving on. All of your skills and experiences will only serve to make you more effective in the long run.

"But No One Else Sees the Opportunity— I Need Some Buy-in First."

This is the one that kills me, that I'll spend the rest of my days screaming about from the rooftops. Opportunities are only opportunities *until* someone else sees them. At that point, there's no first-mover advantage, and little to gain. If you wait to act until others validate your vision, it's far too late.

The founders of Magic Spoon followed their instincts to pivot from crickets to cereal—but if they'd listened to the experts, they never would have done it. The cereal aisle was considered a dead category, no innovation, negative perceptions, and slow growth—the grocery store equivalent of a sugary anachronism. But they saw an opportunity to use what they learned making cricket snacks in a whole new context. What if they combined the nostalgia people felt for the cereals of their childhood, like Lucky Charms and Frosted Flakes, with the current health trends and the move toward keto diets?

Cereals trading on any kind of health angle were typically packaged to look like punishment. What if they made it fun instead? They walked into my office with a bulletproof product vision, and I thought it sounded new, different, and like just the thing to take the cereal aisle by surprise. I wrote them one of their first checks, and just a couple of years later, the business was valued at a healthy nine figures. In June 2022, they closed an $85 million round of funding led by the firm cofounded by Mark Bezos, the brother of Amazon founder Jeff Bezos. Did the rest of the world see this opportunity back when we did? No way. Did that mean they shouldn't have gone for it? Absolutely not.

You're never going to be able to capitalize if you wait until opportunities are obvious and de-risked. I think of it like the difference between lightning and thunder. Light travels so much faster than sound. We see the flash and then there's a long pause before the rumble. Most people don't act on the lightning. They wait for unmistakable confirmation in the sound of thunder.

Except that information arbitrage only works if you're acting alone, not if you wait for the herd. It's easy to follow in someone else's path. It's far harder to start from scratch, to build up from nothing, to create a market where none existed before. That's where you find the biggest chances for breakthrough success. Act on the lightning.

But, you might ask, how do you train yourself to see those big opportunities before everyone else? First, hone your pattern-recognition skills by operating in areas that you already know something about. Put yourself in a position to have what I call proprietary insights. You don't need a unique product to start a business, just a special, actionable insight all your own. Draw a circle around a sector you want to understand, read everything you can, and look for unchallenged groupthink. What's the conventional wisdom, and how can you flip it on its head?

Joe Bayen came to the US from France, and has become a leading Black entrepreneur. He had the insight that the disenfranchised—poor people, immigrants, and others—have a lot of trouble growing their credit scores and end up trapped in a cycle of poverty that they can't escape. First he started Lenny Credit, which extended microloans of one hundred to five hundred dollars to students and millennials over the phone, to help them establish credit histories—but the company had trouble finding bank partners willing to lend and ran out of cash. Undeterred, he pivoted to another approach driven by the same underlying insight, and launched Grow Credit, a company that loans people money for their recurring monthly subscriptions—Netflix, Spotify, Amazon Prime—through a partnership with Mastercard that allows users to build up their credit scores through these even smaller loans. No unique invention, or intellectual property, just the conviction that he was onto something great, and the courage to pursue it.

"It was down to the wire," he told me. "I invested my last $100,000—on a credit card!—and a few weeks later, Mastercard joined us, three more banks followed, and we ended up raising $106 million from more than a dozen investors." I'm one of those investors, and I believe so strongly in Joe's mission. "It's never easy," Joe says, "but when you're acting with a selfless motive, driven by something bigger than your bank account, trying to do something great in the world, it's a lot easier to be relentless, and to never count yourself out."

Joe and the folks at Magic Spoon didn't wait for anyone else to validate their ideas—and, in fact, trusted their instincts to the point that they continued to press onward even in the face of "failure." If you know you have a winning idea, then go for it, despite what you might hear from naysayers.

⊙ ⊙ ⊙

Michelle Cordeiro Grant's story illustrates the transformative power of a proprietary insight. She was working at Victoria's Secret and felt that women were being underserved by the company's marketing approach. Victoria's Secret was owning the space for women who wanted to feel provocative and sexy. But what about women who wanted to feel powerful and competent, who wanted to dress for themselves and not just to look good for their partners?

She knew that a lot of women didn't feel great about lingerie shopping. They didn't enjoy it—and yet they had to buy these products somewhere. Michelle had a proprietary insight, the realization that current brands weren't connecting with women. That's all she needed to start building something revolutionary. Michelle built Lively, a digital lingerie company powered by community and social sharing. She started by focus grouping every aspect of the brand to figure out what women wanted and what would connect with them. "We realized people didn't want to say 'panties' or 'underwear,'" Michelle shared with me as one example. "'Undies' felt comfortable and universal."

It wasn't obvious that this was the right approach. "People asked me why I was investing in community," Michelle says. "They said there was no ROI there. But I knew that we had to think differently from the other brands in the space, and that this community was going to be our differentiator."

Michelle knew they'd hit on a winning brand when her email list went viral. She had 500 people on an initial list as they were building the company's content and voice and she asked readers to refer their friends. In forty-eight hours, 500 people grew to 130,000 people and crashed their servers. Michelle wasn't a designer with a unique new product, and she wasn't trying to invent an entirely new category. Her insight was merely about people and their feelings when buying something every woman needed—and in just a few years, she grew Lively into a giant success and sold the business to Japanese clothing company Wacoal for a reported $100 million.

◉ ◉ ◉

My friend Marc Lore is a serial founder whose massive exits from Diapers.com (to Amazon for $545 million) and Jet.com (to Walmart for $3.3 billion) have made him a legend. Diapers.com was built off the insight that no one was selling diapers online at reasonable prices—largely because they were so expensive to ship. The way he came at it was something anyone could have done: "I just sat down in front of Google and was searching all kinds of random keywords to find out how many times those words were searched," Marc remembers. "I had a newborn baby at the time and just happened to search the word 'diapers' and saw that it was searched for hundreds of thousands of times a month. Nobody was really selling diapers online at the time, even Amazon, and I thought, they're big, they're bulky, people hate going to the store to buy them, so I figured if we could get moms and dads to buy them, low price, delivered over-night, then we would capture them and they'd buy everything else from us, too."

Lore sold the diapers as loss leaders, and then made up the profit margin on the ancillary baby goods he got them to purchase on the site—clothing, strollers, bottles, the whole works. At the start, he'd get orders and go to nearby big box stores like Costco and BJ's, buy the diapers off the shelf (at a higher price than he'd sold them for), and ship them out to customers. He was losing a ton of money on the diapers—but making up for it elsewhere. Eventually, Amazon needed to have it.

"I know a lot of people that want to be entrepreneurs say they don't have a good idea," Marc told me. "But I don't think it's about the idea, I really don't. I've seen bad ideas work well, and I've seen great ideas fail. It's about execution and commitment and drive and tenacity. You just need a little bit of a twist on something that's al-ready working, and that's enough."

Whether we realize it or not, we already have a dataset we're ex-posed to every day as we watch the world go by. How we interpret that data is what makes us unique. Our gift is in recognizing what we see that others don't. Those insights lead to the leaps most worth taking, and if you don't take them now, someone else will—and soon. Don't kid yourself: A dream deferred is actually a decision to relinquish its pursuit to another. If you identify a proprietary in-sight, know that it won't be yours for long.

"I Want to Do It, but I Can't Afford to Go All In."

Taking half a leap—putting a toe in the water, but leaving room to pull it back out—hurts us, and there's research to prove it. A few years ago, researchers at the Wharton School of the University of Pennsylvania gave two groups of subjects the same assignment, and the same plan for completing it. One group was told to think about additional ways they could get to the same outcome—in other words, to come up with a Plan B.[3] That group not only performed worse than the group without a backup, they actually lost motivation to succeed at all. They simply didn't care as much about winning.

Backup plans can make you feel safer and help you cope with uncertainty, but they also reduce the likelihood that your primary goal will ever be achieved. The mere act of contemplating a Plan B sets in motion a feedback loop that dramatically lessens the probability that Plan A will come to fruition. You spend too much of your emotional energy on contingency planning instead of on success.

Arnold Schwarzenegger once gave a speech—now a hit on You-Tube with millions of views—titled "I Hate Plan B."

"Plan B becomes a safety net," Schwarzenegger explains. "It says that if I fail . . . I have something else there that will protect me, and that's not good. Because people perform better when there is no safety net."[4]

This is what I mean when I talk about burning the boats. You can't waste your mental energy looking for a way out or an alternative plan. All of your energy needs to be directed toward your goal or you'll never reach it. At the very moment you should be thinking *What's next?* you undermine your dreams by asking *What if?*

If you are someone who is worried that you won't succeed, trust me, you've already failed.

◎   ◎   ◎

I spent eight years at the Jets before I walked away. It was the kind of job no one left—some of my colleagues had been there for decades—and I had very quickly risen to the top of the organization. I had built a career. But something was keeping me up at night. I looked around and saw people who had been doing this for thirty years and still loved every minute of it, but that wasn't me. Like Sarah Cooper, I had so many people's version of their dream job— but that fact didn't make it *my* dream job.

I started fantasizing about what else I might do. And if you take nothing else from this book, understand this: fantasies are always to be taken seriously. When your brain is telling you something, don't dismiss it. For me, the fantasy was about wasted potential. Not my own wasted potential, at least not entirely, but in large part the wasted potential of the Jets. At a marquee brand like ours, opportunities found us all the time. We were offered a chance to invest in and be early adopters of virtually every major consumer innovation that emerged, with companies like Facebook, YouTube, Snapchat, and Pinterest. But football teams are mature, steady, profitable businesses. There's tremendous inertia under the guise of safeguarding the brand, or in the nomenclature of the NFL, "to protect the shield."

I always found it a bit too precious. When it comes to innovation, sports leagues and teams are usually behind, and never out in front. The bar is simply too high to embrace unproven but promising technologies. Maybe that's smart, given the security of the industry they're in. But it stopped being interesting to me.

Instead, I had a vision of a network of companies and investments surrounding a team like the Jets. Imagine leveraging the fan base and the pedestal on which sports teams are placed to create an ecosystem of standout businesses connected by millions of people. Sure, I had spearheaded the use of Twitter to reach our audience and we had the most followers in the NFL for a hot minute, but I saw all kinds of missed opportunities beyond that. I felt like I wasn't using all of my skills. I wanted to be in a place of perpetual growth and disruption, not presiding over things that were generally fine. No matter what I did, we had our television contracts, and people were still going to buy tickets to Jets games.

So I quit.

Crazy, right? Here I was, in a job that was secure, at least for now. Perhaps I could have just put my feet in the water, and tried investing in a small company on the side to see if I had any talent helping to build businesses. But that would have been half an effort, squeezed in between my real and serious job responsibilities. It wouldn't have worked.

Instead, I left without a concrete plan in mind. I put out some feelers to raise money to start investing. I took meetings. I took a vacation. You might say it was reckless, but what would have been reckless was continuing my life down a path I knew wasn't going to make me happy. We spend so much time trying to preserve what we have that we ignore the potential loss of what might be.

As it turned out, I wasn't alone in my frustration over football's resistance to innovation. Stephen Ross had bought the Miami Dolphins not long before I left the Jets. He had seen me at meetings, and after I left the team, he wanted to know why I had walked away. He needed someone who understood the business of football to help get his front office on the right footing. But, as a business builder, he deeply understood the kind of energy I was craving besides the football work. Just like I would later see something in Jesse, Stephen saw something in me.

Objectively speaking, at the time Stephen met me, there was literally nothing in my background that would suggest I would be a good investor or mentor to other founders. I certainly didn't have the pedigree for a career in private equity. And yet one of the most successful developers in the world and dynamic entrepreneurs I have ever met gave me the opportunity to deploy hundreds of millions of dollars of his personal wealth to create a sprawling consumer portfolio with sports at the epicenter. Not a Harvard grad, or some Rockefeller descendant, but a kid from Queens who started out with a GED. He recognized my potential because he had seen the movie already. Over the long arc of his career, the linchpin of Stephen's success was identifying and deploying talent without regard for the groupthink that all too often anoints the winners in our society. He knew that my background shouldn't trump my talent; he knew that we succeed because of who we are and not where we come from.

It ended up being the perfect combination—I would use what I'd learned at the Jets to help him get the Dolphins' business on track, but I would spend most of my time launching RSE Ventures, where we would identify great brands with great leaders, and partner with them to change the world. It was an opportunity I could never have gotten with the Jets, and would never have found if I hadn't been willing to make that jump into the unknown.

◉　◉　◉

So what's stopping *you*?

Some people tell me they can't go all in because they have to feed themselves. But they're missing the point. Use your common sense to mitigate risk. Have a second job. Have a third job. Going all in is different from having no downside protection. You can have money in the bank. I did when I left the Jets, absolutely. I wasn't going to end up on the street. You don't need to torch your relationships, sabotage your reputation, and make it impossible to ever get a job again. You don't need to put a second mortgage on your house, risk your child's college fund, and live in your car. *But you do have to commit.* When you create backup plans, and then more plans to back up your backups, your hedge becomes your crutch.

You may be wondering, *What about diversification?* We're all supposed to understand the virtues of spreading our risk, of not putting all our eggs in one (unproven, uncertain, unguaranteed) basket. But I believe you dilute your doubt by cultivating your conviction. The degree to which you diversify should have an inverse relationship with how convinced you are of your success. It is counterproductive to spread your energy across a landscape of opportunities such that you can't actually invest your full self into any of them.

I know it's hard to take the leap. Before I decided to launch my special purpose acquisition corporation (SPAC)—and start the journey that eventually had me ringing the bell at the New York Stock Exchange—I vacillated endlessly. I felt like the timing was off, which, in the end, it turned out to be. I believed that my team and I could overcome the hurdles, and had a very distinct vision for building a SPAC team with the kinds of varied expertise (marketing, messaging, some of the smartest business minds I knew) that could unlock value for the company we chose to bring public. In the end, I don't think my strategy was off—but there are some things you just can't overcome. With the fear of inflation growing at the start of 2022, and the NASDAQ narrowly missing its worst January ever (dropping at one point more than 18 percent from its high), the best decision was to pull the plug, rather than push forward on an endeavor destined to fail.

I'm still glad I did it. I learned lessons along the way, and it connected me to Sean Harper, who is an amazing entrepreneur, and who ended up raising $75 million on his own less than a month after we ended our SPAC partnership. I took a risk that didn't pay off this time, but the risks that never pay off are the ones you don't take. I went in with eyes wide open, and I have no doubt that the experience will lead to something greater next time.

◉　◉　◉

I talk about my failure here, because I don't want to pretend that things always work out. I won't tell you that you can have it all, and no one can guarantee success. With every pursuit, something will be lost. Consider everything you might sacrifice: time with your family, your savings, your chance to do whatever else you might be tempted by. But then remember the possible rewards, tangible and intangible. Spend more time on your *why* than on your *how*—at least at first. Decide that this is going to be the journey of your life, and the individual successes or failures along the way are just chapters in a much larger story.

The counterintuitive idea I need you to embrace is that our relationship with risk is fundamentally inverted. We are led to believe that we must identify and develop the theoretical solution to a problem before we assume the risk. This is otherwise known as "prudence." I believe the complete opposite. When we require a fully baked solution to a problem in order to pursue a goal, we deny ourselves a chance to prove the depth of our ability to perform under duress. Problems beget solutions. If you accept the problem with just a vague notion of how you will solve it, and if you always maintain a bias toward action, your primitive mind will do the rest of the work for you.

And then, suddenly, there you are.

You're in the water.

And there's no turning back.

PART II

———

NO TURNING
BACK

CHAPTER 4

OPTIMIZE YOUR ANXIETY

When I think about the power of anxiety to provoke our best performances, Eric Mangini immediately comes to mind. I worked with Eric during his tenure as head coach of the Jets from 2006 until 2008. His detail-focused intensity drove the team to a postseason slot in his first season—coming off a miserable previous year when we had 4 wins and 12 losses—and earned him the impossible-to-live-up-to nickname "Mangenius."

Mangini was always looking for an edge. He was meticulous about every aspect of the Jets' workouts, all the way down to picking the music. His goal was to constantly disrupt his players' routines and pull them out of their comfort zones. He'd have them do ballet, or learn boxing, anything to stretch them out of their normal patterns. Approaching the postseason in 2006, he moved the team's practices into a cavernous indoor football field. The roof, 120 feet in the air, was so high that even the most talented NFL kicker couldn't reach it. And the height created deafening echoes. Was this a problem? Not for Mangini. For him, this was a feature, not a bug. He wanted his players to learn to thrive, no matter the distraction.

Echoes not enough? Mangini blasted heavy metal and rap music so loudly that the players couldn't hear each other at the line of scrimmage. Ears cupped in a vain attempt to block out the noise, the players relied on flailing hand signals to communicate. It was pure chaos—just the way Coach wanted it.

There was a method to his madness. The speakers and the echoes were stand-ins for the ear-splitting crowd noise the team would encounter on their trip to the (now-demolished) indoor Metrodome in Minneapolis. "You play like you practice" was Mangini's mantra. His goal was to subject the players to the right amount of stress to replicate game day, but not so much that performance would be hindered. "I wanted to get them used to discomfort," he told me. "That's how you grow. The noise would force them to communicate nonverbally, which was a critical advantage in the game. And if I could create familiarity with what the gameday environment might be, it could give the team a real edge."

Mangini even turned a Jets training room into a "brain battle-field" run by a former military colonel, Dr. Louis Csoka, who had created the US Army's first performance enhancement center. It was fascinating to have Dr. Csoka in our practice facility. He hooked players up to electrodes wired to computer screens so they could monitor and attempt to influence their own brain waves. The theory was about situational awareness and self-regulation. Players would visualize themselves performing feats on the football field, and watch their minds in real time. With practice, they could use breathing techniques to put themselves in a more relaxed state even at moments of extreme stress.

Did it work? I don't know. It was never meant to make the entire difference. We lost to the New England Patriots in a wild card playoff game, and then collapsed in 2007, our record falling back to 4 and 12 that year. The work Mangini did wasn't magic, or perhaps it just wasn't enough. But the idea—to take players to the edge of their limits while improving their ability to manage the resulting stress—made sense, especially when you look at the science around anxiety. In 1908, two Harvard psychologists proposed what has come to be known as the Yerkes-Dodson law, a proven theory about fear and anxiety.[1] Their research found a bell-shaped curve in terms of anxiety's relationship to our performance. You need a healthy dose of fear—but not an excessive amount—to perform at your best. That makes the trick not to expunge all stress from our lives, but rather to deploy the right amount in pursuit of our goals and use it as a catalyst.

This chapter is about finding that optimal level of anxiety—enough to keep us hungry, motivated, and effective, but not so much as to paralyze us or tip us over into burnout or disaster. There are four steps to making the most of anxiety along your journeys: audit yourself to make sure you're at the peak of the bell curve and in pursuit of the right goals; use the anxiety to effectively drive your performance; beware of the signs that you're tipping over the edge; and cultivate a lifestyle that keeps your anxiety in check with the right coping tools.

Spend the Time to Audit Your Body and Your Mind

Ne te quaesiveris extra. It's the first line of Emerson's "Self-Reliance," and in Latin it means "Do not seek outside thyself." We consult experts, watch YouTube videos, and scan bookstore shelves, all without considering whether we already possess the answers. Self-awareness is the greatest source of value creation entirely within your control. You need only turn inward and ask: *Are you comfortable?*

If the answer is yes, then something is wrong. Being comfortable means that you have excess capacity, and you're not maximizing your potential. Unless you're trying to restore yourself and save up energy for your next journey, you shouldn't be comfortable. Comfortable is how great people plateau.

Professors Kaitlin Woolley and Ayelet Fishbach have studied how personal growth is driven by discomfort. They found that subjects who were most uncomfortable while doing a series of emotionally risky activities—taking an improv comedy class, writing about difficult experiences, or trying to relate to people with viewpoints opposite their own—experienced the most personal growth. "Instead of avoiding the discomfort inherent to growth," they write, "people should seek it as a sign of progress. Growing is often uncomfortable; we find that embracing discomfort can be motivating."[2] Change your relationship with discomfort to feel it as a feedback loop rather than a cry for help.

Only helicopters hover—humans are either ascending or descending. People (and businesses) fall if they're not putting in the extreme effort it takes to maintain their position and keep growing. The most successful businesses deploy a dual strategy of cannibalizing their own waning ideas while at the same time embodying a culture of constant reinvention—and constant reinvention is hard. Being uncomfortable hurts, but it's supposed to hurt. Growth hurts. If you look at your day and see that it's mostly filled with tasks you've already mastered, you're too comfortable. If what you are working on won't force you to update your biography if it succeeds, then why are you bothering?

◉　◉　◉

I always felt robbed of one thing in my life. I love Queens College, but I never had the chance to see if I could compete at the highest level because I was coming to college as a high school dropout who needed to live at home and take care of my mother. That meant night school at an affordable public university, within a few miles of my mother, was the only option. I wondered how my life might have turned out differently if I had grown up in a normal family, with an ordinary childhood, dealing with the kinds of mundane problems most kids face. *Did I do the homework? Do I have a date to the prom?* Instead, I was worrying about whether we could afford dinner that week, or how to give my mother a sponge bath when she couldn't even move from her bed, or if today was the day she was going to stop breathing in the middle of the night, or follow through on the threats she would make in her moments of darkest desperation that she was going to "end it all."

I didn't lack confidence in my own abilities. I imagined that I could have ended up at a place like Harvard, if I'd had the opportunity— but I also knew that was my own ego talking. Anybody could say that. I would never be able to prove it. That fact gnawed at me. I had lived with an unmet desire to show myself that in an academic setting, I was as good as anyone. I craved an opportunity to test whether I belonged on top.

I was never going to be a student at Harvard. I knew that. At forty-five years old, that window had long since closed. But what could be even better than that? I loved teaching and mentoring people, and always wanted to do it in a formal setting. So what if I could *teach* at Harvard? As soon as I thought of it, I wanted it desperately, feeling the kind of butterflies in my stomach that I crave. Only now I had to make it happen.

After months of conversations—a lengthy process to weed out the luminaries who call up Harvard wanting to "give back" but have no intention of putting in the work it takes to teach a successful class—they finally allowed me to propose a course for the winter term, an intensive short session where students dive deep into a specific subject area that is only covered in a cursory way during the regular semesters. The mandate was to find a topic that was contemporary, underexplored, and in which I was an undisputed expert.

"Matt didn't have any of the background typical for an appointment at the school," remembers Len Schlesinger, a full-time faculty member at Harvard Business School for much of the past forty-plus years, and the person who ended up becoming my co-professor for our class. "A large part of the way these conversations go is that I need someone to help me understand why they want to teach a class and why we should be interested. I have a question I started asking years ago, that never fails me: What is it that you know more about in the world than anyone else? When I asked Matt, he instantly said it was the direct-to-consumer (DTC) space. He explained that he knew it as an investor, working closely with other investors and with entrepreneurs, and that he had a strong point of view about what works and what doesn't. Even better, he assured me that if we brought him on to do something in the space, he could deliver on those relationships."

In talking to students, I learned that the DTC space was a gap in the teachings at business school. There were few practitioners on the faculty, and very little chance for exposure to a world that was becoming bigger by the week. Some of these businesses could go from a slide deck to becoming a unicorn in just a few years, and they were far more contemporary than most of the case studies used at HBS. Connecting the classroom to the real-time world of entrepreneurship was something the school was lacking—and something I could absolutely bring to the table, after spending years backing some of the top DTC brands in the world. Ultimately, Len was convinced. Now I had to deliver.

With no preconceived notion of how much value needed to be conveyed in a business class setting, we planned an insane lineup and schedule: four days with almost two dozen DTC founders coming to speak to the students, back to back to back to back in a marathon of valuable conversations with entrepreneurs these students would otherwise have no way to meet, no exposure to at all.

But as the class loomed closer, my anxiety set in. How would I do this? To prepare to go deep with two dozen founders, and really probe their minds for unique and powerful insights, would take so much work. Len told me at the time that only someone who had never taught a business school class could propose something so audacious.

When I prepare now for podcast interviews, I am rigorous about it. I spend hours and hours reading and studying everything I can get my hands on in order to be as ready as possible to talk to someone new. For HBS, I had to invent a process—and do it for twenty-two class sessions. My anxiety in many ways was justified. It ended up being almost a year of preparation on top of all of the other full-time work I was doing. (Of course, you're getting the benefit of some of those case studies in these pages. I didn't know then that I was also beginning to lay the groundwork for the stories I'd share in a book.)

For a hundred students, my guests—Lori Greiner, Jesse Derris, Christina Tosi, and Gary Vaynerchuk among them—broke down the direct-to-consumer space with me from every angle, going as deep as we could. I wanted it to be an immersive experience of sensory overload, so powerful that they would never forget it. One morning we brought in the Gronkowski brothers—four siblings who played in the NFL (and their oldest brother, who played professional baseball), including future Hall of Fame tight end Rob Gronkowski, affectionately known as Gronk—to work the students into a sweat, a metaphor for the grueling life of a startup founder. Another day we brought in the Chainsmokers, live-streamed from Los Angeles, to demonstrate the power of celebrity to supercharge an investment. We had breakfast with Magic Spoon and previewed a new line of cookies with Christina Tosi.

"It's very easy when someone is a practitioner coming to visit for a four-day class like this to just rely on the fact that they're the expert and not actually do the work," Len explains. "But Matt brought a completely different point of view to the course and did more work than I've seen most people do for anything like this."

I left everything on the field. I set up the third floor of my house as a mock classroom, and brought in a huge blackboard, chalk, and erasers. I bought penmanship books to practice my handwriting. I was reworking PowerPoint slides in the middle of the night. Harvard demanded my best effort, and I wanted to deliver. Had I merely provided an okay experience, life would have gone on, even if Harvard never invited me back for an encore—but I wanted to prove to myself that I could do something great.

"Matt was hungry for feedback," Len says, "and he really incorporated it, and could turn on a dime. That anxiety about teaching at HBS would make many people less responsive to feedback, the anxiety paralyzing them—but Matt's anxiety got him hungrier and hungrier."

When the course was over, I told the students to sign up for a time slot to meet with me individually. I wanted to see how I could help them with their lives and careers. As I said goodbye, one student slipped me a handwritten note saying that this was the most impactful course he'd taken at HBS. I still keep it framed on my desk as a testament to what can happen when you embrace your anxiety and give it your all despite your fears.

The class turned out to be one of the most popular intensive courses at the school, and I'm now co-teaching it every year as an Executive Fellow at HBS. "So many students said this was finally a course where they could see themselves," says Len, "especially with two-thirds of the entrepreneurs we profiled being women, and sixty percent of the students signed up being female as well. This wasn't something they were getting anywhere else in the business school."

◉ ◉ ◉

I worked so hard to make the class a success because having it succeed was a goal that really mattered to me. And that's the second question we have to ask ourselves: *Is your goal the right one?*

Being uncomfortable for the sake of being uncomfortable isn't the point. Be uncomfortable because it's worth it. You need to really understand your *why*. What's at stake? Imagine yourself on the other side, having done it, and done it well. Think about the person you'll be, the way you'll feel, and the opportunities that will unfold. Does it make you hungry, willing to sacrifice almost anything in your pursuit? I go through this thought exercise all the time. I transport myself to the future, I imagine walking out of an HBS lecture hall having enriched the lives of a hundred students, and I ask myself what I wouldn't endure to get to that point.

The answer is that for a meaningful outcome on a goal I've set my mind to achieving, I would do almost anything, whether canceling a long-planned vacation, delaying the purchase of a home, or going all in on weeks and months of hard work, late nights, and few short-term pleasures. I'd endure mocking tweets from strangers and doubts from friends and skeptical experts.

The couple that appears on my TV pilot embodies this idea perfectly. Samantha and Edwin had all the ingredients for a fairy tale: Ed's family worked in the jewelry business and was all set to help source a custom wedding ring for Ed to propose with, the couple had saved enough money for a dream wedding, and their corporate jobs provided reasonable security for the future.

"Fuck the ring," Samantha said.

They took the ring money and used it for a down payment on a house instead, with a plan to turn it into an Airbnb to generate some extra side-hustle income. Then COVID hit, so they scrapped the Airbnb plan, moved into the house, and then as the housing market accelerated, they flipped it for a $100k profit. Combining that with the money they decided not to spend on the wedding, they had enough to decide to take a risk and buy a business.

"We were starting to plan a wedding—and I just wasn't getting that excited," Samantha explains. "It felt like it was more about everyone else, and not about how we could really help ourselves, build momentum in our lives and careers, and take a step forward. It seemed so much more rewarding to build a business instead."

If you won't give things up to reach your goal, it's probably the wrong goal. You have to want it—and you have to want it for the right reasons. There have absolutely been times when I've found myself chasing the wrong dream, and those are the times when I've been driven by an impure motive—like vanity or approval, adulation or spite—or when I've been so enamored with the outcome that I've failed to see reality. We're all deluded sometimes, chasing a breakthrough without a foundation that supports it, whether it's because we don't have the skills to achieve it or it's simply something that can't be achieved.

I think about the early days of RSE when I was so eager to prove myself as a budding entrepreneur. One of the first businesses I created was called Leap Seats. I was so convinced that I had a game-changing insight that I didn't want to consider the possibility that it wasn't destined for success. I would go to Jets games and Dolphins games and see all these empty seats in the stadium. The majority of people who sit in the season ticket holders' seats at football games are not the ticket holders themselves, but friends or people who bought the tickets on a third-party resale site. In a stadium with 75,000 customers, we might not have known who 50,000 of them were. This was before digital ticketing, so we didn't have access to these people, and we couldn't merchandise to them.

I had an idea that we could sell the seats in the lower bowl—the ones closest to the playing field—that remained empty after the first quarter. Sign up for our app, and pay ten dollars to move down to a better seat for the rest of the game, maybe fifty dollars for a special moment afterward, like coming down on the field for a picture with a former player. I recruited a rock star CEO, Andrea Pagnanelli, who thoroughly understood the ticketing business, and we built an entire app from scratch. I never stopped to ask myself if I was so enamored with the idea that I was missing something.

I was.

I was missing the reality that this was not going to make sense as we moved to digital ticketing, at least not as a separate stand-alone service. This was a feature, not a business. If I'd worked for Ticketmaster, it would have been the kind of idea to earn me a promotion . . . but I didn't. If I wasn't going to use the app as a bridge to become a ticket seller—and I definitely didn't want that—then this was not an idea worth investing in.

There's a fine line between confidence and delusion, and entrepreneurs need to live right on it. If you don't delude yourself just a little bit—like, sure, I could pull off my HBS class without a hitch—then you'll never embark on something on the periphery of your capabilities.

But you can't fool yourself forever. You need the self-awareness to know who you are, how the world works, and what can actually be achieved. I ended up pulling the plug on Leap Seats. Andrea was going to be perfect to fill a need in another business—and I didn't want to lose the opportunity to redeploy her. I saw the light, and didn't let the fear of admitting I was wrong stop me from making the right decision.

Let Fear Drive You to the Next Gear

I was petrified when I walked into Congressman Gary Ackerman's office at age sixteen to start my $9/hour job. I knew I had to prove my worth. I was afraid, every day, of being exposed as a kid who didn't know a thing about . . . well, almost anything. That fear drove me to do whatever I could to add value.

One afternoon, Ackerman's campaign manager—a gruff, old-school, Camel chain smoker in his mid-fifties—needed help with a mail merge. He needed to print out (on an old dot-matrix printer) thousands of personalized letters to supporters. It was 1991, and computers were still a mystery to anyone over age twelve.

I had never owned a computer in my life—we didn't even have a dishwasher—but I wanted to be the hero, and I was too afraid not to be. I told him I'd take care of it. "I know something about computers," I volunteered, assuming that I was certainly smart enough to figure it out. Everyone left for the day, and I stayed up all night testing, trying, learning how to do it, choking back tears as letter after letter wouldn't line up with the clear plastic address window on the envelope. By morning, I'd cracked it. The campaign manager arrived to find the job done—and me, sprawled out, fast asleep on a stack of boxes.

"He claimed vast computer knowledge, which I needed for demographic lists," Ackerman's campaign manager told *PR Week* years later, in one of my first press clippings. "[He overstated his ability,] but he learned it. He taught himself, which impressed me."[3]

At the end of the primary season, leading into the general election, there were no jobs left. Everyone was fired—except for me.

I was young, but fear had driven me to learn an important lesson when it comes to achieving professional success: make yourself indispensable at whatever task you are assigned, no matter how menial or seemingly trivial. If someone found a job important enough to give it to you, then it's important enough to do it well. Even when I worked on the clean-up crew in the kids' party room at the local McDonald's when I was thirteen years old, I knew I needed to find a way to make myself irreplaceable. Getting on my hands and knees to inspect the undersides of the mushroom-shaped tables for dried chewing gum (which wasn't just left there by the kids!) quickly got me a promotion to party room maintenance manager—now tasked with making sure, by the end of each day, that all of the McNugget fragments had been removed from every crack and crevice of the restaurant. (At the time, chicken detritus felt like a step up from gum.)

Fear can do all sorts of great things for you. Marc Lore talks about how fear drives him to the next level. "When you have a life-or-death kind of situation where if something fails, you might not be able to feed your family, you'll find that sixth gear and you'll wind up doing things that you never thought possible," Marc told me. "Even when I had money, I still put myself in that kind of situation. When I was building Jet, the e-commerce business I ultimately sold to Walmart, I put every friend and family member I knew into the deal, to make myself fight for it. I couldn't lose my mom and dad's money, or the money from other relatives and friends. I had a lot of pride on the line and felt like there was no Plan B."

In order to win big, you'll need to be able to turn your fear into action, using anxiety like a tool, letting it drive you higher and higher.

But You Can't Let Fear Push You Over the Edge

Comedian Gary Gulman had spent more than twenty years doing stand-up comedy, making a living but never quite breaking through. What no one around him knew is that he'd been battling anxiety and depression since childhood, and it was about to overtake him. In 2015, filming a Netflix special at the Highline Ballroom in New York City, he thought this was finally going to be the moment his career took a giant leap forward. "I thought it was my best work," Gulman has said, "but the reception was lackluster. It just didn't work. And then it took a year to sell the special to Netflix and it didn't get a good reception there, either."[4]

Gulman's father died soon after that, and those two situations sent him into a paralyzing depression that lasted over two years. He could barely work. He was forced to move out of New York and back home to his childhood bedroom in Peabody, Massachusetts. After one gig, alone in a hotel room, he came close to killing himself. "Comedians are known for being slobs, so what would the poor cleaning woman think when she came in Monday morning and had that to contend with?"[5]

Eventually, with time and treatment—checking himself into a psychiatric hospital and receiving electroconvulsive therapy, on top of an evolving medication regimen—the depression lifted. But rather than going back to the comedy routines he'd honed over the course of the past twenty-five years, he channeled his anxiety into his work. He wrote a new show, *The Great Depresh*, talking about his struggles publicly for the first time . . . and ended up selling it to HBO, with the backing of comedy producer and industry superstar Judd Apatow. The show received massive critical acclaim. "For such a dark subject, it has no business being as hilarious as it is. Gulman is just that talented," wrote one reviewer.[6] Gulman's career hasn't just been resurrected—the show has taken him to new heights. It was all possible because he embraced his flaws and harnessed his anxiety, finally putting it to work for him instead of against him.

◉　◉　◉

Baseball pitcher Zack Greinke was the youngest player in the major leagues, just twenty years old, when he made his debut with the Kansas City Royals in May of 2004. He showed signs of brilliance during an inconsistent rookie season, but appeared to be a future star with an unlimited ceiling. "From the start he could do magical things with a baseball," wrote Joe Posnanski in *Sports Illustrated*. "He was the Royals' pitcher of the year as a rookie, the youngest in franchise history, and that's rare enough—a quick glance through history shows how few twenty-year-olds there are who have been ready to retire big league hitters."[7]

But inside, Greinke was battling a terrible case of social anxiety. His teammates found him shy and awkward, so much so that after Greinke struggled in 2005, the Royals sent him to live with gregarious Hall of Famer George Brett for the winter to work on his social skills.[8]

It didn't help. Greinke returned to the team for spring training in 2006, but ended up walking away from training camp due to his mental state, and nearly left baseball altogether.

"He endured one bullpen session where he was so vexed he couldn't throw a strike," wrote the *Los Angeles Times*, "winging each pitch with increasing recklessness and speed. Afterward, with on-lookers staring in sad confusion, he walked off the mound and—he thought—out of the game forever. 'Why am I putting myself through this torture when I don't really want to do it?' he recalled feeling. 'I enjoyed playing, but I didn't enjoy anything else about it. I was like, 'I'll go do something I really want to do.'"[9]

For two months in 2006, Greinke was away from the team, before returning mid-season and pitching mostly in the minor leagues the rest of the year. He credits Zoloft with treating his social anxiety and making it possible for him to pitch again. Now, more than fifteen years later, Greinke is still pitching (back with the Royals in 2022 after stints with the Brewers, Angels, Dodgers, Diamondbacks, and Astros) and has had a superstar-level career. He's likely on his way to the Baseball Hall of Fame, with more than 220 career wins—second-most of any active player as of this writing, and tied for 73rd most in all of baseball history—and having earned more than $330 million in salary.

◉ ◉ ◉

Gulman and Greinke reached rock-bottom—but even without being faced with the realities of ending up in a psychiatric hospital or walking away from a multimillion-dollar sports career, you can still suffer substantial effects from anxiety when it crosses the threshold from driving you forward to hurting your capacity to perform. When it moves from optimal anxiety to what I call derailing anxiety, it can easily sabotage your dreams.

For my entire life, I've struggled with anxiety, insomnia, and obsessive worries about things I can and can't control. My friends chide me as the most paranoid risk-taker they know. Sometimes it helps me, but sometimes it absolutely doesn't. When I'm facing a big moment, I can become paralyzed and completely unproductive. My body rebels, putting my success at risk simply because my brain won't shut off and let me get rest. It's a fight-or-flight response, a constant need to be at high alert—to look for danger. This became an acute issue when I was about to have a huge professional breakthrough and appear for the first time on *Shark Tank*.

I was in a hotel room in Los Angeles, and, for the second night in a row, I was wide awake. At eight a.m., I was expected to walk onto the set at Sony studios and share that very special row with Mark Cuban, Lori Greiner, Daymond John, and Kevin O'Leary. It was my first appearance on the show, maybe my only appearance depending on how it went. I had no doubt in my ability to do the real work of investing, but I had no idea if my day job would translate to being able to grill entrepreneurs on television. I feared that I would embarrass myself in front of a few million strangers—or, even worse, the people I actually do business with every day.

None of this concern was rational. It wasn't a fear of being unprepared, for sure. I was overprepared, just like I was for my HBS class. My son and I watched every single episode of the show in advance—almost 200 of them, which amounted to nearly 800 investor pitches. I wrote copious notes to distill everything that I believed about business into pithy soundbites.

I had also prepared myself physically. I was fifty pounds overweight when I first met with the *Shark Tank* producers almost a year before my day on set—and I willed myself to lose every last one of them in the months leading up to my appearance, so that I wouldn't cringe when I saw myself on CNBC reruns for the next decade. I didn't stop there (though maybe I should have): to fight my tendency to slouch in chairs, I bought a $99 piece of posture-correcting plastic that I wore on my back for a month, which would zap me whenever I dipped low in my seat. (And, as ridiculous as it sounds, it actually worked.) Was it vain? Maybe, but if worrying about my appearance was something that was going to hold me back, it was worth addressing. Understand yourself and your motivations—fighting against who you are is never the answer. Accept yourself, and do what you need to feel ready to be your best.

Still, in that hotel room, I was wide awake asking myself *why?* This was a choice. Why had I voluntarily put myself in this position, and put my career and my business in harm's way? That morning, after a sleepless night, I found myself crouched down on the tile floor, head in my hands, unable to catch my breath. In my mind, I went back to the days after 9/11, when I was working insane hours and wouldn't sleep for three or four nights in a row. I put on my headphones and listened to Eminem's "Lose Yourself" on repeat for two hours, trying to get myself in the mindset of the scrappy, hungry kid from Queens I was (and still am). In the green room when I arrived at the studio, I couldn't hide that I was barely keeping it together.

I pulled Daymond John (another Queens native) into my dressing room and asked for a piece of advice, anything. He said, "Look, you got here. You belong here because you are here."

Kevin O'Leary told me, "The camera doesn't lie. Don't try to be one of us, be whoever you are." Great advice, by the way, from both of them. And then I walked out onto the set . . . and I froze.

There's no scripting on the show, no advance preparation, no handlers, no one to turn to for help. The entrepreneurs walking through those doors are as fresh to the Sharks as they are to the audience, and the questions come rapid-fire. I used to wonder what the Sharks were writing on the pads in their laps—it's the numbers, because you have to do the math in real-time.

The music started and the first entrepreneur came in. I heard, "Hi, Sharks . . ." and then for about a minute and a half, I was lost in the fog of war. It was chaos as the Sharks immediately started talking—shouting—all at once, over and past each other, and of course made no effort to pull in the newbie. No, it wasn't life-or-death, I knew that, but that didn't stop my fight-or-flight instincts from kicking in. I needed to toss out the fear and trust myself, trust that I could shine. I took a deep breath and I thought, *I can do this.*

◉   ◉   ◉

Remember that self-talk from back in chapter 2? It worked. In that first pitch of the day, I found myself competing against Kevin for a deal with a business I understood, and a founder who seemed like he knew what he was doing. I looked him in the eye and simply painted a picture of what life would be like with me: that I could help bring his business to the next level, cover his weaknesses, be there to help him work through the struggles, be the hero I never had.

Kevin tried to steal back the entrepreneur's attention, but I had him. He was looking directly at me. "You've got a deal!" he said. I pumped my fist in the air, and as I ran up to hug him, I heard Kevin growl, "Well, I guess I'm out."

In between pitches, once everyone settled back into their chairs, Lori Greiner, the most nurturing of the Sharks, turned to me, put her hand on my forearm, and whispered, "Matt, on a scale of 1 to 100, that was a 95—and nobody gets a hundred. In ten years, no one has ever walked onto the set like that and acted like they've been there since the first day." I'd burned the boats . . . and now I was swimming with the Sharks.

Afterward I was overjoyed, but that level of anxiety was not where I wanted to live. I don't advise you to ever let your anxiety get that bad. Instead, I want to give you a tool kit to prevent you from ending up in the same dark places as I have, or as Gary Gulman and Zack Greinke have found themselves.

Here are my top four tips for getting through anxiety.

Find a Study to Reassure You

There's a reason there are moments in this book when I call out things like the Yerkes-Dodson law, the proven anxiety theory I mentioned at the start of this chapter. The truth is that I'm obsessed with the science of the mind. Data is power. If I can find a study to show that I'm actually doing something right, in whatever I'm trying to pursue, then that knowledge can be enough to move me past my doubts.

I have no better example than when I ran a marathon in Paris. I hadn't slept at all the night before—for forty-eight hours, really, because of the jet lag. What do you do when sleepless in Paris, staring at the Arc de Triomphe, and waiting for a marathon to start? I called the team doctor for the Jets, Dr. Damion Martins, to ask for any hacks to get through an extreme endurance event. I woke him up in the middle of the night in New Jersey. "You're calling me for *this*?" he asked. He told me to chug orange juice throughout the race. "Your brain will love you and your bowels will hate you, but you'll get through the race with the energy you need." (I realized by mile twenty how right he was.)

Wanting even more, I started googling. I hoped to find advice about how to correct for my lack of sleep—or, better yet, scientific proof that a lack of sleep wasn't a problem, and that others in the same situation who thought they were in for disaster turned out just fine.

I found a compelling piece of research that while *mental* performance is absolutely impacted by a lack of sleep, *physical* performance can withstand thirty to seventy-two hours of being awake.[10] Bingo—I was reassured, and all was once again good in my head. I ran the race and improved my time by ten minutes over my speed when I ran the New York City Marathon.

Will there always be data to reassure you, in any situation? Of course not. But with eight billion people in the world, someone, somewhere, has gone through what you are going through right now. Find that study, or find that person, and save yourself the trouble of repeating their mistakes. Inform your decisions and overcome your worry with facts.

Meditate Daily

I have found that most of the wildly successful CEOs I know practice transcendental meditation. From Ray Dalio to Bill Gates to Arianna Huffington, there is no shortage of successful people who rely on this tool to relax their minds.[11] Meditation has been shown to boost resilience, emotional intelligence, creativity, relationships, and focus—and I'm going to be another voice telling you that it should be a key tool in your anxiety tool kit.[12] I believe really strongly in this, and think it's one of the greatest gifts you can give yourself.

I'd be lying if I said I'm perfect about meditating every day, but I do make an effort as much as possible, and hold myself accountable, because self-care is incredibly important. I tell my founders and employees over and over again about how treating yourself well is critical to maintaining peak performance. For me, personally, it's an area where I often fail. I deny myself when things get busy. My blood pressure is too high, I struggle with my weight, and I don't sleep well at night. But while some people see these kinds of things as badges of honor, proof that they're working hard, that's the wrong way to look at it. Denying ourselves the gift of self-care is not helping our professional pursuits, it's hurting them, and it's making life harder in so many ways. The sooner you form good self-care habits, the more likely you'll stick to them in the long term. Start small, but be consistent.

There are people I admire who talk about habituating their behavior and removing as many decision points as they can in order to maximize efficiency and their ability to access their creativity. Steve Jobs and Albert Einstein wore the same outfit day after day so they didn't have to think about their clothing at all. There are people who shower at the same time every morning, drink their coffee, meditate daily as a rule, and block out the first hours of their day for the most intense work they have to accomplish.

I marvel at them in some ways—and yet, at the same time, I know we all approach life differently and take varying routes to excellence. Nothing in my life is a routine. My wife is amazed at the fact that I have no shower routine, no breakfast routine. I check email at all hours. I jump from emergency to emergency. I hate to be pigeonholed into routine, out of fear that I won't have the brainspace for spontaneous insights, which are the most important outputs I need to stay attuned to.

I think you should meditate, but at the same time I want to assure you that not meditating will not be the reason you don't burn the boats. Try different things, figure out what works best for you, and stick with it. Do what you can, forgive yourself when you don't achieve perfection, and keep trying.

Pick the Right Person to Join You in the Foxhole

My wife, Sarah, is my secret superpower in all ways, the calmest and most rational person I know, the key to me controlling my anxiety—and my complete and absolute partner in everything I do, as we help each other unleash our fullest potential on the world. She's one of those rare people who has seemingly internalized every How To book ever written. I have every chance of coming home to find her underneath a car replacing a muffler, or on the roof laying shingles. My Instagram videos celebrating Sarah's crazy skills garner hundreds of thousands of views; she has a life hack for everything. The point is, a partner is either a force multiplier or an energy vampire. There's no in between.

I think it's so underrated. We don't talk nearly enough about relationships and how important the right partner is in achieving success. None of us can do it alone. But the conventional wisdom that you should choose a partner to bring you down to earth, to mitigate your weaknesses—whether in life or in business—is a myth that leads to combustible relationships more than compatible ones. We talk about how opposites attract in love, or how cofounders should bring different, complementary skills to the table—but similarity is often much more lasting and powerful than difference. In my Harvard Business School class, I asked every founder who came through our most recent cycle why they picked their personal and professional partners, and what has made those partnerships successful. Almost unanimously, they talked about value alignment, and how a successful partnership was less about dividing labor between people with complementary skill sets and more about value overlap, and heading 100 percent in the same direction. Skills don't matter if you don't have the same vision of the future, and the same ideas about what's important.

I make it a point to meet someone's partner in the course of doing my due diligence on an investment, because you can often tell so much right away. How's the relationship—is it a source of strength or a source of conflict? If I see signals of contempt such as undercutting jabs or subtle eye rolls, I know there's trouble coming. What we need to look for is one sensibility, one voice, one unified passion. And if someone has picked the right life partner, frankly it tells me a lot about how they choose their business partners and employees, too. Great people can identify that same quality in others. On the other hand, when I hear someone say about their partner, "They ground me," I think of planes stuck on a runway and ask myself, *Why is this a good thing?* Planes are meant to fly, and so are you.

Expose Your Achilles Heel— and Ask for Help to Fix It

It's the simplest strategy, but the one we don't always think to pursue, worried that others will judge us or penalize us for admitting our weaknesses. My friend Mike Tannenbaum, now a highly praised football commentator on ESPN, was the general manager of the Jets before we hired him as executive vice president of the Dolphins. I respect Mike immensely. He's a wonderful human being, the son of a Boston transit worker who built himself up starting as an intern for the New Orleans Saints in 1994.

Mike had a crazy dream of working in sports at the very highest level, and went step by step to make it happen. He went to Tulane

Law School as a means to an end, graduating with honors, and then got a job after graduation working for Coach Bill Belichick and the Cleveland Browns, researching contracts and driving people to the airport. From there, he moved with Belichick to the Jets, and in four years rose from negotiating contracts to becoming assistant general manager—and then five years later was named the youngest GM in the NFL at just thirty-five years old.

He worked so hard—and, in the end, fostered so much success—that everyone around him just had to respect him, and he kept moving up the ranks. In his sixteen years with the Jets, the team went to the playoffs seven times, and played three times in the AFC Championship Game.

But it wasn't easy. Mike's anxiety about creating and maintaining that success fueled his rise, but also manifested in extreme intensity. Mike would get a rabid look in his eyes when the pressure was on, only to end up targeting anyone and anything that rubbed him the wrong way. If he ever noticed a player laughing on the sidelines during a losing game, he would call the player out the next day. "So you think losing is real funny?"

Sometimes when I talked to him after a loss, Mike would seem like he was gripping his pen so tightly in his fist that I stayed two feet back so he couldn't plunge it into my eye. It killed him if other people didn't approach winning with the same passion as he did. I get it, even if I tried to rein in that same impulse in myself. Mike vocalized what many of us feel when we are dying to win and those around us are perceived to be phoning it in.

"I still remember pounding on the glass window of my suite if I would see you on the field talking to someone from the other side," Mike remembers about our pregame routine, when fraternizing with the enemy was a capital offense. "It was game day. We weren't there to be friends. Small talk before the game would make me so angry."

I admired the depth of Mike's commitment, but I also knew that this fiery intensity, his greatest asset, might one day sabotage his career. Our greatest asset can also become our fatal albatross. Eventually, I had to intervene. I told Mike that his anxiety was presenting in a way that was jeopardizing his success, and perhaps even his job. What did he do? No, he didn't poke me in the eye with a pen—we got him help (from my go-to industrial psychologist, Dr. Laura Finfer).

"You used words like 'this will be the greatest gift,'" Mike remembers, "and I don't know if I believed you at first, but you were totally right. It's really hard to hear things about yourself that you might know in your soul to be true but don't realize that others are also seeing. Getting help gave me so much more self-awareness, made me more comfortable in my own skin, and enabled me to finally let people see my vulnerabilities."

A couple of months after we talked, I walked into Mike's office, and there was a massive fish tank built into the wall. The lights were dimmed, and he had '80s music playing softly from a boombox. He had learned coping mechanisms and put them into practice. For Mike, a change in his office environment worked wonders, and relaxed him enough that he wouldn't be consumed by his rage.

"When you get these kinds of jobs," Mike explains, "there's some imposter syndrome going on. I was the youngest GM in the NFL, on the big stage in New York, and I was fearing that I wasn't worthy. I had always been balancing two ideas in my head—one, *How come I'm not in charge already?*; and, two, *Will I ever really be ready?* I got my ambition from watching my father work so hard in his career at the transit agencies in Boston and New York. I wanted an easier path for my kids, and I was willing to fight to make it. But when you stepped in, I knew I needed to find a better way to express all of that."

He was still the same intense Mike T., but he was able to conserve his intensity for when it mattered, and his overall performance improved dramatically.

"My ambition and my insecurity have together been such a blessing and a curse, all at once," Mike explains. "Wherever I've been, I want to go higher. I know, even now, that I still have a million miles to go, and I'm working my hardest to get there.

"I'm still not great at calibrating it," he admits. "I'm on the board of a company and if someone is one minute late for a call, it bothers me. I grew up in the hard, dispassionate, unempathetic world of football, where the standards were the standards, and it affected how I saw the world. But I try to remind myself it's not always so binary. There are shades of gray. Not everything has to make me angry."

Mike is now excelling across multiple platforms. After stints as an agent, and then again in the general manager's seat when we hired him at the Dolphins, in 2019 he became a front office insider for ESPN, driving much of their NFL coverage. Beyond ESPN, he also started The 33rd Team, a football think tank and online platform powered by experts with more than 500 combined years of coaching and front-office experience, offering deep analysis, commentary, and insights. As if that isn't enough, Mike mentors students and tries to connect them with opportunities in the game. But most importantly, he understands the power of asking for help, and keeps growing his skills, becoming better and better at everything he does.

⊙ ⊙ ⊙

These tips can work no matter your organization. They can keep you on the right path after you've set out on your journey. Most of us can't avoid dark emotions—however, if they can drive us to work harder and smarter than everyone around us, we've used the fear to put ourselves in an unmatched position to succeed.

But that's just the internal fight.

We're also battling a world that inevitably tries to intrude on every path to success.

I wish it was as easy as dealing with your own demons, and emerging in a siloed atmosphere where you were completely in charge of your destiny. It's not. Things will happen. And when they do, you have to not just be prepared to deal with them, but prepared to use them, to look for them, to love them. When bad things happen, I feel a sudden charge and borrow a page from Rahm Emanuel, the former mayor of Chicago: "You never want a serious crisis to go to waste. And what I mean by that is an opportunity to do things that you think you could not do before."[13]

CHAPTER 5

EMBRACE EACH CRISIS

The morning of 9/11, I was only a few months into my job as press secretary for the New York City Mayor's Office. I was setting up for a press conference just blocks away from the World Trade Center site when the second plane struck the towers. I didn't know where the mayor was, and I headed back to City Hall to figure out how to reach him. I had just gotten through the gates when there was the massive sound of an explosion and everyone began screaming. The towers were falling—and when I returned to the crash site two days later with President George W. Bush, on his first tour of the area, we recovered the equipment I had been plugging in just moments before the collapse. It was completely crushed. The area right where my colleagues and I had been standing was obliterated.

I spent the next hundred days managing the media response to the worst terrorist attack in history, with barely any time to sleep. I shepherded every major world leader through Ground Zero, from the emir of Qatar to the prime minister of Great Britain, to witness the atrocity and marshal support for the US military response. We put up a viewing platform overlooking the site, and a mural with the flags of all ninety-one countries that had lost a citizen in the attacks. We needed allies to let us use their bases and airspace— and our boat tours for world leaders around the tip of Manhattan, bringing me right back to the fiery inferno, became an almost daily occurrence. We coordinated closely with the White House, with an unspoken goal to shock and guilt every head of state. Gallows humor kept us sane. We called these trips with world leaders "Liberty Tours" amongst ourselves.

It was so much more than hard. It was tragic beyond belief, and many days I wanted to hide under the covers and pretend it had all been a horrific nightmare. But being there, helping to bring New York City back to life, and learning that I could survive in a situation like this, ultimately changed everything for me. I realized that my traumatic upbringing, and perhaps even my mother's death, had given me the ability to manage my way through anything.

The lessons of this chapter are twofold. The first part is about fostering the skills it takes to not just deal with crises, but use them as opportunities to reach new heights. The work of Barbara Fredrickson, a psychologist at the University of Michigan, bears this out. Her research has demonstrated that positive emotions during crises do more than just help in the moment; in fact, they lead to superior long-term resilience, and an increased ability to cope and thrive in the future.[1] Looking at college students' responses to 9/11, Fredrickson found that those with negative emotions suffered lingering effects as compared to those who made an effort to concentrate on the positive. Thinking positively had a lasting benefit, helping subjects buffer themselves through future crises in their lives.

We are protected against depression and stress by focusing on the positive, and by actively looking for moments of hope, gratitude, awe, and contentment. Resilient people can thrive merely by extracting the positive from every negative situation. In other words, seeing a crisis as an opportunity can make it so. Almost every uncomfortable situation can be reframed by substituting two little words—*have to*—with *get to*. The most powerful example is the rut we all fall into in our relationship with work. I remind myself every day, I don't *have to* go to work, I *get to* go to work, which is a privilege millions of migrants around the world risk their lives to pursue.

The second part of the discussion involves crisis management even in the absence of crisis. What do I mean by that? A true Burn the Boats mindset harnesses the clarity that comes in a crisis without needing the walls to come crumbling down around us. Crises force us to limit choices and focus on what really matters. But we can do that anyway. We can iterate before we're forced to, pivot because it's the smart thing to do and not the only option left. We can do the creative, flexible, and ultimately wonderful things we must do when fighting to save our business in the midst of disaster—even when the danger isn't real.

Here is your guide to crisis management.

Face Everything—and Then Work Backward from the Worst-Case Scenario

The first thing you have to do in any crisis is find a way to live another day. When we find ourselves without answers, we tend to overlook the most obvious next step in any crisis situation: just survive. Past persistence is a very strong predictor of future viability and longevity. When I come across a company that seems to have nine lives, I know it's no accident. Someone at the helm made a conscious decision that they simply will not die; they will find a way. So what do you do when you don't know what to do? Just show up.

Those first ninety days after the Twin Towers were attacked were all about showing up, and constantly demonstrating to the world that we were not withdrawing in fear. We organized events immediately—a press conference as soon as we could get our equipment plugged in, our tours for world leaders and then events for the larger public, a prayer service at Yankee Stadium less than two weeks after the attacks, with Oprah Winfrey as the program's host, the New York Philharmonic performing for Lower Manhattan on the one-month anniversary, and so much more. Rudy Giuliani earned the nickname "America's Mayor" because he showed up constantly, fearlessly, and tirelessly. It's sad to see him now as a shadow of his former self. I choose instead to remember him during those impactful days after 9/11, when his forceful persona had a calming presence and I learned the symbolic importance of being on the ground when all hell breaks loose.

◉ ◉ ◉

When I think about surviving even when it all feels lost, my mind actually turns to, of all places, pizza. The East Coast chain &pizza is a proud RSE investment, run by Michael Lastoria. Lastoria has stepped up over the years in so many ways for his workers, particularly during the COVID-19 pandemic. Within days of the virus beginning to rear its head in March of 2020, he didn't act out of fear, shut down stores, and merely hope the threat would pass. Michael knew this was a once-in-a-lifetime opportunity to live the values the company claimed in its marketing, and to actually demonstrate that the fight for a living wage wasn't just the empty rhetoric of sunny Instagram posts.

Instead of freezing wages or cutting jobs, &pizza provided an instant one dollar an hour pay raise to its staff; free unlimited pizza for employees, their families, and hospital staff; reimbursement of commuting costs when mass transit stopped running; an expanded sick leave policy to cover caring for children when schools closed; health and safety pay for anyone diagnosed with COVID-19 or who came into contact with someone who was diagnosed; and, later, as the Black Lives Matter protests spread across the country, paid time off for every employee to pursue their own personal activism. In November 2020, the company announced a $15 minimum wage for every employee across the country—and in June 2021, they announced a $500 bonus for every employee or new hire fully vaccinated against COVID-19.

All of this came at a price, of course. The company stopped expansion plans. They cut expenses where they could. But they did this all because Michael knew that the best way to survive the crisis was going to be to double down on his people and make sure they stayed with him. "My philosophy," Michael told me, "and the philosophy of our shareholders is that the financial health of a business and its employees' needs are inextricably linked. We focused on our employees—and at the same time converted our shops in city centers into kitchens for our charitable efforts."

For Michael, the pandemic put a spotlight on issues that have been problems in the restaurant industry for decades—low wages, lack of benefits, dangerous working conditions, and the cyclical nature of laying off and rehiring staff when it's convenient for employers. He now had an opportunity to do something about all of it. "Raising wages is the single clearest way to say to our workforce, 'we value you,'" he told me. "All of our work counts for nothing if our people cannot live on the wages we pay them. If you make sure that your staff's basic human needs are met, they'll give more to the business because they want it to succeed. We did everything we did because we had the conviction to take bold action in the face of adversity."

Lastoria was the right leader for the right time; of course, we all need to strive to be the right leader for whatever crisis we face.

◉   ◉   ◉

Imagine the truest and fullest disaster playing out, and then get practical. What do you need to put in place to make it through? Are you concerned you'll be strapped for cash? If so, think about if there are any assets you could sell in a pinch. Are you worried your employees will revolt? Consider bold strategies to maintain their loyalty. Are you scared your business partners will bail? Don't let fear stop you from sitting down for an honest and real conversation.

Thinking it through gives you a plan, and frees your mind from focusing only on the fear. Once you contemplate the worst, and envision yourself hobbled but still standing, the fear becomes manageable. You are no longer consumed with the unknown, because the worst-case scenario has been processed. You can unlock so much excess mental capacity if you do your best to free your mind from worry.

All of this can happen even without the nightmare coming true. Accept that it might, act appropriately, and move forward. Protect yourself against the loss and then take the energy that was directed to prevention and reallocate it toward pursuing something bigger.

But what to pursue?

Ask Yourself: "If I Were Starting from Scratch Today, What Would I Do?"

Milk Bar founder (and my partner) Christina Tosi is a rock star of a human being, full of far more light and sunshine than I can ever summon. To know her is to love her. And yet, even with a growing collection of beyond-delicious products, the COVID-19 pandemic could have meant the end of her business. We had always envisioned migrating her products beyond the brick-and-mortar stores where she started out, but we worried about losing what worked.

Faced with mandatory store closures after the virus hit, we could have panicked, tried to mitigate losses, and held on until we could open up again. Instead, Christina asked herself a simple question: If I was starting out today, what would I do? Forced to close her stores, the automatic response didn't need to be "How do I get them back open?" Instead she asked, "Why do we even have stores?"

Within days—literally days—Christina doubled down on e-commerce. She launched a new baking show on Instagram Live, stepping into kitchens around the world at 2 p.m. each afternoon to show people how to bake with a hodgepodge of household staples. She made deals to start selling her unparalleled cookies in the supermarkets that were making their own pivots to home delivery— every Whole Foods in America, every Target, and beyond. She began sending care packages to frontline workers in hospitals around the country.

"I wanted to figure out how to be there for people," Christina told me. "That's what my business is built on. Dessert can save the world, and I wanted to come as close as I could to literally baking a cookie for everyone on the planet. Bake Club was my way of showing up. We tried a bunch of different types of content, and they didn't feel authentic, and so I just listened to my gut, and went on

Instagram and said, 'Here's what we're going to do, we'll start a baking club tomorrow—what time works for you?'"

It sounds obvious now, but the genius of Milk Bar's pivot is that it was obvious to Christina even as things were all crashing down around her. Even eighteen months after the pandemic began, her Instagram Live show was still getting more than 50,000 views each episode. Throughout, she could have focused all of her energy on reopening her brick-and-mortar locations, but she looked to reimagine instead of merely reclaiming what she had lost.

"You have everything you need," Christina says. "Even in a crisis, you might be looking for answers, but inside of you is already everything you need, and you just need to figure out how to leverage it. The more voices you have in your life, the more complicated it can get, the more you might question yourself, but you can't forget—you already have the answers inside."

Yes, a crisis brings destruction, but it also brings the potential for so many new opportunities that couldn't have otherwise been realized. Christina emerged from the pandemic with a far bigger, far stronger business than she had before, a worldwide fan base, and the full realization of a strategic move from the fast casual space (which trades at a multiple of three times top-line revenue at best) to consumer packaged goods (with a multiple instead of five to ten times revenue). She embraced the crisis, and Milk Bar is thriving.

◎   ◎   ◎

How you manage through crisis is how you ultimately demonstrate the quality of your decision-making. At RSE's fast casual coffee chain Bluestone Lane—a burn-the-boats business where Nick Stone, armed with a vision to create an Australian-inspired coffee chain (believing American coffee culture paled in comparison to what he had experienced in his native Melbourne), quit his job in corporate finance and went all in. The pandemic became a catalyst for action. Nick used the crisis to bring his overhead in line, shift his operations to digital, renegotiate every lease, and buy supplies from businesses that were forced to downsize and could use our cash. He asked himself the questions that you have to ask in any crisis, the follow-ups to the big question about what you'd do differently if you were starting out today:

◉ Are you moving decisively to survive longer? Or are you merely hoping things get better before you have to make hard decisions?

◉ Are you pivoting to meet the current needs of your customers? Or are you wedded to what's now an outdated business model?

◉ Are you leading from the front, talking to your customers, lifting up your team, grabbing the flag, and charging up that proverbial hill? Or are you burying your head in the sand, feeling sorry for yourself?

◉ Have you given yourself the freedom to act?

For that last question, as much as possible, especially in a crisis, you don't want your decisions to be encumbered by having to get approval from others or having to convince someone else that your intuition is right. When you're truly innovating, the reality is that overreaching checks and balances on your decision-making—

buy-in from others or anything that curtails your ability to follow your instincts—often have very little benefit. They mostly inhibit success and put a premium on form over substance. I know this goes against conventional wisdom, but it's true: Collaboration merely for collaboration's sake often results in regression to the mean, diluting exceptionalism in the name of feel-good consensus-building.

To get people to be as early as you, to transport themselves into your dream, and understand your stream of data—that's where we all go wrong. When you decide to abandon your ideas because everyone else decides that they don't see what you're seeing—that's how innovation is suffocated. Crisis isn't just the life-or-death, fight-or-flight moments we all experience. It's also the quieter moments when opportunities pass you by because you don't have enough autonomy to act on them, or when change doesn't happen because you don't have the freedom to execute.

◉　◉　◉

Under the banner of RSE, my partners and I cofounded a company called Relevent Sports Group, and, starting more than a decade ago, invested well over nine figures getting an international soccer tournament off the ground. The entire International Champions Cup story is a lesson in reinvention in the face of crisis. We built a tournament that couldn't generate enough revenue for us to eke out a profit as the teams demanded more and more money. No matter how hard we tried, traveling the world to develop relationships and grow a fanbase, we didn't crack the code. And we were burning cash.

We brought in the most dynamic dealmaker I knew, Danny Sillman, and flipped the entire business around. Danny actually turned out to also be one of the best operators I've ever worked with. Forget the tournament—instead, Danny realized we could leverage the relationships we had built into becoming partners with top soccer leagues to sell their media rights in the US.

This behavior in pursuit of a viable business became a Harvard Business School case study on our eventual joint venture with La Liga, the top division of the Spanish football league, securing for them a record $2 billion North American rights deal with ESPN. And then Danny leveraged the success with La Liga to pull off a coup. We entered into a partnership with the institution that oversees all soccer in Europe—UEFA—to sell their media rights in the United States. The idea that a US-based company would represent European football was once unfathomable. But Danny, Stephen Ross, our other cofounders, and I had spent years crisscrossing the Atlantic and traveling all over Europe to understand the customs and idiosyncrasies of European football. We flew tens of thousands of miles, hosted endless late-night dinners in Spain, and navigated bureaucracies and fiefdoms at every major European football event. We paid our dues. Our tenacity and American bias toward disruption earned the respect of the greatest change agent in the game, Aleksander Čeferin, the president of UEFA. Čeferin, a principled man I have come to deeply admire, didn't stand on ceremony. He cared only about maximizing the fan experience and generating more revenue to support the growth of the world's most popular sport.

The *New York Times* wrote about the shock of us winning out over some of the top sports agencies in the world: "The [big] surprise . . . the lucrative rights to the United States. Those were won by Relevent Sports Group . . . the latest chapter in its efforts to pivot toward a new strategy geared around selling premium soccer rights after a decade in which its highest-profile asset was the loss-making International Champions Cup."[2]

In August of 2022, our work paid off. Relevent sold UEFA's rights to Paramount (which owns CBS and Paramount+) in a record six-year, $1.5 billion deal. Just like Danny, we can't be afraid to retreat and reinvent the entire endeavor if we know in our heart that the road ahead is doomed no matter how hard we try. That's true leadership.

◉　◉　◉

Switching strategies isn't just about business. For me, the COVID-19 pandemic became personal early on. When I came down with the virus the morning after ringing the bell at the New York Stock Exchange, I was hit hard. I spent almost a month in isolation. There were moments I didn't know if I was going to come out the other side. But once I did, I realized that I couldn't waste this opportunity. Yes, there was so much tragedy, of course—but nothing in life is binary unless you choose to see it that way. You can acknowledge huge disaster while at the same time trying to find your own best path forward. It's hard to admit this to myself, but this book was never going to get written if not for COVID. Prior to the pandemic, I was on the road for what felt like eight days a week, racing from meeting to meeting, flying to Dolphins games, on the phone with entrepreneurs, batting away e-mail after e-mail. I was putting out too many urgent fires to ever find enough time to dive deep.

With face time no longer a concern, and commuting and travel time back in my pocket, I was able to unlock a whole new set of possibilities—this book among them. Part of the push emerged from fear. The day after my office shut down, I sat on my couch and pulled out a piece of paper. I worried that the stress and uncertainty would mean that I wouldn't take full advantage of the gift of time that the pandemic was giving me.

I was inspired by Isaac Newton, who did some of the best work of his life during the two years of the Great Plague in England in the mid-1600s. Forced into isolation, Newton found himself freed from the demands of teaching and with the capacity to devote himself to study. He asked himself the most fundamental questions about how the universe worked—and then he found answers, developing theories about gravity, light, and calculus that would end up marking the most productive period of his career. His "Year of Wonders," it is often called—and yet it took place in an environment of disease and danger.[3]

I'm no Isaac Newton, but I knew I would forever regret wasting this idle time. Truth is, to waste any time—to waste ideas, insights, or any fleeting instincts—is to squander the scarcest resource we are granted. The universe affords us a finite number of opportunities. Sometimes these opportunities are obvious—a job offer or a business proposition—but other times they're just thoughts that float in and out of our consciousness. We've all read an article or heard something in passing and had the realization that there is potential opportunity lurking.

No one would blame you for not dropping everything to invest all of your life savings in Bitcoin the first time you read an article about it, maybe a decade ago at this point, even if it crossed your mind that there might be something interesting there. And yet imagine if you had done exactly that. You'd be a billionaire as of this writing, like a handful of early Bitcoin speculators have become.

I started mining Bitcoin in 2013. I rented server space to do it. I had three hundred Bitcoin, but then I got impatient. I sold it to buy an apartment—and if I'd kept it, I could have bought the whole block. I do this sometimes: I know enough to act, but then I abandon too soon and move on. Or, worse yet, I don't act at all. (That said, when it comes to Bitcoin specifically, I do think that eventually, perhaps even just several years from now, it will be consigned to the dustbin of history, seen as fool's gold. I suppose we'll see how well that statement ages.)

My list of failures on this front is long. Marketing mastermind, entrepreneur, and all-around-Internet-visionary Gary Vaynerchuk told me in early 2021 that NFTs—non-fungible tokens, unique digital assets, original audio, video, or image files that can be bought and sold on the blockchain, just like physical artifacts are bought and sold traditionally—were going to be the next big thing. He told me it was going to be life-changing, and that I needed to buy some JPEGs known as CryptoPunks before it was too late. I laughed at him. None of it made sense to me and I thought it was all too silly to even contemplate. Gary is a genius and a mystic and I know it, but I still didn't listen.

He went on to create VeeFriends, an NFT collection and community around Gary and the business advice he gives to fans—and it has become a runaway success within a year, valued at more than $1 billion, and even spawning a VeeFriends collection carried at Macy's and Toys"R"Us. What was just an idea in Gary's mind when we talked a few months earlier has made him a billionaire—because he listened to his instincts and made it happen.

Eight months after Gary told me to do it, I finally immersed myself into the web3 community, and he and I launched a metaverse fund. I worry I'm late—but I imagine the reality is that I'm only late compared to Gary. When someone who has a track record of seeing the future gives you a glimpse of what's to come—listen.

◉　◉　◉

We don't have to take every risk that crosses our path—but we need to understand that these epiphanies are not endless. If you squander them, they are gone forever. Never be limited by what things look like today. You can always reverse course tomorrow. At the same time, if you let an opportunity pass you by due to indecision, don't spend too much energy lamenting the miss. Learn from it, and commit to being twice as nimble next time.

Who Is to Say What Is Bad and What Is Good?

There is an old Taoist parable about a farmer whose horse runs away.[4] The villagers express their sorrow, but the farmer says, "Good, bad, who's to say?" After a few days, the horse returns with two more horses behind him. The villagers congratulate the farmer, but again he responds, "Good, bad, who's to say?" His son tries to ride one of the horses, but it throws him off and he breaks his leg. The villagers are sad again, but not the farmer. "Good, bad, who's to say?" War breaks out, and the son is the only village boy unable to go fight. The other boys die in battle. "Good, bad, who's to say?"

Who is to say which events in our lives will turn out to be good and which will turn out badly? Things that seem like crises we can't possibly endure may very well end up being the catalysts that unlock our full potential. My childhood struggles were awful . . . unless you look at them as exactly the circumstances which delivered me the power to thrive in difficult situations, and which led directly to my professional successes.

I was giving a chat late one night on Clubhouse when Taylor Lindsay-Noel caught my attention with her story. In 2008, she was a fourteen-year-old gymnast in Canada, bound for the 2012 Olympics. And then she fell off the high bar and broke her neck. She's now a quadriplegic, wheelchair-bound, unable to move her body below her neck.

And she's happy.

Gymnastics dreams gone, she went to college, hoping to become an entertainment reporter. But the work was too hard with her disability. She explored different career options online, and eventually started a podcast, talking to influencers while having a cup of tea. Unable to land a tea company as a sponsor, she ended up creating a line of tea herself. She launched a business, Cup of Té, and eventually made it onto Oprah Winfrey's list of Favorite Things.

Her tea set was in the gift box at the 2021 Grammy Awards and the Oscars, and Taylor is on her way to her first year with more than a million dollars in sales. She has a thriving career, love, and a rich and fulfilling day-to-day. None of this would be the case if not for the terrible accident she endured. If I didn't hear it from Taylor directly, I wouldn't believe it, but she insists she's happier now than she was before her accident. "It almost felt like a rebirth," she told me. "I was completely stripped of my identity as an athlete and an Olympic hopeful and was forced to reexamine who I am, and re-architect my life. I reevaluated my passions, long-term desires, and the things that would truly make me happy. Every day I wake up I'm grateful for the opportunity to do more, be more, and give back."

Good, bad, who's to say?

There's no end to the people we can point to who not only came through crisis, but went on to thrive in new and unexpected ways. And I don't just mean accidents and circumstances beyond their control. This applies as much to people who made their own crises, through bad decisions, awful mistakes, even criminal acts. Look at Martha Stewart. She served five months in prison after a highly publicized case of securities fraud, where she sold stocks on insider information and then tried to cover it up. Did she go into hiding after her release from prison, retreat from the public eye, and give up? Not at all. She built her empire back to where it was, and beyond. She has launched countless new television series, written books, and partnered with everyone from megacorporations to Snoop Dogg to introduce new product lines across the home cooking and design industries. Martha did not let a crisis destroy her.

Michael Milken's story is perhaps even more dramatic. He was at the top of the financial world in the 1980s, credited with the development of the "junk bond" industry that grew to be worth billions of dollars. And then he ended up in prison for almost two years, indicted on ninety-eight counts of securities fraud and racketeering. He had to pay back more than a billion dollars to defrauded investors and the government. After all this, upon his release from prison, he was diagnosed with prostate cancer. What did he do? He started a charity to fund prostate cancer research, which has grown to become the largest philanthropic source of prostate cancer research money in the world. He then launched a think tank to fund research into cures for other diseases, and in 2004 was called by *Fortune* magazine "The Man Who Changed Medicine."[5]

In 2014, George Washington University renamed its public health school after Milken, thanks to $80 million in gifts to the school from his foundation and others in his name. The world is almost surely better off because Milken went to prison and became a changed person.

Good, bad, who's to say?

We Don't Get to Choose Our Moments to Shine

My friend Lauren Book has served in the Florida State Senate since 2016 and was chosen unanimously by her fellow Democrats to serve as minority leader in April 2021. She has met with Presidents Obama and Biden, and is seen as a leading future contender for

Florida's governorship. And her entire life's journey has been built on overcoming adversity and finding ways to shine despite the incredibly challenging hand she was dealt. Starting at age eleven, Lauren was sexually, emotionally, and physically abused for six years by a live-in nanny, who was trusted by her family and swore Lauren to secrecy. The price Lauren paid was tragic—an eating disorder that dropped her to just eighty-four pounds, insomnia, and post-traumatic stress disorder. The nanny was sentenced to twenty-five years in prison after the abuse came to light. The trauma could have derailed anyone's path to a productive future.

But Lauren didn't succumb. In fact, she used her experience to motivate a career and create opportunities to help others that she never planned for. Lauren went to college and graduated with a degree in elementary education, setting out to become a schoolteacher, and then went on to earn a master's degree in community psychology. But that wasn't enough. She wanted to share her story, and use it to inspire the world—and help lift up others facing similar circumstances.

Lauren started a nonprofit, Lauren's Kids, to educate children and families about sexual abuse. For more than a decade, she has led an annual 1,500-mile walk across the state of Florida, called "Walk in My Shoes," more than forty-two days of walking to honor the 42 million survivors of child sexual abuse in the US alone. Lauren wrote a memoir, *It's OK to Tell*, and a children's book, *Lauren's Kingdom*, to help pass along the lessons of her experience and give kids permission to reveal the secrets damaging their lives. And, still, she wanted to do more. She ran for the Florida State Senate in 2016 to help pass legislation to protect kids from abuse and from anything else that might be holding them back. In 2018, in the wake of a deadly mass shooting at Marjory Stoneman Douglas High School in Parkland, Florida, Book sponsored the bill requiring schools to implement a mobile panic alert system. She became an invaluable resource for the students involved, attending funerals, meeting with parents, and helping the survivors advocate for change.

In early 2021, the pediatrician for Lauren's four-year-old twins was arrested on child pornography charges. This of course hit so close to home for her, and she couldn't believe that under Florida law he was able to continue practicing medicine even while the case was pending. She pushed for a law to ensure that medical licenses are suspended immediately upon a doctor being charged with a serious crime relating to sex or violence. On this issue, and so many others, Lauren has become a hero. Not because she set out to be, but because she listened when a voice inside told her that she could use her trauma to help others instead of sitting idly by. Now, as Senate minority leader, she is helping to set the agenda for Florida, and I'm in awe of her limitless future.

I wanted to use Lauren's story in this book in part because I wanted to make sure that the lessons here weren't all about making money. That's not what burning the boats is about. We go all in and push ourselves so that we can make a difference, make an impact, and achieve our goals—whatever they might be.

"I'm honored to do this work every single day," Lauren told me, "and I feel so lucky and proud to use my voice and use this experience—which I know that some people would not want to lean into, because it's tough and painful. But I figured out that instead of just being a victim, I could use my story to really try to make a change in the culture, and a shift in how we look at protecting children and survivors."

Her journey has ended up making her an unmatched advocate. The universe chose her, even if she would have never chosen herself.

◉   ◉   ◉

When I talk to Lauren about our difficult childhood experiences—difficult in very different ways—we both end up circling around the same ideas, of leaning into the discomfort and fear instead of away from it, and how by doing so you unlock potential you otherwise can't. "It's a journey," Lauren says, "and you need to understand that whatever happened to you already happened, and so it's a matter of finding a way to move forward. It's a process, constantly evolving, not a destination, and you have to be patient and kind to yourself. Life is fluid, life is messy, life is gray, but there will always be opportunities out there to make an impact and to help the world."

Ultimately, Chase the Threat

Why was Taylor Lindsay-Noel able to reinvent her life in the aftermath of crisis? Why was Michael Milken able to pivot to become a difference-making health care philanthropist? Why was Christina Tosi able to expand her brand so phenomenally during a worldwide pandemic? Crises force us to act. They give us no choice but to summon all of our strength and will because we know that the alternative is that something will be lost.

It is often much, much harder to make these big moves when things are humming along and there's no immediate impetus to change. When nothing is pushing us to urgently move in the direction of survival, we make a fundamental mistake. We think it's okay to do nothing. But we can look at it another way. In crisis, our choices get limited. We have to survive, and the list of things that will lead to survival can seem short and finite. Outside of crisis, our choices feel endless. Christina Tosi could have pivoted to the supermarket shelves at any point over the past decade. She could have also moved beyond baking cookies and also started her own clothing line. Or converted a warehouse into a cookie factory to make products for other brands to sell as their own. Or launched an interactive Broadway cookie-baking show to entertain thousands over the holiday season. Her business was strong enough that none of these choices, unexpected as they may sound, would have destroyed what she had.

We can all do bold things, all the time. But usually we don't, because the world of options feels too large. What should we choose? It isn't clear, and maintaining the status quo is easier—and so we choose nothing.

It's easy to tell ourselves that more choice—more options—is always good, but research tells us that alternatives can paralyze us and make us much less effective. Psychology professor Barry Schwartz has written about the paradox of choice: customers at an upscale grocery store were offered a coupon for $1 off the price of a jar of jam. Some customers saw a table with twenty-four jam varieties. A different group of customers was shown just six. "The large display attracted more interest than the small one," Schwartz writes. "But when the time came to purchase, people who saw the large display were one-tenth as likely to buy as people who saw the small display."[6] In other words, having too many options paralyzed the shoppers.

There is a dark side to having options. Professor Francesca Gino of Harvard Business School has counterintuitive research in progress on people working in a call center in India. Divided into two groups of employees, one of whom had other options for where to work, and the other where this job was their only choice ("no other income opportunity"), you might think that the ones with potential alternatives would have more confidence and outperform the rest. But that's not how it turned out. While the starting level of performance was the same in both groups, the ones who had no backup plan ended up performing at a higher level. This, according to the researchers, "defies conventional wisdom that potential employees with more job options have the highest potential to perform well on the job."

"Plus, with options comes potential regret," Professor Gino adds. "If you have five choices and can only pick one, you spend lots of time asking yourself, 'Was that the right choice?' But if you had no other options, you're more likely to be grateful for what you have."

◉ ◉ ◉

So what can we take from the stories in this chapter? Bad things will happen—to our businesses, in our lives, and in the world. It is all too easy to be derailed, to lose track of our goals, and to stop burning boats. But crises can also provide opportunities to shine, prosper, and make giant leaps.

If we run toward these challenges instead of away from them, we can ultimately not just stay on course but find new and even greater paths.

Be sure to continuously ask yourself, both in good times and in bad times:

◉ What's the worst that can happen?

◉ What would I do if I were starting from scratch today?

◉ How can I extract value from this otherwise bad situation?

Christina Tosi surely wishes the pandemic hadn't happened. But is she happier with her business now than she was in February of 2020? No question that she is.

And am I happy to have finally found the time to write this book? Absolutely—and I hope you're just as happy to be reading it.

It shouldn't have taken a worldwide pandemic to make it happen, but it did. It won't next time, because we learn, we get better, and we realize that things that once seemed impossible can actually be achieved. We break the patterns that stand in the way of our victory, and unlock our true potential.

CHAPTER 6

BREAK THE PATTERNS THAT STAND IN YOUR WAY

Some of the best preparation for my career goes all the way back to my early days as a reporter. The reason? Pattern recognition. A reporter sits in the stream of information seeing the patterns of life play out over and over again. Watch people being people for enough time, and you cultivate your ability to spot trends and forecast the future.

It's these patterns that help us succeed, and it's these same patterns that stand in our way. I've made some big moves and done some blockbuster deals in my life, and the worst buyer's remorse is when you realize, only in hindsight, after everything has gone wrong, that you could have spotted an issue—whether in a company, in a partner, or within yourself—if only you'd scrutinized the facts a bit more. Even worse is when you spotted the issue but talked yourself out of it due to cognitive bias or arrogance that you could muscle your way past it.

We have to become adept at not only identifying but acting on the behavioral patterns that strongly influence the outcomes of our efforts. Sometimes they're external—circumstances we should recognize that we need to manage against. Other times, they're internal—modes of thinking that can trap us into making bad choices, or ways in which we inadvertently sabotage our success. This chapter will focus on teaching you how to spot those patterns, and then learning how to overcome them.

Navigate around the External Obstacles . . .

Wrong Partners

As I've said before, the right partner—both personally and professionally—is so important. I see a particular pattern frequently: a founder assumes that because they're new to an industry, they need someone with subject matter expertise. So they recruit a cofounder grounded in the same industry they're looking to upend . . . but the cofounder is too steeped in the status quo to allow the company to stray far enough out of the box. The partnership gets stuck, one partner pushing hard in one direction and the other trying desperately to hold them back. This happens within established companies, too. Somebody wants to innovate, but at some point the innovation starts to feel too different, and too scary, and it's easier for the innovator to give up than to keep fighting.

This is why control is so important to hang on to if you seek to do something truly novel. In anything we do, we have to look very closely at whether it's a partner we need, or merely an employee with a particular skill set. I often see founders give away too much equity and power to someone they could have instead hired as an employee, rather than bringing them on as a cofounder. Yes, you might have a problem, and you might need help. But do you really need to enter a partnership that you're going to be stuck with, even after the issue that drove you to seek that person's help gets solved?

Lively's Michelle Cordeiro Grant had a brilliant approach—and the confidence to stick to it—that I think about every time I see someone going down the road of partnering when they don't necessarily need to.

"The first thing I did was write a list of all the things I was terrified of," she told me. "What are all the spaces in the business I knew nothing about? Fulfillment, customer service, digital marketing, all of these blind spots that I needed to fill. And then I went through my network and started creating my bench, the people I could turn to if I had problems or questions. There are so many mini-moments that you have to get through in a startup. But I could bring someone in to consult as a CMO or a CFO. I could bring someone in to solve a discrete problem, and still retain control of my business. It doesn't have to be permanent. You can test things out and see what you need in those moments."

I love that attitude. Indeed, a 2018 study by two scholars at the University of Pennsylvania looking at thousands of Kickstarter projects found that solo founders were more than twice as likely to have their businesses survive than teams of two or more.[1] And yet, I don't want to make the case that you should necessarily go it alone. The data actually does show that businesses with two or more founders are more likely to become billion-dollar companies than those with just one. Eighty percent of those billion-dollar unicorns have had founding teams at the top.[2] So a partner can be a great thing—but it's only a great thing when born of necessity and not insecurity.

When you're evaluating potential partners, you also have to evaluate yourself: Are you going to be someone who actually values contribution from others, or is there going to be constant friction? For instance, when I'm looking to invest in a business that's built on a partnership, I look for certain red flags:

◉ **Tension tells.** No one is foolish enough to reveal to an investor that a partnership is starting to sour, but if I detect subtle friction percolating into partners' interactions with me as a potential investor, when they ought to be on their very best behavior, then what's going on behind closed doors is surely ten times worse. Sorry—for that reason, I'm out.

◉ **Divergent theories of change.** Often there's one partner who drove the idea, and then there's the domain expert with experience in the space. But that domain expert needs to buy into the same theory of industry change or else it's never going to work. If your domain expert is stuck in the traditional thinking of the industry, either afraid to do something different or not truly convinced that something different is needed, then they shouldn't be a cofounder.

◉ **Lack of differentiated roles.** Who's doing what, and why? Yes, complementary skill sets are subordinate to a unified vision, but if there's overlap in expertise, or it's not clear why each partner owns their particular domain, then there's a flaw at the core of the partnership. Each person needs to have a reason to own their piece of the business.

- **Mismatched temperaments.** Companies can be like families, but partners can't be like dysfunctional parents—where one is a pushover and one is a disciplinarian—to their employees. If the employees know that one founder is more malleable than the other, or they can pit the partners against each other, then the whole company is destabilized and exploitable. Partners need to speak with one voice and be on the same page, and not foster a situation where employees (and therefore clients and investors) know which partner will cave to their demands, and which partner to avoid.

- **Misalignment of effort.** Sometimes one partner is working so hard, and the other . . . not so much. And that's a huge problem for any team. Just ask former Navy SEAL Curt Cronin. Before becoming an advisor to businesses and organizations around the world, Curt spent twenty years as a SEAL and is a former leader in the Naval Special Warfare Development Group. He's my guru when it comes to peak performance—physical, mental, and emotional—and I brought him in to train the Miami Dolphins on getting into the zone and remaining there for as long as possible during a game. Curt talks about how everyone on a team needs to be fully committed, or the entire effort falls apart. "The only reason any of us—SEALs or otherwise—can do superhuman things is that everyone knows that each person is fully invested. The moment one person hedges, no one can commit, and the flywheel stops turning." Everyone has to be all in, or resentment builds, and things fail. I see this scenario sometimes when partners' motives are different. One has family money sitting in the bank, and the other is much hungrier from a financial perspective, and looking at this as their big score. It never works. It's not sustainable if everyone isn't maxing themselves out.

Bad Investors

Partners aren't the only stakeholders you have to worry about. Investors matter, at least in efforts that require outside money, and a pattern I see again and again is that hesitant or demanding investors can get in the way. When choosing investors, your first principle should always be: *Do no harm.*

You may or may not have heard of the failed startup Juicero—a Wi-Fi-connected juicer that would deliver customers freshly packed bags of chopped produce ready to be juiced via a subscription service. Their downfall was a video from a *Bloomberg* reporter showing customers being able to squeeze the bags themselves, with their hands, making the $699 machine seem, well, unnecessary. CNET called them "the greatest example of Silicon Valley stupidity."[3]

We can debate the merits of the machine—frankly, they're not really much different than the coffee pod systems that have exploded in popularity over the past twenty years. You don't need anything more than some hot water and coffee grounds to make a cup of coffee—why should juice be any different? But the company's downfall began months before the viral video, when investors forced out Doug Evans, Juicero's founder and CEO, in favor of a former Coca-Cola COO.

When you meet Doug, within ten minutes it's clear who he is and what you're getting when you write a check into one of his projects. His strengths, but also his limitations, are on display with that first handshake. He doesn't hide his cards or what drives him and what he hopes to build. This is someone who, post-Juicero, is now living in a yurt and advocating that sprouts are the future of civilization. He runs from meeting to meeting; he's a staple at Burning Man. Anyone investing in Doug should have understood what they were buying—vision and passion above all else—and to jettison

MATT HIGGINS ⛵ Burn the Boats

Doug for being Doug meant that they never should have made the deal in the first place.

Doug saw Juicero as the start of a long game—not just a juicer but a community, the machine being the entry point into an Internet-connected lifestyle supporting people's health and wellness goals. Doug believes the investors didn't get it. It seemed they wanted discipline and safety. That was never going to be Doug. It was a mismatch, pure and simple. "The right investors will support the founder through the end," Doug says, "and I look back at Juicero and think that we made a few critical mistakes, and we were ahead of our time. The investors made the decision that they were done, but I felt the business wasn't done yet."

Stakeholders of any kind are a potential roadblock between your instincts and your freedom to execute. If you don't have their support, the energy leakage in trying to pander to the needs of others is going to doom your chance of success. Don't give people power unless you really need them.

Not Enough Money

My advice about limiting the influence of investors bumps up against a real problem for most companies: they need investors because they need money, and that reality can't be ignored. When the money runs out, the business is done. I saw that firsthand almost twenty-five years ago. The best job I've ever had was at Kozmo.com, a way-ahead-of-its-time startup, pre-smartphone, that promised to deliver goods and groceries in under an hour to customers in nine cities around the US. They raised hundreds of millions of dollars, and lost every penny. But in 1998 and 1999, they appeared to be on an unstoppable rise. At one point when I was working at the mayor's office, Kozmo offered me an impossible-to-resist jump in salary to come on board as director of crisis communications. I'd end up

142

back at the mayor's office eventually, but when Kozmo came calling, I decided to take the leap.

Joe Park, the CEO who founded the company when he was just twenty-eight years old, had an incredible grasp of the future. He knew that eventually e-commerce would be all about the last mile, but the reality was that the world wasn't ready yet. Back in 1997, people were still reluctant to enter their credit card number online—"sixty to seventy percent of our customers were still on dial-up connections," Joe told me recently. To support the massive warehouse and delivery infrastructure that Kozmo needed to scale, they had to reach a critical mass of customer density in each territory as quickly as possible. Otherwise, each new unprofitable order of a pint of ice cream would actually hasten their demise.

To do that, they raced to build brand awareness, investing so much in advertising and expanding their delivery zones far faster than the numbers could justify, but mindshare wasn't the same as profitability. "The thing we should have done differently," Joe says now, looking back, "is to recognize that we needed a lot more runway to wait it out until the market was ready. Even Amazon went through its death moment early on, raising $1.8 billion in convertible debt in 1999 and 2000. Tesla was walking on thin ice a few years ago, too. Kozmo was one of the three or four biggest startups of our time, but we just didn't have enough money to survive."

There's a point Joe makes about the market not being ready, and it gets to the next pattern I see over and over again.

You Can't Predict the Timeline of Success

Joe Park knew where e-commerce was headed before pretty much anyone else, which is why Jeff Bezos ended up hiring him a few years after Kozmo folded, to run the company's advertising division and then its gaming unit. But the world wasn't there yet. I see this so often. All of us expect reward far too early. We are seduced by the thoughts in our own heads, and we imagine that others are thinking them too, even when they're not. I often think I'm late to an idea when I'm actually incredibly early. When I'm looking to invest in a business or an industry, I'll obsessively read everything I can find, and immerse myself in the space. Sometimes that can delude me into thinking that everyone else is right there with me, when in fact they're not.

I had an opportunity to make an early investment in what became a wildly successful business—an electric vertical take-off and landing (eVTOL) aircraft company—but I passed. Part of what held me back is that I saw dozens of other companies already in the space. I thought maybe I was too late and the bump had already happened. But, to tell you the truth, I wasn't sure. And the reality is that when you've passed the tipping point, you won't wonder about it—it will be incredibly obvious. If you don't know whether you're early or late, I'll bet almost every time that you're early, and that there's still plenty of upside. Just ask the people who invested in Facebook back when it was valued at $15 billion in 2008. (It's worth fifteen times that as I write this.)

Along the same lines, when you're tempted to bail on an idea, hold off and ask yourself if you're reacting to your own boredom and impatience, or if there is actually a reason to exit. Familiarity breeds contempt. We get burned out and sick of hearing our own stories, even if most of the world hasn't come close to hearing them yet.

You need to structure your big bets in life to give yourself time to be right. It's hard enough to be right; it's impossible to predict exactly *when* you'll be right. Maybe you're very wrong in micro-terms, but Nostradamus when it comes to the macro. I tell people it takes at least three years for a startup to stabilize, five to reap the harvest—and almost never less, no matter the product.

◉　◉　◉

This same kind of timing uncertainty played out with my investment in RESY, a restaurant reservations service that we eventually sold to American Express. Along with Ben Leventhal, the founder of the food website Eater, and Gary Vaynerchuk, who both drove the idea, we began with the notion that restaurants were not effectively monetizing their prime inventory. Why should a table at a top restaurant on Friday night at 9 p.m. cost the same as one on Tuesday at 5:30? We thought there should be a way to capture value. But the market didn't see it the same way, and still doesn't.

Instead, Ben realized that what top restaurants really needed was an alternative to OpenTable, the juggernaut in the space that was using paid search to intercept a restaurant's demand—and then selling it back to them every time someone booked a reservation. Many restaurant owners ended up resentful yet dependent on the loop that OpenTable created through its role as the dominant player.

Top restaurants didn't need OpenTable's services—they controlled their own demand—and in fact wanted something more robust than what OpenTable was able to provide with its aging technology. Based on these findings—and realizing that the world wasn't ready for the initial RESY model—Ben pivoted the company into a superior back-end system for the world's top restaurants, looking to destroy OpenTable's monopoly in the space.

The truth is that it wasn't smooth sailing from there. When the team went out to fundraise, they fell completely flat, and nearly ran out of money. We moved the team into our offices at RSE to stabilize, kept iterating, and eventually sold to American Express for nine figures. I still believe in our original value proposition, but the world just wasn't there yet, and still isn't.

● ● ●

Talking to Joe Park made me remember another piece of Kozmo's story. It wasn't just that the market wasn't ready for us, it was also the case that we were being compared to companies that were a step ahead of us in the journey. Webvan was a grocery delivery company that eventually got called one of the biggest dot-com flops in history, losing nearly a billion dollars.[4] Kozmo's model was different (Webvan blew much of its money trying to open its own warehouses and buying delivery trucks), and its path to profitability much shorter, but once Webvan collapsed, no one was willing to give Kozmo any further investment.

I saw the same pattern with Kin, the insurance company I tried to take public. Yes, the broader stock market drop was a problem, for sure, but more specifically, the company's closest competitor, Hippo, saw its stock price collapse 90 percent in less than a year. Even though Hippo was backed by LinkedIn founder Reid Hoffman, the market violently rejected its public listing. There were real distinctions between Hippo and Kin (which I believed had a vastly superior business model and the numbers to prove it), but institutional investors couldn't get past the comparison. It was just too early in the evolution of the insurance technology market for subtleties. This all leads to a lesson: If you're early, you need to make sure you are your own market maker and not being benchmarked against other players. You need to be the first mover, craft your story, and live or die on your own merits—not be caught in the crossfire when a lesser version of your idea falls apart.

These external obstacles—partners, investors, money, and timing—can be fatal, for sure, but the patterns that are not always quite so obvious are the ones that are more about you than about the rest of the world.

. . . But Don't Forget to Look Within

You Can't Do It All

I see this pattern so often: you're a CEO, and you're a highly capable individual. You understand your business exceptionally well, and if there was no limit to your capacity or the number of hours in the day, you'd gladly handle every piece of it yourself. You're hiring people because you have to, not because you want to. So you end up holding your employees to an impossible standard, micromanaging them, and stepping in too soon when you're worried they'll fail. You end up bogged down in operations instead of doing what a CEO needs to be doing—scaling yourself up, leading with vision, and directing the ship. It's a recipe for failure, and the single biggest trap I see smart leaders fall into.

There's no better example of this than the head coach of most football teams. Head coaches almost always come up the ranks as offensive or defensive coordinators, calling the plays, and becoming truly excellent at it. Then they get promoted and suddenly they're supposed to abandon the skill that made them successful? Many of them can't. They still want to call the plays, which means they don't step back and see the bigger picture. And yet, the culture of the NFL places such a high premium on the mythology of the natural born leader that there is no on-the-job training for the newly minted head coach. You're expected to either have it or not. It's no surprise that so many new coaches are fired within three years.

Even the best play callers need to transcend and occupy the complete role as head coach of the entire team. "They need to evolve into the job," says Mike Tannenbaum.

"They need the confidence to hire great employees," adds Rex Ryan. "Once I got the head coach job, I had no fear of hiring the best people I could below me. I kept a guy who interviewed for the job up against me, because I knew they chose me, so why should I feel threatened? I brought in young guys, guys I knew, and some guys I didn't know, with amazing reputations. I absolutely wanted the best."

But Rex is unusual. Many head coaches refuse to hire someone better than they are, because they're worried that their job will be threatened. Don't fall into this common, ego-driven trap.

◉ ◉ ◉

In the business world it's even harder, because it's not just about calling offensive and defensive plays. There are endless roles that need to be filled, and good leaders need to render themselves obsolete at doing virtually all of them.

Ask yourself: If you're in the hospital for a week, will the business still function? It needs to. And if you're afraid of people outshining you, get over yourself. You have to hire people who are better than you at every task, and you need to celebrate that, not be resentful of it. People don't want to work for leaders who can't rise above micromanagement. People want to work for leaders who value them, appreciate them, and trust them. The biggest job of a leader is putting great talent in place and helping them shine.

To scale, you need to understand your own strengths and weaknesses. In the political space, Lauren Book has talked to me about making strategic alliances. You find someone you can align with, who brings different strengths to the table, and the combination works. You use your relationships and your skills to help them reach their goals, and they use theirs to help you. But, whether we're talking politics or business, that's the way it is in every arena. Know what you can do, and know where you need others to step in.

Nicholas Horbaczewski from Drone Racing League provides a

perfect example here, of fearlessness when it comes to giving others the opportunity to shine. "It's definitely easier to try to just keep doing it all yourself," he admits. "I did that for a long time—too long. But at some point, I had to acknowledge I was making the wrong tradeoffs. I knew I had to hire a president, but hiring senior leaders into a company is just about the hardest thing you have to do. A bad hire in a senior position is a catastrophe."

Nicholas hired Rachel Jacobson as DRL's president in the wake of their C-round of financing. It was a big decision for him to step back. But it was necessary. "She was exactly what we needed to supercharge our trajectory," Nicholas explains. Rachel jumped in and helped take the company to the next level, closing new partnerships, helping to get drone racing legalized for sports betting, expanding their video game to top consoles, and more. Without her, I'm not sure DRL would have lasted another year. One person can't do it all alone.

Don't Play Small

One of the many things I admire about my business partner at RSE, Stephen Ross, is that he understands that you have to go big. Forget downside mitigation. When you have a winner, you have to remember: Winners are so rare. It's the ultimate Burn the Boats point. Go all in on a winner, because "the less you bet," as Stephen says all the time, "the more you lose when you win."

It's really difficult to double down if you feel like you're alone on an island. We are all afraid to be wrong. My rational brain often gets in the way of my emotional brain. My rational brain can't understand why everyone else, when presented with the same exact facts as I'm seeing, isn't jumping up and down at an opportunity. My emotional brain realizes that love is in the eye of the beholder, and that we need to follow our hearts.

When our heads and our hearts are fighting, it's easy to try and split the difference. We make a small bet, so we won't feel too bad if it turns out we're wrong. But if it's worth going in at all, then I would make the case that it's worth going all in. I know there are investors who like to "spray and pray," throwing a little bit of money everywhere and hoping a few things pay off to cover the failures of the rest. I've tried that and realized there's another name for this philosophy: spinning wheels. Investors who are playing small aren't the ones driving breakout success. If you want to be a leader, you have to actually take a risk and lead.

Not wanting to be stuck playing too small is why loyal viewers of *Shark Tank* always hear the Sharks insisting on more equity. We know that whether we have 2 percent or 42 percent, to engage is going to take significant energy, and if we only have 2 percent of the upside to gain, we can't justify the time. There's an opportunity cost to everything you do, and putting your time into one venture inevitably means passing up others.

You often have to look at hundreds and hundreds of potential businesses or potential deals in order to find a winner—that's absolutely true. You wouldn't necessarily marry the first person you ever date, and so you shouldn't write a check before exploring if there's a better use for your money. The best decisions are always relative decisions. You should never make a choice in any context in isolation, without juxtaposing it against a viable alternative. But if and when you do find those winners—the ones that hold up to comparison and to scrutiny—don't waffle and don't let go. Playing small is the best way to ensure that you won't ever achieve big dreams.

Don't Buy the Hype

It's hard to go all in when no one else is seeing what you are. But don't let that fear steer you into following the herd and thinking that others know best. Investors fall into this trap when they see a market getting crowded and they can't resist jumping in, too. They sell themselves on a business idea because they're afraid of missing out.

Look at Theranos, the health tech company that raised $700 million and achieved a $10 billion valuation before being revealed to be a fraud. Founder Elizabeth Holmes claimed to have developed the technology to revolutionize blood testing, eliminating needles and enabling a finger prick to power more than 240 tests off a single drop of blood (cholesterol, chlamydia, cocaine . . . and that's just a small selection of the Cs).[5] This would have been great if it worked, but it didn't. That didn't stop Holmes. She put together a shiny board of directors of luminaries and octogenarians, including Henry Kissinger, Bill Frist, James Mattis, and David Boies, and used their fame to lure investors.

Honestly, when I saw the Theranos board populated with those big names, I knew something was rotten in the state of Denmark. I wasn't sure it was fraud, but it was clear to me that Holmes was running a misdirection—a play in football meant to divert your attention away from what the quarterback actually plans to do with the ball. I asked myself, if I was assembling a board to help me revolutionize blood tests, would any of these people even make the list? She did have one person from the world of science, Dr. William Foege, former director of the CDC (who, as it happened, never wavered in his support for the company, even after the fraud was revealed!), but the rest of the board were outsiders to the industry. As the website TechCrunch wrote while Elizabeth Holmes went to trial in the fall of 2021, "Except for Foege, nobody knew the first thing about diagnostic testing, the technologies behind it, the challenges, the logistics, economics or even the biology. . . . [Board members like James Mattis] took the word of Holmes and the senior leadership team that the technology worked."[6]

Elizabeth Holmes told a great story, and got a lot of great press.

From all reports, the company tried to turn its science fiction dreams into reality . . . but they couldn't, and they lied about it, and no one figured it out until far too much money had been lost. In 2022, Holmes was found guilty on four counts of defrauding investors, with her trial revealing the depth to which she faked demonstrations, falsified reports, and overstated financial results.

The story of Theranos is a phenomenal lesson in not being seduced for the wrong reasons. If something triggers an emotional response in your brain, trying to soothe fears you may not have even realized you had, you have to ask yourself, before being lulled into complacency: *Am I being manipulated?*

This is a proven trap for our flawed human brains. We can look at what's called the *availability cascade*, the vicious cycle that drives fake news, where a story gains more credibility the more it spreads, with prominence substituting for accuracy, and people becoming more likely to believe something just because they keep hearing it. Professors Timur Kuran and Cass Sunstein have written about this phenomenon, where even false information can get traction just because people imagine that if they're hearing about it, it must be true.[7]

Shady entrepreneurs can use this to their advantage, hyping up their company in the press, getting big names behind it, and making it seem like all the "cool kids" are backing them. You don't want to be left out, and you assume that others must know what they're doing, so you jump in. The research talks about "availability entrepreneurs," who understand this dynamic and use it to promote their agenda. There is certainly money to be made betting on the greater fool theory, the idea that there's a new sucker born every day who will prop up a company's valuation and give you a handsome return. But I promise you, karma is real, and even if such an investing strategy might work for a while, enabling the unethical choices of others will poison you in the end. I prefer to stick to entrepreneurs who actually deliver value and don't just try to convince me that they're the real deal.

Sometimes We Have to Let Go

We all love our businesses, and we don't want to admit failure— to ourselves, or to the world. There's a temptation to chase too long even when all evidence is saying otherwise. Entrepreneur Danny Grossfeld went on *Shark Tank* selling ready-to-drink hot coffee in cans, accompanied by a hotbox to keep them warm. It was apparently all the rage in Japan, but simply had not taken off in the US. He had been trying to sell to bodegas, movie theaters, anywhere he thought the product might make sense—but in six years, he'd had no sales, just inquiries. Danny had invested more than two million dollars from friends and family, including over half a million dollars of his own money.

It did not go well for him on the show. Robert Herjavec pointed out that the US was filled with coffee shops, and the product may not be filling the same need as in Japan. Mark Cuban said he liked the concept, but hated the business. "That boulder is going to fall and squash you," he said.

The clear lack of interest from the market was a deal killer for everyone. Lori Greiner said Danny should "stop the bleeding," and Kevin O'Leary said that if a business goes more than thirty-six months without turning a profit, it was time to "take it into the barn and shoot it." I think Kevin's rule of thumb may be a little bit simplistic—it took Facebook five years to turn a profit, and Amazon nine years—but at least they had users, revenue, traction, all evidence that people cared. Danny had nothing.

We stick with ideas too long in part because of the sunk cost fallacy, the notion that what we have already invested in a flawed endeavor justifies our continued investment. This is also known as throwing good money after bad. Don't do it. You need signs of traction. You have to recognize when the market has spoken. I find there's a tipping point on fundraising rounds that tracks this point. If you've gotten to a Series E round and the business still needs to raise money, you're getting to the point of no return. Seeing too many letters in those rounds is a visible signal that something has gone very wrong. By the time you get to F, G, and beyond, you should have either become profitable or exited, with rare exceptions. Frankly, it's also the reality of how these funding rounds work that the stakes held by the CEO and the management team are getting diluted with every successive round, with terms potentially more desperate with every investment. When you're that far down the road, you aren't burning the boats—you're battening down the hatches and looking for an escape.

At some point, you just have to ask yourself a few more of the hard questions:

- Is this a solution in search of a problem?

- What else could you be doing with your time and money? (Opportunity cost!)

- Is future effort truly leveraging the effort and money you've already put in, or are you just convincing yourself you're making progress in order to justify staying the course?

- If you were starting over—just like I asked in chapter 5—is this the business you'd start today?

People worry that if they abandon their dream, they will never have another great idea. But winners don't have one great idea in their lifetime. Ideas are just like homes in real estate; there's always a new one coming on the market tomorrow.

Sometimes it's actually not as dramatic as letting go of an entire idea, and it becomes more about figuring out the right pivot, just like when Emmett Shine and his team decided that Pattern would buy existing brands ripe for acceleration rather than incubating their own from scratch. Winners iterate. The universe is benevolent, and always gives you one more chance to course correct before it's too late. What sets the most successful people apart is that they're not only able to make those course corrections, but they do it before they are forced to. They eagerly use what I call their small rockets.

I like to think about the pursuit of any major goal like the launching of a spacecraft. Large booster rockets harness the power of seven million pounds of thrust to send the ship on its initial trajectory through Earth's atmosphere. That's the big decision to go for it. But a ship is fitted with smaller rockets too, called sustainers. At launch, they are of little use getting off the ground. However, along the journey, these sustainer rockets make all the difference. If the spacecraft is off course by even just a few degrees, it will end up as a fireball over the ocean. Small blasts from those little rockets will bring the spacecraft back on course. Great leaders use their small rockets way before everything goes up in flames.

Maybe You're the Wrong Leader for This Business, No Matter How Incredible It Is

We're up to the heavy hitters now, the patterns that will doom you to failure even if everything else is perfectly in place. I see lots of situations where the business might be great, and the leader might even be great, but it's not the right match. One of my favorite investors, Ben Lerer, calls it founder/product fit. Sometimes the leader knows it's not a fit, but they're afraid to let go of their baby. You have to remember, just because you *can* do something doesn't mean you *should*. Is this really the journey you want to spend your next three, five, ten years following? We are not all the same. We do not all have the same passions, interests, and desires.

I know not everyone agrees with me, but I don't like to back people who aren't living their dreams. I would much prefer to back someone who feels like this is their calling, even if it's for reasons they can't explain. That mystical impulse will sustain them through the drudgery of building a business—and there's always drudgery, even in the best scenarios. You can be a great operator, but if you aren't the one person on this planet destined to do what you're doing, I'm not interested. I want to feel as if God, or the universe, or some divine being, whatever you want to call it, put you on this earth at this exact moment so that you would be in a position to pursue this dream, whatever it might be. I want you to radiate inevitability.

Call it hobby insurance, perhaps. There are going to be so many twists and turns along the way, so many challenges, so many crises, so many times when it's easy to make the wrong choice, that a company needs a leader who is crazy enough to sacrifice themselves to make their business work. When I hear, "If only you back me, we can do this together," I run away in fear, because if you don't have the conviction that you can do it without me, you are not The One.

The biggest mistakes I've made are when I imagine that the power of an idea goes beyond the power of the individual. I want to see airtight alignment between the business and the leader. Like Freddie Harrel of RadSwan, or Christina Tosi. So I ask, every time I'm looking at an opportunity: Does this founder have a passion for the underlying space, enough to drive them through the darkest days? You'll need it. A friend of mine recently approached me with an idea. She said she wanted to create a national network of electric car charging stations, like gas stations on steroids, with upscale shops and businesses. It's a capital-intensive business, with a need to understand site planning and zoning, and you have to want to spend years building that up.

She said she wanted me to run with it, and make it happen. I laughed. An idea is nothing. I'm going to reorient my life to work on this idea just because it might work? Like everything, it's all about the execution, and the execution is only going to be successful if I live and breathe electric charging stations. I don't. "But if you do," I told her, "then go for it."

Along the same lines, I write people off as soon as I get a whiff of paranoia from them that someone is going to steal their idea. Unless we're actually talking about an invention that needs to be kept under wraps until adequately protected, there is nothing to be afraid of. You can't steal a successful business. If you're worried about theft, it means you have nothing built, nothing proprietary, nothing worth a dime. There's a great line in the movie *The Social Network* in which Mark Zuckerberg's character turns to the Winklevoss twins and tells them, "If you guys were the inventors of Facebook, *you'd have invented Facebook.*" Execution is everything, and if you aren't the one person on the planet able to best execute the vision, well, pick another business, because this isn't the one.

Or Maybe You're Not Yet Ready to Lead . . .

Not everyone is ready to be a leader at the moment the opportunity presents itself. The lessons in this book might help you get there, or at least that's the goal, but most of us aren't born perfect performers. We need to grow ourselves to get there. I have backed companies even though I knew the jockey wasn't up for the task, thinking that the power of the idea would be enough to compensate for a weak founder. It never happens. A great founder can overcome a weak idea but a great idea will buckle under the weight of a weak founder. I've made the big mistake of thinking an idea is so revolutionary that it will manifest itself. Not true.

On the other hand, the opposite does happen—a great leader will absolutely iterate their way to a world-class business. What does it take? It's easy to articulate and almost impossible to cultivate in people who can't see it for themselves. You need the right blend of confidence and humility. You need to know you can do it, and be unafraid to pivot as needed. You need to be able to admit when you're wrong, and then instantly act on that information and move yourself in the right direction. I can predict CEO failure based on how quickly a leader makes a decision after the need to make that decision becomes objectively inevitable. If you need to see the iceberg portside before you start steering to avert it, you are too late, and you will fail.

The right blend of confidence and humility ensures that you're not going to be embarrassed by the need to change. When the leader doesn't have that, I conclude (as the saying goes in Italian: *il pesce marcisce dalla testa*) that the fish rots from the head—and I move on to a new company, looking for the right people at just the right inflection point, following their dreams. Once found, I back them with no reservations.

◉ ◉ ◉

In my HBS class, I told the story over three sessions of immi, a good-for-you ramen company whose story is still unfolding as I write this. The question I asked my students was to help me decide whether or not to write immi a check for $250,000 and be the company's first outside investor. The students were excited . . . until I informed them that the beta version of the product tastes terrible, and the reviews are almost uniformly awful, to such an extent that the company literally had to stop marketing, and stop selling the ramen, because it was getting trashed on social media. Of course, hearing that, no one raises their hand to write the check. Who would back a food company selling food that no one wants to eat?

And then I bring in the two cofounders, Kevin Lee and Kevin Chanthasiriphan, and it becomes immediately apparent that these people were put on this planet to sell protein ramen. They have self-awareness, they know where things have gone wrong, and they're back in the test kitchen, putting together version 2.0 with all of the right data behind them, and all of the right instincts.

By the end of the class, hearing the two Kevins talk about how Asian food hasn't yet joined the better-for-you trend that so many other indulgences have found success exploiting, and outlining their path to get there, everybody's hand is up. They would back the company—and so did I. (And fifteen months after that class, a new-and-improved immi landed a deal with Whole Foods, and they can't restock the product on the shelves quickly enough.) Not only do winners iterate, they have a magnetic power to enlist others to the cause. Self-awareness telegraphs to supporters that it's safe to believe. When you meet someone with high self-awareness, even if you consciously surmise they're on the wrong path, you subconsciously think, "They'll figure it out." You instinctively trust that they will course correct when the ship runs aground.

◉　◎　◎

What's the opposite of self-awareness? Ignorance, maybe. Delusion, perhaps. The biggest thing that scares me away from investing in a particular person is feeling like they're hiding something, or failing to understand that you can't actually hide anything. Problems will all ultimately be revealed, and that's why you need to get ahead of them and find them before they own you.

Curt Cronin talks about the missing conversations, and how we need to get everything out on the table, no matter how hard, and no matter how uncomfortable it makes us. "The most difficult conversations I ever had in the SEALs," he told me, "were when I decided to say out loud the things that I was assuming about why something had gone wrong. We can't rely on our assumptions. We have to actually get things out in the open."

"People are terrified of having hard conversations," Curt explains, "because we imagine the worst-case outcomes. But we don't think about the cost of not having those conversations, and the inefficiency of guessing what someone else is thinking and feeling instead of actually knowing."

I see bad leaders trying to avoid conversations all the time. They want to brush past things they think I won't see in their business, instead of working together with me to fix the problems. I first learned about the human tendency to hide all kinds of things when I worked at McDonald's as a kid. When no one's looking, people will make mischief (so much gum under the table) and leave it to others to clean up the mess. I saw in that filthy party room that you can make anything (or any business) look polished, but what's just below the surface tells you the larger story.

In the best circumstances, the leaders are right there with you, scoping for the flaws with eagerness. Good leaders are intellectually curious—about themselves, and about their businesses. I tell people, don't look for the holes to poke, look for the holes to plug. Great leaders get excited about the opportunity to plug holes, about the chance to expose themselves to smart investors and figure out how to make their business better.

If I feel like someone is hiding the truth, or not being fully authentic, it doesn't actually matter if I find out what they're hiding, because I've already learned what I need to know. I can't work with someone who is going to feel threatened by discovery, and who isn't completely present, completely open, and ready to do the hard work. I look for signals of transparency, like being able to admit when you don't know something. No one has the answer to every question—and investors understand this. I don't want someone just trying to placate me, because then I know you're just doing everything you can to get a deal and not as concerned as you should be about whether it's actually the right fit.

◉　◉　◉

One of the ways I confirm my instincts about people, before I decide to go in on a deal, is something I'm shocked more people don't do. It's a common mistake in private equity to spend tons of money and energy on experts to look at the financials of a business, but no money on psychologists to do a deep dive on the leader. When I was being promoted to the executive level at the Jets, they asked me to submit to a full-day grilling by an industrial psychologist, a combination of interviews and a paper-and-pencil test to probe my mind and get at my leadership style, my flaws, and my misconceptions about the world. I was deeply offended at first, as I find some people are. Why should I have to meet with a psychologist before getting a promotion? Hadn't I proven my worth already? Mostly I was afraid that the tests would validate the voice in my head calling me an imposter.

But it was life-changing.

I learned so much about myself, and by the end of it, I knew—this was a tool to separate the winners from the losers. I now bring in my favorite industrial psychologist, Dr. Laura Finfer, for major deals anytime I have the leverage to make it a condition of writing a check. I don't like doing a major deal without her. Give a trained professional three hours to probe the dark recesses of someone's mind, and they will put it all on paper in black and white. The ones who resist, incidentally, are generally the ones who perform the worst. They don't see feedback as the gift it truly is.

The biggest misses of my career have been when I ignored the report or decided to glide past the two or three critical sentences that revealed the hidden truth. In more than thirty analyses, it has always been in there. So, to close this chapter, I decided to talk to Dr. Finfer, who is principal at Leadership Excellence Consulting, about the patterns she most often sees in her work, and what she looks for when she's evaluating leaders. Here are five patterns Dr. Finfer often sees derailing the people she works with, at companies large and small:

- ◉ **Relying too much on raw intelligence.** On the one hand, it's absolutely the case that intellectual horsepower is a prerequisite for success, driving the ability to solve problems, think strategically, and form a real vision for a company. But along with intellect has to come emotional intelligence—the ability to work with others, and the ability to work on yourself. You need a willingness to adjust and change. You have to be able to take feedback, and, to be a good leader, you have to be able to deliver feedback, too.

- **Being too deferential to authority.** Of course, you always want to listen to all of the stakeholders, no matter your role, and you never want to be a bully in your interpersonal interactions. But you do need the confidence to stand up for what you believe in. Strong performers speak their minds, and aren't afraid of causing a bit of conflict. "I'm sometimes shocked," Dr. Finfer told me. "Some people are way too afraid of disagreement." You do have to know who you're dealing with, she cautions, but if someone—a boss, an investor, a partner—can't tolerate an opinion different from their own, you're not going to solve that problem simply by agreeing with them all the time.

- **Failing to understand workplace politics.** "Lack of political savvy is a huge derailer as you move up in an organization," Dr. Finfer says. "You need to package your words and choose your moments. You need the interpersonal awareness to know how to deal with each individual in an organization, because everyone responds differently." In other words, you need to think about what will motivate a particular person, and what will push them away.

- **Not distributing credit.** Dr. Finfer pays careful attention to language when she's evaluating someone. She notices when people use "I" instead of "we" when talking about successes at work. "There's usually no way it's only them, so it speaks to how much they're valuing the people around them," she says.

- **Evading questions.** Dr. Finfer also notes when people try to evade questions or barrel forth with an agenda of their own instead of really listening to her and responding to what's being asked. "They don't want to show weakness, or they're hiding something."

It comes back to the fatal flaw I just discussed: not being honest and authentic. You can't spend your time trying to fool people. It's obvious, and it will come back to bite you.

The good news is that improving on all of these fronts is possible. Mostly, it takes recognition of your weaknesses, and a willingness to grow and improve. And what happens when you do, and you break these patterns, is that you finally get to the opposite shore. You burn the boats, and you keep reaching for your dreams.

But then what?

Life is not a single journey.

We all understand how satisfying it feels to complete something—to achieve. But we can sometimes forget about how much joy there is in beginning, how much anticipation, excitement, and hunger. Revel in those moments when you lock in on something new, when you *want* so desperately that you feel like you can bend the universe.

When you get to a finish line, before you even take a breath, you should be looking ahead. Appreciate the victory, but in the very same beat, ask the question that animates life: "What's next?"

PART III

BUILD MORE BOATS

CHAPTER 7

CONSOLIDATE YOUR GAINS

When I think of leveling up, I think about Marc Lore, and his incredible serial exits. In 1999, Marc started The Pit, an Internet marketplace for collectibles that he sold to sports-card giant Topps for $5.7 million just two years later. Then, in 2005, Diapers.com, with its massive exit to Amazon, and then Jet, a shopping club designed to compete with Amazon with a lower annual fee than Amazon Prime and optimized pricing algorithms, which Walmart bought for even more.

Lore left Walmart in January 2021 and has announced plans to build "a city of the future."[1] "He believes that no worker should have to commute more than 15 minutes," writes Jim Souhan in the *Star Tribune*.[2] "That all trash should be stored underground. That all vehicles should be autonomous. . . . [Lore's goal is] a city that would look to blend the best of New York, Stockholm, and Tokyo." But the ambition is bigger than just the city itself. "I'm trying to create a new model for society, where wealth is created in a fair way," Marc told *Fortune*. He calls the new economic model Equitism, "giving back to the citizens and the people the wealth that they helped create."³ By 2030, he plans to seed this new city, named Telosa (Greek for "highest purpose")—built on inexpensive land in an underpopulated part of the country—with fifty thousand diverse citizens looking for a new way of life.

On top of that, Marc also recently founded Wonder (which I invested in), a new company that brings fine dining directly to people's homes—with vans outfitted with kitchens, and chefs that will finish and plate Michelin-quality meals right outside the customer's door. It's on-demand home dining, with a roster of top-quality chefs—like Bobby Flay, Marcus Samuelsson, Nancy Silverton, and Jonathan Waxman—already signed on to let Wonder re-create their menus and deliver their meals. Flay told the *New York Post*, "They figured out how to emulate exactly what I do."⁴ Wonder just raised $400 million on a $4 billion valuation.

In the meantime, as if that wasn't enough, Marc has just become the coowner of the NBA's Minnesota Timberwolves and the WNBA's Minnesota Lynx, along with my fellow guest Shark Alex Rodriguez.

What's fascinating about Marc is that he goes and does it. He builds and builds and builds. Did his lessons from Diapers.com inform his work building Jet? Absolutely. Will his experience with Jet inform what's next? No doubt. But he takes those lessons, he consolidates his gains, and he launches his next journey. What do you do when you've reached the end of one journey? Burn the boats and do it all again.

To embrace this perpetual growth mindset, I have four principles to guide you.

Use Every Advantage You Currently Possess

I give talks to football players about preparing for their postplaying careers. So many of them have dreams—to invest in real estate, to produce movies, to become a commentator on ESPN, to make their money grow—but they don't want to think about any of it until they're done playing. I tell them they're missing an opportunity to leverage their biggest asset: relevance. People love to say they're in business with an NFL player—a *current* NFL player. Once they retire, their convening power (the ability to catalyze action) drops precipitously. They are no longer nearly as interesting or as relevant to the world. Is that harsh? Absolutely. But my job is to give them the smelling salts so that they wake up before it's too late.

How can these players take advantage of their current status? By figuring out what they want their lives to look like after they retire, and then putting the pieces in place now. Lots of these football players get inbound calls from people who want them to invest in their business or get involved in an opportunity, but I tell them to ignore the inbound calls and focus on making outbound calls instead. What do *they* want to do? There's almost no one who won't give them a call back, and there's almost nothing out of reach.

I know of football stars who follow this advice, reaching out to people as notable as Warren Buffett to mentor them and help strategize about the future. Would a billionaire take anyone's call? Surely not. But stars have status—and they can use it to their advantage. Take Byron Jones, a 2015 first round draft pick who in 2020 signed a contract with the Dolphins making him the highest-paid corner in the NFL at the time—$82 million over five years, with more than $50 million guaranteed. Byron lives with a philosophy of preparing for the future, and making a game plan to be ready not just for what's happening now but for what's yet to come. He knows that being a football star is not going to last his entire life; it's only the first step. "I always knew I was going to be in the NFL," he told me. "But I actually did two internships in college, one at the state capital and one in Congress, to prepare for life after football."

Byron was planning for the future well before most players would even think to. In fact, he called me up shortly after he signed to pick my brain about investing, wanting to know how to turn his guaranteed $50 million into $100 million, or even more. He told me that he lived on $10,000 a month before he signed his deal, and had given himself a raise—to $13,000 a month. Seems like a lot, until you realize that there are millennials in New York City living on far more than that, who definitely aren't NFL stars with eight-figure guaranteed deals. "I lived on the same budget for my first four years after being drafted," he told me.

Even Byron's journey to the NFL was very much the product of a focused plan. Before being drafted, he paid special attention to the skills he knew would be evaluated at the NFL Scouting Combine, where the league puts the top college players to the test. "I was actually rehabbing my shoulder in the months leading up to the Combine, so I couldn't train. But that didn't mean I couldn't prepare in other ways. I focused on nutrition, weight management, and watching film. I wanted to know what it would look like at the Combine, what elements they'd be evaluating us on, and what movements we would do."

One element at the Combine is the standing long jump. Byron had always been good at jumping, making it to a national track and field competition when he was eight years old, but he decided that if he channeled his energy particularly on the standing long jump, he could excel at that one skill and use it to stand out from the pack. "The Combine was three days of intensity, the most exciting time in my life," he remembers. "There were X-rays, MRIs, and then the final field events. In training, I had been jumping 11 feet 3 inches, maybe 11 feet 4 inches. My first jump was 11 feet 6 inches. And then, my second jump: 12 feet, 3 inches. I had never even been thinking about 12 feet, but I tried to keep my cool, act like it was normal for me."

Byron may have tried to make it seem normal, but that jump was 8 inches farther than any NFL player had ever jumped. In fact, he jumped farther than any standing jump in recorded history, and he currently holds the unofficial world record.

So how might he turn his $50 million into $100 million? Here's one plan I pitched to him when he asked. There you are, I said, with this one-of-a-kind leverageable asset. That long jump record could totally make him a star. Imagine a TikTok campaign where he jumps over a series of crazy things: eight TikTok stars lying on the floor, a gap between two skyscrapers, a couple hundred of Christina Tosi's cookies (always looking for ways to grab press for my businesses). He could go crazy on social media, build up a following, and become a social media hero.

Byron interrupted me. "I don't want any of that social media stuff," he said. "I want to be a serious investor." As Byron continues to become a bigger and bigger football star, he's got time to figure out his future—but in today's world, I told him, the lines are blurred. You're a better "serious" investor, with access to the greatest deal flow, if people know who you are and want to be in business with you. Byron's advantage is the platform that can make him relevant and current as a prominent figure who can pull the levers of influence on behalf of the companies he backs. That's incredibly valuable. Maybe that'll end up driven by his long jump feats, or maybe it'll be something else—but I know Byron's thinking about it, and being smart when it comes to his future. His life is going to be a massive success way beyond football.

● ● ●

The advantages of a football star are obvious, but that doesn't make the point any less relevant for the rest of us. We may not be football stars, but football stars almost surely don't have the unique assets that *you* bring to the table. The reality is that *everyone* has a leverageable asset—a quality, a circumstance, a story—that can move them due north to their dreams. When I was working at McDonald's, my advantage was my willingness to be the best gum scraper anyone could be, and do it with a smile. I tell people who just got laid off: Your edge is that you are now untethered to fixed assumptions. You're free. It's hard to look at the world with clear eyes when you're trapped within a system. With all options on the table, you can start anew and really figure out what ought to come next. What are *your* leverageable assets?

Think about it:

● **What do you do better than anyone else?** Byron Jones jumps. Christina Tosi bakes. How about you?

● **Who or what do you hold special access to?** You might not think you have an answer here (especially if you don't know any billionaires). But everything we do gives us access to particular worlds that few others see. When I was helping to build the 9/11 Memorial, my insight into zoning issues and land use made me the perfect hire for a football team looking to build a new stadium. Was the connection obvious to everyone? No, but the knowledge I had made me unique. Keep an eye out for opportunities in your broadly defined wheelhouse, and don't let lack of domain

expertise deter you when you know you have the insights you
need.

◉ **How does your reality—past or present—give you a special
perspective on the world?** I only thought to drop out of school, get
my GED, and go right to college because my mother had done
exactly that as an adult. It almost surely never would have crossed
my mind if I hadn't already seen the fact pattern in a different
context.

It's really all about the framing. I could look at my childhood
struggles as something that could hamper me for my entire life,
or I could see them as having opened my eyes to the struggles people experience in the world, giving me particular empathy for those
who have overcome and insight into what someone needs when
they're at their lowest. I can use that knowledge to help build brands
that transform the lives of those who require the most help. That's
not my only leverageable asset, but it's absolutely one of them, and
you have plenty of your own, too.

◉   ◉   ◉

The very same principle applies to businesses themselves: you find
their leverageable asset, and you extend out. Although I don't have
a sweet tooth, my years as an investor in Milk Bar have given RSE
valuable experience scaling a bakery brand. When we heard that
Magnolia Bakery was for sale, we knew we could draw upon our experience with Milk Bar to restore this beloved American institution
to its rightful place. Once the darling of pop culture in the halcyon

days of *Sex and the City*, the place where Carrie Bradshaw would indulge her cupcake cravings on a bench in the West Village, Magnolia had since fallen somewhat off the map. And yet, walk down Bleecker Street on any Saturday morning and you will see tourists from all over the world snaking around the block in pursuit of banana pudding. The love affair with Magnolia Bakery has sustained itself for more than two decades.

My team and I acquired Magnolia Bakery in the middle of the pandemic. And we knew that our Milk Bar experience, turning bakery wonders into consumer-packaged goods that could be enjoyed by customers nationwide, was the asset we needed to turn around the business.

The brand had remained frozen for two decades because it was under-resourced, and now we had the ability to finally give it the rollout it deserved. We ended up hiring a chief marketing officer and building our own infrastructure to sell banana pudding to anyone in the country, expanding e-commerce sales from $900,000 to $10 million. Up next? Going to retail in stores across the nation. The advantage? Name recognition. The play became simple because we already knew the playbook: get product into people's hands through as many channels as we can while preserving the special experience that draws long lines of people to NYC's West Village—and now, to Stephen Ross's Hudson Yards project, too.

Big Leaps, Not Incremental Progress

Everything we do has an opportunity cost. I see so many people who think they need to earn their next move, to pay their dues, to wait for the world to recognize their potential and pluck them from their current role into some dream future that I can assure you is never going to manifest itself.

I shake my head when I see friends who are waiting for one promotion after the next, thinking they are on a ladder to the top—and then one day the organization hires someone from outside instead. That loyal employee isn't the boss's darling anymore, the career trajectory stalls, and they are left to stagnate. I left the mayor's office twice rather than wait for them to one day decide that I deserved a promotion. By leaving, I accelerated my path, because I was no longer beholden to their hierarchy and could come back at a new, higher level.

Forgoing the incremental path sounds counterintuitive, especially when we're scared. We imagine we should take things slowly, make small changes, and eventually it will lead to meaningful progress. But all that does is extend our journey and give us more and more opportunity to turn back.

Jesse Derris and I debate this point all the time. He proposed raising a small fund before we raised a big one—but why? What skills was he going to learn raising $10 million that were standing in his way from raising $100 million? The most impactful conversations I have with people are when I take away their misconception that everything they think is necessary actually isn't required at all. *No one will take me seriously as a founder unless I have ten years of experience. No one will hire me to run a project this big if I haven't already run three smaller projects in the same industry. No one will give me money unless I already have money.* I'm here to tell you that these are all lies and they're holding you back. You can go straight to the goal—just like I went straight to college. Who needed the rest of high school?

I'm not denying that experience is critical if you need to develop a new skill. We can't all jump right to the apex of our careers. But I believe we each have an innate understanding of whether we truly need experience to grow—or if we're ready, and just hoping the world will grant us our turn. Waiting in line is for kids; as an adult, you need to take your turn. So often, it's the people in our lives with the most compromised motives who tell us to be patient. The jealous spouse. The insecure boss. The frenemy we can't seem to live without. Approach all such counsel with healthy skepticism. The stakes are so high. One bad piece of advice to bide your time could shave years off your growth trajectory. When you know you're ready, you're ready—and you shouldn't let other people's notions of how slowly you ought to be moving ever hold you back.

◉ ◉ ◉

Alexander Harstrick was a rock star, a former military intelligence officer who had worked in the Pentagon, served in Iraq, and was now getting his MBA at Harvard. He had a dream to launch his own investment fund in the defense industry—and the knowledge to do so—but assumed he didn't have enough experience.

Alex had an ironclad thesis centered around military innovation and the connections and experience to produce phenomenal deal flow. It should have been easy. Yet, sitting in my office, he was nervous. Alex had bought into conventional wisdom and felt like he had no choice but to take a subpar offer from a private equity shop in New York and "pay his dues." I questioned his incrementalist mindset.

"But who is going to back me?" he asked. "Who is going to write me a check fresh out of school?"

"No one," I said. "Until someone does."

I didn't hear from him for a few months. One afternoon, he

called to ask for my address. He wanted to send me some swag—a hat, a pen. "Swag from what?" I asked.

"Oh," he replied. "From the fund I started after I walked out of your office."

I had assumed Alex had settled into a mundane existence at that big private equity shop in New York City. Turns out, the day after we talked, he rejected the job offer. Instead, he pounded the pavement to find an anchor investor for a new fund. *His* fund, J2 Ventures.

"Not only did I find one, after more *no*s than I can remember," he told me, "but I closed a ten-million-dollar fund, and now I'm raising fifty million."

I'm one of his investors, and proud to be.

"The most surprising thing I've found about starting something new," Alex continued, "is how un-scary it has been. This is not to be confused with thinking things have been easy—far from it—but the value I've received from the work I've done and the business that my team has built, relative to the actual work we put in, has never been more balanced. Since we got started, the only scary thought I've had is that there could ever be a world where I would go back to working for someone else."

One simple decision to adopt a step change mindset changed the entire trajectory of Alex's life. We are wired to believe our lives evolve like colorful stacks of sedimentary rock, each achievement gently layered upon the last. We think there is some preordained sequence to success, that you have to have the lemonade stand before you build the global lemonade business, that you need to raise $10,000 before you can raise $10,000,000, or that you need experience as a CEO before you allow yourself to lead. None of it is true, if you look at how the world really works. The notion of incremental progress is just our attempt to impose order onto the chaos of life and reduce success to some kind of discernible formula. *Pay your dues and you'll be rewarded with upward mobility.* In reality, the greatest spoils usually go to the ones who refuse to submit to a typical road map.

We presume slow and deliberate incrementalism when there's not necessarily a reason to. Skip the steps you don't need, and make the jumps that will put you on the highest ground so that your next leap can take you even higher.

"The research actually shows that if you center your decision-making around passion instead of the normal trajectory of a career, you end up learning faster and being more successful," says Francesca Gino from HBS. "A lot of our MBA graduates end up going to consulting firms. They think they'll be there two years and then jump to a venture of their own, but the timing is never right. There's never the moment to get to that."

Before deciding you need to take a small step instead of a big leap, ask yourself: What makes you think this is the necessary sequence of events? Do you actually think these incremental steps are giving you skills you need to succeed, or are you just trying to satisfy an imaginary external audience and needlessly delaying the inevitable?

◉　◉　◉

The incremental approach is why I urge people to escape corporate hierarchies whenever they can. Traditional business models try to organize people at scale, keep them in bands and move them slowly up the chain. This is the trap of places like law firms or consulting firms. You're part of a class of similarly situated employees and there are few ways to stand out and rise to the top more quickly than your peers.

Expedient for the firm. Soul-crushing for you.

For someone who aspires to more, it becomes a long waste of time. You need to resist attempts to lock you in place or limit your growth. I tell people not to be afraid to quit their jobs if they know they deserve more and don't see a path to getting there—it's much faster to take a leap up the ranks in someone else's hierarchy. When you move to a new organization, you are born anew and get a fresh start. And, yes, of course, stay at a job if you love it—but only if you love it. You don't have to leave, but you need to always remember that you can, and should, if your growth is being stunted. Never look to one job to satisfy every career aspiration. If you're ambitious, that's not realistic, as you will almost surely evolve faster than the corporate world can accommodate.

◉ ◉ ◉

I make this point, and then I catch myself wondering if I'm making it sound too easy. It's hard to stray from the typical path, I know. And it's made even harder by all sorts of considerations, both within our control and entirely outside of it. I find myself wondering if I could have made the leaps I've made in my career if I was carrying the kinds of weight that a lot of people in our society are forced to shoulder.

On the last day of my Harvard Business School class in January 2022, I had an incredibly frank conversation about race—as important as anything we had covered in the course—with a remarkable student, Tracey Thompson. After a session with a white male entrepreneur whose crass language and casual style were integral parts of the image he projected to the world, Tracey, a Black woman whose mother immigrated to New York from Jamaica, confided in me that she would never be able to present herself in the same way in front of an audience.

"Why not?" I asked.

Her answer was that it wasn't just that she would worry that others wouldn't respect a Black woman who spoke that way. It was that she felt like she carried the reputation of her race and gender on her back wherever she went, and that she had a duty to represent them well—or others who followed in her footsteps would be judged accordingly. In her mind, there was no margin for error.

This weight—this burden—is something that, frankly, I've been privileged to avoid my whole life. I've never worried that I was representing anyone other than myself, and I know that I've surely been given the benefit of the doubt so many times because of my gender and race.

I'd like to think that as a society we're moving in the right direction on these issues, but I also recognize that people have burdens that I don't, and that their ability to make bold choices is affected by how they're perceived in the world, and the obligations they carry with them. That's why Tracey's career aspiration—to tear down the barriers of institutional racism and back diverse founders and diverse businesses as a venture capitalist—is so inspiring to me.

"It's not even just about investing in Black-owned companies," Tracey explains. "I want to help get more people of color on boards and cap tables, even if they're not minority-owned. I want to support companies that have diverse supply chains and employ a diverse set of people. I want to train more venture capitalists of color, and foster a new generation of companies that are more equitable and at the same time more financially successful. I want to prove that people of color can run great businesses and that diversity and success can feed off each other."

We can only do that if we recognize that the barriers standing in the way are different for everyone—and that society has stacked the deck unfairly against certain people. If everyone is to have the fullest amount of agency over their lives and power over their destinies, then the ultimate goal should be a quest to level the playing field for everyone, so that outcomes are not distorted by factors outside of our control.

Every Journey Is Easier than the One That Came Before

Exiting a job, or leaving a secure-but-limited-upside role, especially to go out on your own, is inevitably going to be intimidating the first time you do it. You don't have a bank of experiences in your mind to reassure yourself that you can do it, and that it will all turn out okay. The second time, it's easier. The third time, even easier than the second. And by the time you've become a master at burning the boats, you don't even have to think about it. The research around habituation supports the obvious proposition that things are easier when you've done them before. Taking risks is simpler when you've already taken risks.

But habituation can also hurt us. I worry that even if habituation might make my life more efficient, the price of that efficiency would be a loss of creativity—the very creativity that fuels the insights necessary for continued growth and success. Habituation can be a great tool, but beware of becoming a robot.

Studies have shown that we get used to workplace distractions— phone calls in the background, a coworker's strong perfume—and notice them less and less.[5] But that same research says that we also stop noticing how systems keep us down, and how the structure of an organization can limit us. In 1974, Harry Braverman wrote a seminal work on the psychology of the workplace. In *Labor and Monopoly Capital*, he devotes an entire chapter to "the habituation of the worker to the capitalist mode of production." His point: organizational hierarchy trains us to accept terrible working conditions.[6] We cannot let ourselves get habituated to boredom, to monotony, and to the crushing of our entrepreneurial spirit. (That could have been Jesse Derris, if he hadn't made the leap to start his own firm.)

The first time I taught at Harvard, it was all-consuming. But the second time, it was much less of a lift. We get a real increase in efficiency the more times we do something. That enables us to do so much more simultaneously. On the other hand, the challenge becomes how to perform at your best when performance becomes automated.

Dwayne "The Rock" Johnson gave a great talk on this topic to the NBA's Los Angeles Lakers. "Keep your back against [the wall]. . . . Play angry."[7] My biggest struggle is how to summon the demons that drive me when I start feeling too confident. My mind is always on fire, and I often have to resist the temptation to move on to the next thing before the last one has reached a steady, self-perpetuating state. I forget that the point isn't to keep moving, but to maximize the heights you can reach in every pursuit.

In the blunt words of my partner Stephen Ross: *Don't be a grasshopper.* "If you have a great idea, you need to stick with it," he says, "and not just run to somebody else's great idea. You have to actually see an idea through to execution, and make sure there's the right team in place, before you let yourself jump." If you leave too soon, you don't let yourself reap the rewards of your insight and your work. You exit before the windfall, before the world matures to see what you created. You feel like you need to chase the rush, find the pressure again, but you miss the opportunity to truly capitalize. Eventually the grind will wear you down. A litany of half-finished projects will be left in your wake and they will chip away at your self-esteem.

To keep performing at your best, even when the pressure may feel like it's off, you have to shift motivational systems, from the optimal anxiety of chapter 4 to the pursuit of greatness. You give your all not just to get through it, but to chase the ever-rising ceiling on your potential.

What Can You Do Today That You Couldn't Do Yesterday?

Every time I achieve something new, I immediately look for something to build on that success—often in ways that weren't necessarily obvious beforehand. Once I started investing in companies, suddenly I had the kind of experience that could land me on *Shark Tank*. Once I had the *Shark Tank* seal of approval, I could teach at HBS. Once I taught at HBS, I could write a book. What can you do today that you couldn't do yesterday that moves you closer to what you want to do tomorrow? If you've still got a pulse, then there's always something else you should want to do tomorrow. And every new thing you achieve in life puts you in a better position to secure whatever that next milestone is.

An exciting and freeing thought experiment: If you ignored the limits, and assumed you could do anything, what is it that you would do with your life?

◉ ◉ ◉

Jesse Palmer was a backup quarterback in the NFL, but he saw something in himself beyond just football. "It wasn't until I got really lucky getting drafted in a media market like New York that my eyes were opened to possibilities and opportunities," Jesse told me.

Jesse ended up as the first professional athlete to appear on *The Bachelor*, back in 2004—and audiences recognized something special. From there, Jesse has continued to find success in television, using a love of food to end up as the host of baking competitions on Food Network, spending two years as a correspondent on *Good Morning America*, and hosting his own show called *DailyMailTV*. "I didn't say no a lot," he remembers now. "Early on, I said yes to a lot of things to really give myself an opportunity to decide whether or not I like doing something. Never in a million years would I have expected to be in the food space, a former NFL player talking about cupcakes and pastries."

Jesse actually wasn't forced to walk away from his life as a backup quarterback. He still had opportunities. But he saw his potential on the media side and made the decision to jump. "It's never easy to walk away, so as much as I was excited about the opportunity to be on TV talking about my passion, it's so hard to replace the rush you feel, the high you get from playing professional football . . . but I had an offer to be on television, and there are only a finite number of those opportunities, so I decided I needed to ride the wave," he says.

Jesse is still riding that wave. He is now the host of TV's *The Bachelor* and *The Bachelorette*. He's nobody's backup anymore.

◉　◉　◉

Picture your highest ambition—and then take the first step. Make the call, build the website, prototype the product, write the book, give the talk, apply for the job, ask the crush on a date, whatever it is—marshal your strength, your courage, and everything in your past that has led you to this point, and start moving.

You might think this is easier for celebrities than the rest of us—

that someone like the incredible actress, my friend Scarlett Johansson, would have no trouble getting a new venture off the ground. But you'd be wrong. There's an entrepreneur inside of her that had been trying to get out for years, but given her prolific acting career, she'd never had the time and energy to invest in really making it happen.

Like many entrepreneurs, Scarlett's vision for her skincare brand, The Outset, was born from her own pain point. Most people would never know it, but Scarlett struggled with acne and "problem skin" into her adult years. She found her solution in a simple, consistent beauty routine of cleansing, prepping, and moisturizing skin every day. While the market was touting trendy but aggressive ingredients and complicated routines, Scarlett believed that great skin starts with the basics, and she knew that people could benefit from a similarly easy and nourishing approach.

"As an actor," she told me, "I've had working skin since I was eight years old. I've tried what feels like every product out there and have worked with the most renowned experts in beauty. As I've matured, so have my expectations of products and the beauty ideals they represent. I saw a gap in the market for clean and effective skincare that simplified and elevated the everyday. But most importantly, I felt that I finally had the confidence to share my point of view."

There was a clear opportunity. It made perfect sense. The big leap for Scarlett was to accept that she wasn't going to be able to do it alone. She couldn't go all in on a business, as many of us can't—so she needed to find someone who could, someone who shared her passion and could turn her idea into a company.

Jesse Derris and I worked with Scarlett to recruit Kate Foster, an entrepreneur whose first startup was acquired by a large media company and who had a track record of success as a beauty and fashion executive at top brands like Victoria's Secret, Ann Taylor, and Juicy Couture. Together, the smart and committed duo raised millions to support their vision for an everyday skincare collection that would be like "the perfect white tee" of skincare.

The Outset was born, and as I'm writing this, they have just launched online and at every Sephora store in the US. I'm so proud to be advising them along the way. Scarlett's path is different from mine, and certainly very different from most people's. But the thinking is exactly the same:

◉ How can you make your dream happen?

◉ What ingredients do you need to get from where you are now to where you want to be?

◉ How can you consolidate the gains that came before to give you the best chance of success on your next endeavor?

Of course, just like Scarlett's partnership with Kate, we rarely leap alone.

CHAPTER 8

SUBMIT TO THE GREATNESS OF OTHERS

I met Gary Vaynerchuk when I was still working for the Jets, back in 2009. At that point in his career, Gary was a wine entrepreneur in suburban New Jersey—or, more accurately, a YouTube wine critic with a growing audience, a star on the fledgling platform, trying to expand his family's wine business by taking it online. I was meeting with Gary—a rabid Jets fan—to try to extract some of his newfound wealth for the team's benefit and sell him a suite at the stadium.

I didn't know Gary, and as I prepared for our lunch meeting at a bagel shop in Springfield, New Jersey, I assumed we were going to have a pleasant chat about our favorite reds and whites, and I might learn something about the wine business. I couldn't have been more wrong. What I didn't realize until we sat down was that wine might have been Gary's business, but it wasn't his destiny. It was just his entry point into the Internet, and an online world he saw unfolding in ways that sounded crazy at the time but ended up being exactly right.

In our first ten minutes, he was telling me about the seismic shifts soon to be unleashed by the Mark Zuckerbergs and Jack Dorseys of the world, predictions about where the world was heading, identifying patterns, and seeing years into the future. Twitter was showing us all that we have the ability to be content creators, he was insisting, and it was going to leave corporations flat-footed because individuals could make one-on-one connections and move quickly in a way that organizations couldn't.

He pitched out his idea for a firm that could bring companies into the new world of social media, show them how to beat the system before their competitors even understood there was a system to beat . . . and it all clicked. His frenetic bravado punctuated with obscenities in every breath, Gary would have been easy to dismiss. In fact, that's exactly what most "serious" people did when Gary spouted off: they disregarded him. Instead, they should have listened far more carefully.

I knew that if we properly resourced Gary, he could change the way the Jets reached our fans. He didn't buy a suite, but we cut a deal to make the Jets the first client of VaynerMedia, his yet-to-be-launched marketing firm, trading him four fifty-yard-line Jets tickets (that he still owns to this day) in exchange for him developing our social media vision.

Gary and I have been working together ever since. When I moved to RSE, Stephen Ross saw Gary's genius, too, and knew that he could be a differentiator as we built our portfolio of businesses. We became his only partner and acquired a significant stake in his company. VaynerMedia now does a quarter of a billion dollars in annual revenue, with clients like TikTok, Unilever, and PepsiCo, offices around the world, and awards too numerous to count. The scrappy agency that started out managing Twitter accounts for anyone who could write a check now produces Super Bowl ads for Fortune 100 companies. Gary has also written five bestselling books, and I've been along for the whole ride. The guy I listened to ranting in a bagel store in New Jersey hasn't changed his methods— except that when he talks now, he reaches 20 million people with a single comment.

I saw it, and others should have, too—if only they'd ignored the unlikeliness of a profane hustler of a wine salesman understanding the online world better than anyone else on the planet and jumped in with both feet.

◉   ◉   ◉

A friend of mine recently asked me what the one key to my professional success over the past decade has been. "It's not like you've invented a great product or built a great business," he told me. And he's right. But what I have done is made an incredibly important transition from believing that I had all the answers and could get to the top myself to realizing that the key to success at the highest levels and the largest scale is to find people who are better than you at everything one could possibly need to do, and submit to what makes them incredible.

It's inspiring to be humbled every day. It's easy to get bored with yourself, and far more interesting to bask in the glory of others, to sit in the reflection of the awesome people around you. This has been the single best pivot in my life, to realize that it didn't all have to be on my shoulders, and I could instead devote myself to elevating others and then harnessing their gifts for our mutual benefit.

This chapter is about serving and empowering others. To do it effectively, it's a pretty simple formula: identify their gifts, don't hold them back, and then do whatever you can to unlock their potential. Follow that blueprint, and you'll realize the lesson I've learned over and over again: It's not about ideas, it's all about people.

Identify Greatness

We've already discussed many of the qualities I look for in others. First, there are the pragmatic optimists I covered back in chapter 2, who will help you nurture and nourish your ideas rather than tearing you down. I've never met a wildly successful pessimist. And then there are those who combine confidence and humility, the perfect combination to be a founder worth investing in.

Four more characteristics that I've found to be predictive of success:

- **Empathy.** You have to feel for other people, understand their needs, and appreciate their pain. You need to step outside of yourself and put yourself in other people's shoes in order to see the full picture of a situation, get a 360-degree vantage point, and solve problems.

- **Defiance.** I'm not talking about being bullheaded or angry—by "defiance," I mean insisting on your picture of the future and refusing to be swayed. As Jeff Bezos has said about Amazon, "We are stubborn on vision. We are flexible on details."[1] You can't be a pushover. Just like Dr. Laura Finfer said in chapter 6, you can't be too deferential to authority. If you know you're right, you have to advocate for your position, and not stand silently by as someone else makes the wrong decision, or pushes your organization in

the wrong direction. At the end of the day, we are all empowered
agents, even if exercising that power ends up meaning that we
choose to walk away.

⦿ **Detail.** There are a vanishingly small number of people who truly
   subscribe to the idea that incremental effort, however slight, can
   make a disproportionate difference—but it's absolutely true. I'm
   not talking about the negative spin we often put on the notion
   of perfectionism, wasting endless time without clear benefit just
   to avoid a mistake. But I do think there is unappreciated value
   in getting the details right. "How you do anything is how you do
   everything," Mike Tannenbaum would often chide slackers when
   we worked together at the Jets and Dolphins. It's an old trope;
   true, nonetheless. I freely admit to caring about the details more
   than many, but that's because the details matter. I call them
   proxies of competence. If you make small mistakes, I bet you'll
   make big ones, too.

⦿ **Finish.** I first appreciated this concept while working with Eric
   Mangini on maximizing players' efforts on the football field.
   Mangini drilled the notion into his team that you need to apply
   maximum effort at all times, play through the whistle, and never let
   up. But it goes far beyond football. In everyone with breakthrough
   talent, no matter their domain, I see that desire to be a little extra
   at the end, that hunger to finish strong. My very favorite keepsake
   from all my professional and personal accomplishments is a
   video of me finishing the Paris Marathon. I have no athletic gifts
   whatsoever—running marathons was an exercise in learning how
   to pace myself. I needed to use a different kind of mental muscle
   than I ordinarily relied upon, finding patience to deploy my energy
   over a long duration instead of in one burst. I had a singular goal

that morning in France: don't just finish the marathon, but finish strong and run the last quarter-mile faster than the first. It meant I had to hold enough gas in my tank to sprint when I saw the twenty-six-mile mark in the distance. I'll never forget the sensation of my chubby self, whizzing past a throng of other finishers for those brief final minutes. There's a tendency to get tired or sluggish when we see the completion of a goal in sight. The challenge is to fight that urge, and instead do your best work right up to—and through—the finish line.

⊚ ⊚ ⊚

So if those are the characteristics that tip the scale in someone's favor, the next question to ask is how you ought to apply them. How do these traits translate into winning on the ground? What I've found is that in any organization, you need to fill four distinct domains, archetypes that make an organization structurally sound: the Visionary, the Catalyst, the Executor, and the Communicator. It isn't necessarily that one person needs to fill each of these roles, but a talented individual must be accountable for every domain—and the founder can't be responsible for all four. We need to recognize which role best fits our skills and temperaments, and then hire and partner with geniuses for the rest.

The Visionary

The Visionary is the person who can see around corners and predict the way the world will unfold ten steps into the future. Gary Vaynerchuk and his magical brain are the perfect example. "The way to see the future is by paying attention to the current," he told me. "I listen to data points, whether I'm looking at the top downloaded apps, going to Reddit, 4chan, Discord, reading Twitter, watching who's emerging on TikTok. In a lot of ways, I see myself as an A&R man at a record label in the 1970s—the guy who had to find the next great artist. Back then I would have been going out to the bars and seeing how the crowd reacted, noticing how they're responding differently to one band than another, then going to show after show to confirm it. No one would ever believe the amount of homework I do to get to my conclusions. People think I'm wasting my time—but spending that time is exactly what you need to do to understand the world, see patterns, and predict the future."

◉ ◉ ◉

Kelsey Falter was the recipient of the first check we ever wrote at RSE. She was a twenty-three-year-old engineer and designer who had recently graduated from Notre Dame, and she had started a company, Poptip, that used natural language processing on Twitter to gauge sentiment around companies or ideas by the nanosecond. By scraping and analyzing unstructured text from tweets and deploying short instapolls, she could see what people liked, what they didn't, what made them excited, angry, sad, or emotional—and then she could use that data to shape strategy for brands and individuals. She had early adopters who loved the product, and a big vision that her software could be used for applications as diverse as selling sneakers or helping someone who might be suicidal before they even realized it. She imagined that data could reveal triggers enabling proactive interventions that could get people help they desperately needed.

Kelsey was so far ahead of the curve on many of her ideas, but what was most challenging about setting her company up for the long haul was getting enough people to see that vision, too. Kelsey's imagination might have made Poptip a billion-dollar business, but the world wasn't quite there yet—in fact it took Twitter and Instagram nearly seven years to launch the functionality that Poptip provided. Vision, even with early product adoption, isn't enough.

What makes Kelsey's story so unexpected is that she understood this, even at such a young age. She knew that it was going to take more than what was there now, and she knew that meant her company was vulnerable. "We had a product that was used and paid for and loved by huge companies on a regular basis," she remembers. "But it was built on risky partnerships."

Kelsey had the confidence to realize that the world might not play out exactly how she hoped and expected. "We were closely embedded with Twitter and Facebook, and had access to their data," Kelsey explains, "but it was a constantly changing landscape, and it was difficult to bank on the trust of a partnership. We didn't know if they were going to cut off data access tomorrow, and that lack of control worried me. We needed to find another way forward, and I knew there was uncertainty there. The iteration that Poptip would have required in order to become a high-price-point software-as-a-service product was too risky to continue with."

At the same time Kelsey was thinking about how to de-risk the landscape ahead, the data analytics company Palantir Technologies, floored by Kelsey's data engine, offered to buy the whole company. "It wasn't my vision to sell," she says, "but I did want to keep my word to my employees and stakeholders. I wanted to return capital to my investors. I knew we could make something great, but it wasn't there yet."

Kelsey had the self-awareness to make what is for many founders an impossible decision: she sold her company before she needed to, in order to avoid a potentially worse fate. "I was talking to investors at the same time as I was talking to two different possible acquirers," Kelsey says. "I was going into pitch meetings the day before I agreed to the Palantir deal, because I wanted to have those options, and be able to make the very best decision. I was directing all of my energy at a positive outcome for the company, even if I didn't know what shape that positive end result would take."

Kelsey stayed at Palantir for a couple of years after the sale to help see her vision through. She was rockstar talented, and shortly after she got to Palantir, she won the company-wide hackathon, competing against some of the most senior engineers around. Palantir went public, and Kelsey never has to work again—but of course she'll be on to something else before you read this, and I'll be right there with her, because I believe not only in her gifts as a Visionary, but in the confidence she has to see the range of future possibilities and operate in a way that maximizes the end result. Our investment in Poptip returned seven times the check that RSE first wrote. It was my earliest lesson in backing the jockey, not just the horse. The lesson here is that when hitching your wagon to someone's star, you'd do well to find yourself a true Visionary.

The Catalyst

If the Visionary is like the writer of a screenplay, that writer needs a producer to actually figure out how to make the movie. The Visionary needs a Catalyst to bring the pieces together and achieve the vision. This is usually a distinct individual. Visionaries rarely have the tools to bring together the people necessary for execution. Catalysts need to be organized motivators, who can identify the right team members, get them excited, and bring them on board. If the Visionary sets the overall agenda, the Catalyst divides it into workable pieces, puts together the actionable plan, and runs the organization on a day-to-day level.

Sean Harper is one of the greatest Catalysts I've encountered. I introduced Sean earlier as the cofounder and CEO of Kin Insurance. Kin has taken on an industry dominated by hundred-year-old giants and shown that better data can change everything. Sean spent five years reengineering how insurers underwrite homes, reducing the calculations to the variables that matter most, and then reinventing the home insurance customer experience for the twenty-first century, going direct-to-consumer and eliminating middlemen. It adds up to an amazing story of industry reinvention—and Sean is the perfect person to be at the helm.

Sean has this calm passion that very few people can hold within themselves. His superpower is to constantly lower the temperature in the room, give people the benefit of the doubt, eliminate anger, and see the forest for the trees. The insurance industry is highly regulated. There are lots of detailed requirements, and at the same time there are constant shifts and changes. To organize and manage a team that can thrive through such complexity is a significant challenge.

"My emotional regulation is a big advantage in business," he told me. "It makes people like to deal with you. It's work to have to massage people's emotions, there's a tax on having to keep someone motivated, or having to process their feelings for them. If you can process your own feelings instead of forcing others to do it with you, then you become so much easier to work with. If other people can feel confident that you aren't going to have an irrational emotional response to things that are going on around you, they will trust you, and be eager to work with you and for you."

It's a remarkable point. Sean talks about the times when crises have been near, and his investors have asked him, "Why aren't you worried?" "Part of it is that I might have more data than they do," he explains, "like if we needed to make payroll and didn't have the cash, but I knew what was in the pipeline, and trusted that the money was on the way. But part of it wasn't about the data at all, it was just about being in control of my emotional response. 'Do you want me to be running around in a panic,' I would ask them, 'or do you want me to be calm and focused?' Faced with that question, the answer is obvious. Of course it's better if I'm calm and focused. It's better for the business, and it's better for everyone who has to deal with me."

If this sounds like someone you know, keep them close, because a Visionary can't make dreams come true without a Catalyst to get them out of bed.

The Executor

Where a Catalyst has to see the forest for the trees, a good Executor can see the trees and ignore the forest, focusing on their particular role and knocking it out of the park. A lawyer is an Executor of one particular silo of a business. The CFO is an Executor. The CTO is often an Executor. These people are sometimes unhappy with those jobs and want to toggle between being Visionaries and Catalysts instead of being content to dive deep into their expertise and use it to find competitive advantages. The Executors in these cases have what I call vision envy. This messes up organizations, because you end up with competing visions, arguments over the division of responsibilities, and a gap in execution.

Part of the problem can emerge when there is a weak link in the

Visionary or Catalyst roles. Someone has to fill those roles, and if the people assigned to do so are failing, then Executors will inevitably feel pressure and obligation to step up, even if it's not a natural fit. Or, if praise is lavished on the vision and the Executor is ignored or deemed an interchangeable commodity, there is potential for envy and struggle. Great Visionaries and great Catalysts will shower recognition on good Executors, because they know they need to communicate appreciation for the role and not inadvertently encourage mission creep. After all, someone has to do the work!

When I think about great Executors, I think about Rachel O'Connell. Before going to Harvard Business School, she worked at a bank by day, but spent her nights volunteering in the fashion world. "It felt so energizing and fulfilling to help creative people bring their vision to life," she told me later. Taking my Harvard class, Rachel didn't necessarily see herself as one of the visionary creators I covered in our sessions, but she did get so excited by the idea of supporting those creators' dreams and adding value wherever she could. Her plan had been to find an internship at a big, traditional retailer or manufacturer, hoping to work her way up the ranks, but the class inspired her to find a way to speed up that journey.

"Hearing entrepreneurs share their passion reminded me that it wasn't working in fashion or beauty that moved me. It was serving and deeply connecting with creative people. I wanted to find that connection right away in a creative-business partnership from the get-go." It's the step change point from chapter 6—don't be afraid to think big instead of plodding along an incremental path.

Talking to her after class, I knew that Rachel was just as much of a special talent as the entrepreneurs I had brought to HBS, because the willingness to serve visionaries is a gift. Rather than resenting them and wishing their success was hers, she leaned into an equally important support role. In fact, in a flash of insight, I knew exactly the right job for her. I happened to know that the cosmetics legend Bobbi Brown, a brilliant creative who admits to having no interest in the numbers, was looking for an analytical brain to help her with a new product line. Rachel said she loved Bobbi Brown, and I couldn't help but think it was fate. I pulled out my phone, put it on the table in the Harvard cafeteria, and said to Rachel, "If Bobbi picks up, it's meant to be." She did, and by the end of our conversation, Rachel had lined up an interview.

"It was such an incredible chance to get the deep learning and personal meaning that only comes from working alongside a creative leader and helping bring her vision to the world," Rachel says. She helped Bobbi Brown launch a new cosmetics line—the creator and the quant, both soaring to new heights—and now works at Estée Lauder, with a limitless career ahead of her because she knows how to serve and how to execute.

In all things business, be sure that you're being honest with yourself about your strengths and weaknesses, and never try to fit a square peg in a round hole. If you've always dreamed of being an entrepreneur, but instead find yourself flourishing in support roles to entrepreneurs, don't let your ego sabotage your success. Be a world-class Executor.

The Communicator

Even when all of the other elements are in place, we underestimate the importance of being able to explain to others what the mission of an organization is, and why the organization has the ability to actually implement the vision. Storytelling is critical—to a range of audiences, from investors to employees to customers to the media—and not just an add-on skill that anyone should be expected to possess. I've worked with companies where executives try to make themselves the company's storyteller, but if they're not great at it, the entire enterprise never gets off the ground.

My friend Tom Carroll is my secret weapon in storytelling. I bring him into companies that have trouble surfacing and articulating their own story. Tom was the CEO of TBWA\Chiat\Day, the global advertising agency that launched Apple in the 1980s, and then relaunched the tech giant with the company's revolutionary "Think Different" campaign when Steve Jobs returned as CEO in 1997. Working with some of the most talented storytellers in the world, Tom is passionate about how to create big, iconic brands—but his skills aren't just important when it comes to reaching consumers, they're important for everyone.

We all intuitively grasp the power of storytelling when it comes to the B2C (business to consumer) world, but the opposite is true when we think about B2B (business to business) marketing. The phrase *B2B* is itself a misnomer, since behind the ones making the purchase decisions at a *B* are simply more *C*s. Everyone you sell to is ultimately a consumer. Every sale is an attempt to transmit belief from one individual to another. Note that I didn't say "transmit necessity." Selling is about feeling. Underpinning all belief is an emotional imperative. To paraphrase the humorist Finley Peter Dunne, great storytelling will comfort the afflicted, and afflict the comfortable.[2]

You can't forget about stories, even in industries where storytelling doesn't seem like the most natural fit. Kin had an incredible insurance story, using data to manage risk better than any of its competitors and thrive in the "new normal" of climate change—while at the same time going direct-to-consumer and enabling self-service and communication via text and social media in the "new normal" of what customers expect in pretty much every industry. But their team was bad at explaining it.

I brought in Tom Carroll to rebrand Kin—the "new normal" phrase comes right from his work—and we helped the company tell its story more effectively than before. The ability to distill and disseminate a message can absolutely shrink the amount of time it takes for the world to understand and buy in. If you're too early for the world, communication is the critical tool needed to close that gap.

I was recently commiserating with legendary investor Cathie Wood about how it can often take longer than you anticipate for others to see what you see. She engineered her own Burn the Boats move when she quit her job as chief investment officer of Alliance-Bernstein in 2014 to go out on her own and start Ark Invest, placing big bets on innovation through several actively managed ETFs, at its peak holding nearly $50 billion in assets under management.

Cathie reminded me that she had been evangelizing for Tesla for a long time before the company's trajectory became obvious to the market. In August of 2018, she went on Twitter to effectively declare a $400 price target on the company, which at the time would have meant an improbable $670 billion market cap. The audacious call was met with derision. The marketplace wasn't there yet.

"We couldn't believe that no one wanted to listen to us," she told Bloomberg in 2020.[3] "They made fun of it. And it made me feel more strongly about Tesla, because what we saw happen over time as the naysayers were growing was that Tesla's barriers to entry were increasing."

Cathie was ultimately proven wrong on her price target, but in the best way—Tesla reached a $1 trillion market cap in 2021. "The market is very inefficient and many of the people who are making the assessments around innovation don't have direct experience with that innovation," she explained to me. Her office is the antidote to that, populated with young analysts who can't wait to figure out what comes next. That culture of intellectual curiosity has propelled her to the pantheon of investor royalty and even spawned a line of merchandise.

People do eventually catch up and understand. But you help yourself immensely with the right Communicator, who can translate your vision and bring it to life.

⊙ ⊙ ⊙

Together, these four domains make up the core competencies of a great organization. And, of course, the humans accountable for each of those competencies need to be incredible players themselves—whether as employees or as founders.

As I said at the top of this section, you can't do it all yourself, and I'm as good an example of that as anyone. People ask me all the time how I manage to run companies, do all of the deals I do, teach at Harvard, and be on TV—and the answer, plain and simple, is that I couldn't do it unless I had a dream team working alongside me as partners to make everything happen.

Uday Ahuja, RSE's Chief Investment Officer, has been with me almost since day one. A graduate of the University of Michigan's Ross School of Business, Uday landed prestigious jobs at Goldman Sachs in investment banking and then private equity before eventually coming to RSE. Uday takes the lead when we decide to move forward on an investment, structuring creative deals, negotiating terms, and managing our entire team through the diligence process. Some days, it seems like Uday's entire job is to deal with the petulant needs of difficult personalities, and yet he is unflappable no matter the problems thrown his way. He's exactly the steady hand I need to counterbalance my enthusiasm. On the legal side, Corrine Glass is my general counsel, a Harvard-educated lawyer who scrutinizes every word of every agreement. She loves structure as much as I do, has a steel-trap memory, and is always finding clever ways to work around problems I haven't even considered. Nothing gets past her. And while Corrine is a tough lawyer, she always acts with the big picture in mind—like the best lawyers do—and never lets partisanship get in the way of a deal.

Together, their ability to execute the end-to-end investment management process unleashes my ability to do what I do best.

The most important thing we all can do is understand our own gifts and where we fit in the mix. But it's not enough to recognize the greatness in ourselves and those around us. We also have to recognize the opposite—when people are causing an organization's demise or limiting its potential for success. Problems generally boil down to one simple fact pattern: someone at the top is holding back the entire organization by being difficult, unsupportive, and short-circuiting the power of everyone around them. Difficult people—Withholders, Hijackers, Victims, Martyrs, and Gaslighters—stand in the way of others reaching their full potential, and become toxic in the pursuit of victory.

Don't Hold People Back

We all end up having to deal with difficult people at times, especially when we find ourselves trapped in other people's hierarchies and subject to their whims. That's part of why I push people to get out of hierarchies and embark on their own. One of my biggest rules is that, whenever possible, I don't deal with difficult people. If you witness someone being rude, dismissive of other opinions, hostile, or disrespectful, even if it's not directly aimed at you, avoid it. Any behavior you see directed at others will eventually be directed at you.

The exception I make, very carefully, is for situations where art is at the center of the activity. I define art broadly—visual arts, performance, culinary arts, writing. Art attracts tortured souls, so I have a higher tolerance for artists being difficult characters. That doesn't mean I ever tolerate meanness or cruelty, but idiosyncrasies, even those bordering on petulance, sometimes need to be indulged for the right person.

The thing you have to remember is that when you're first negotiating with another party—whether it's an investor, a partner, or an employee—you are seeing their best selves. No one leads with their worst. So if their best selves are difficult, or display behavior you can't explain, can't forecast, and can't tolerate, then you need to get out quickly. Please believe me when I tell you that it will never get better—it will only get worse.

There are five patterns of behavior I see over and over again that bring people and organizations down. You want to avoid being one of these, or interacting with them. If you meet any of these toxic personalities, run away.

Withholders

Withholders are unable to deliver praise or feel happy when someone else steps up and contributes to success. These people are wired by insecurity or the need for domination. They resent anyone who possesses skills they don't have, or anyone who doesn't feel the same self-loathing that they themselves are plagued with. If you are thriving, they see it as their mission to bring you down.

If you are too dependent on mentorship, you are susceptible to encountering Withholders and finding yourself in a vicious pattern where you seek approval from someone who will never offer it. Most of us assume people come from a rational place when dealing with others. We assume a job well done will be recognized and rewarded. Withholders trade on those assumptions, and torture the people around them.

If you work for a Withholder, you can't win. You have to leave. I have to admit that I hold two seemingly contradictory views on patience and professional advancement. On the one hand, I've seen how increased responsibility is a leading indicator even as increased compensation may lag behind. Good performers will be rewarded with growth opportunities, and eventually increased pay should come. That's how it ought to work. But not when it comes to Withholders. They will take advantage forever as long as you are a willing accomplice. If you have even the tiniest sense that you might be a Withholder, before you take any other lessons from this book, you must stop withholding. Praise the people around you. Recognize their gifts, whatever they are, and help maximize them. Let gratitude into your heart and whatever ails you will finally begin to heal. There is only good to unlock when you support the people around you.

Hijackers

I get tons of messages on Instagram and LinkedIn, and I feel guilty that I can't realistically respond to most of them. I read them, I really do, and I scan them for signs of serious struggle or depression, where a kind word from me might make an impact on someone. Being surrounded by Hijackers tends to bring these kinds of emotions out in people. They get really desperate, and don't know where to turn.

A young entrepreneur I had never met sent me a direct message on Instagram not too long ago that caught my eye because of her exceptional art. She owned a small business, creating bold designs to elevate cars into statement pieces—wraps that transformed and protected at the same time.

She was messaging to pitch me on wrapping my car like a shark after my *Shark Tank* appearance, but also to ask for advice. She explained that she knew the value of the work she was doing, but somehow she kept finding herself in situations where people simply wouldn't pay her for the product. Someone had commissioned her to do a wrap, and she meticulously labored over it, day and night, for weeks. The customer was satisfied with the work. But not satisfied enough to actually pay her. This was a recurring fact pattern. People would commission work, and then they would find minor flaws to blow out of proportion, and refuse to pay—or simply ghost her.

She was so conflict-averse that she couldn't confront these thieves, and had been unable to summon the confidence to adjust her business to demand payment up front, for fear that it would mean she would never get any orders. She lacked the self-worth to avoid the Hijackers in the world who wanted to steal from her.

I assured her that her work had value, and these people were mistreating her. I told her to be unafraid to demand they pay, and unafraid to demand they pay up front. It's a lesson she had to learn for herself, and over time, she did. She's thriving now, with new-found confidence, and if you're in the market for a wrap, hit up Christina McKay at Curvaceous Wraps and tell her that I sent you. (And pay for it!)

It's not always so brazen and extreme but, essentially, Hijackers are Withholders with the added bonus of aggression. They want to take what you are great at and claim it for themselves, trading on your vulnerability. If you want to honestly extract value from creative genius, you need to be empathetic to the deficiencies of those around you, not looking to exploit them. A great leader will pay someone a fair wage even if they know that person will never have the courage to ask for it. I'm reminded here of &pizza's Michael Lastoria, and the advocacy he has done in favor of raising the federal minimum wage—"the single clearest way to say to our workforce, 'We value you,'" Michael says. In fact, a great leader will go out of their way to compensate the people least able to ask, because that leader sees the immeasurable benefit of people feeling secure, and how that security will bring out their gifts to the maximum extent.

Victims

Generally, good performers live in a place of gratitude. They don't feel entitled to success and so they are thrilled and thankful when it arrives. Victims live instead in a place of constant injustice. They are the people who never overcame their demons and enemies. Victims will see every bump in the road as confirmation that they are being unfairly targeted. This is useless to growth and success. If something bad happens, you can acknowledge it, and learn from it, but you shouldn't build your identity around it.

When I got cancer at thirty-two, I went to a support group and everyone was just so angry that we were now part of the unlucky seven thousand men a year in the United States to be diagnosed with testicular cancer. Keep in mind, we were the lucky ones, being treated for a cancer that has a 95 percent survival rate. We were likely to go on and live long and otherwise healthy lives after treatment. To each his own, but I couldn't relate to my fellow survivors in the group who lamented the unfortunate aesthetic of having one testicle. (I never thought that was the most flattering region of the male anatomy anyway.)

After my cancer surgery, while I was getting radiation treatment every day for almost a month at Memorial Sloan Kettering, I had an epiphany during a *why me?* moment. The inverse of *Why me?* is *Why not me?* I didn't have a good answer as to why someone other than me should take my spot and contend with this misfortune, yet I had plenty of reasons to believe I was better equipped to handle it than most of my peers. Plenty of money. History of relatively worse trauma. Gallows sense of humor. Yeah, why not me? Maybe I was rationalizing, but I derive pride from my work, from my accomplishments, and even my scars. I'm so grateful to be different—to be other than, never less than. Testicular cancer was just another form of exceptionalism. Overnight, I became quite possibly the only GED recipient in America who both graduated from law school and has only one testicle. (And if I'm wrong and there's another one of us out there, please hit me up on Instagram—let's grab a beer, friend!) I spend no time at all lamenting my situation, and you shouldn't either, no matter what that situation is. You are never destined to be a victim. You will always have the last word until your last breath.

I really do think people are the same before a crisis as they are during it. The crisis only amplifies everything that makes them strong or weak. In a crisis, victimhood comes out like never before. Victims see crises as validating everything they believe about the world. Everyone is out to get them. They can't possibly succeed. And then, the prediction comes true, and they fail.

Don't fall into this trap.

Martyrs

Martyrs are kind of like victims who actually do the work—but don't do it well enough to justify the psychological drain they place on an organization, and tend to spread themselves too thin to optimize their performance. Martyrs take on as much as they can possibly handle—and more—but they don't do it to help the team. Instead, they do it to confirm the narrative they carry around about themselves as unjustly forced to take on the burdens of others.

The good news is that Martyrs are coachable and don't necessarily have bad intentions—just like Nick Stone of Bluestone Lane, who went from trying to do everything himself to learning how to delegate, enabling his business to reach new heights. If you can convince someone that the greatest service they can do in pursuit of a cause is to delegate to people best suited to perform the individual tasks, then they can redirect their energy to deploying others instead of taking things all on by themselves. CEOs sometimes become Martyrs due to a lack of maturity or experience or a desire to avoid conflict. If the company has been bootstrapping for a time, it is hard to switch modes once resources are available to hire help. The CEO fails to evolve the definition of the job, and clings to the hero status of having all of the responsibility resting on their shoulders.

Bad leaders can end up rewarding Martyrs as hard workers willing to do anything, but those leaders fail to recognize that doing isn't the same as accomplishing. Martyrdom and victimhood are really two sides of the same coin; to Martyrs, the universe is forcing them to carry an unjust burden, and to Victims, the universe is making it impossible for them to ever succeed. In both cases, it's the universe's fault, and they refuse to take agency over their destiny.

Gaslighters

We typically think of Gaslighters in personal relationships, but they exist in the corporate world as well. Corporate Gaslighters make up the final category of negative influence I regularly see. They will spend their energy trying to rewrite reality, to the detriment of everyone around them, and they often possess narcissistic traits. They combine the qualities of Withholders, Hijackers, Victims, and Martyrs in one, attempting to convince people that they are not seeing what is going on right in front of their eyes.

Back to Elizabeth Holmes and the story of Theranos. She is a classic corporate Gaslighter who tried her best to deflect blame

209

in the face of accusation, and insist that everyone else was seeing something that wasn't really there. Eventually, of course, her fiction crumbled, not unlike the story of Enron, where CEO Jeffrey Skilling used to attack members of the media and make them think they were stupid if they couldn't understand his business—until one intrepid reporter from the *Wall Street Journal* refused to be intimidated.

⊙ ⊙ ⊙

These five archetypes cover what not to do as a leader, and the kinds of people to avoid whenever possible. But how can we turn this on its head? Instead of keeping people down, what can you do to harness the potential of others and ultimately bring order to the universe?

Unlock the Full Potential of Others— Giving You the Freedom to Reach Further

The greatest leaders rise to new heights because they surround themselves with people better than they are at every piece of the puzzle, and then they empower them to maximize their potential. The biggest reward of achieving great things is finding the people on this planet meant to do exactly what they're doing and bringing them along with you. We can all be talent-spotters as well as enablers and fans, helping the people around us shine in whatever capacity they're meant to.

You can do this selflessly and selfishly at the same time. You can support others so that they themselves succeed, but you can also make sure you have a stake in their success. I love when entrepreneurs I back become wealthy beyond their wildest dreams—and I love it even more when I have a 20 percent stake in their business, and I see tangible reward for the work I've put in to help them grow. The honest truth is that you can get very wealthy drafting behind talented people.

This is why one of the biggest indicators of success I see is when there are phenomenal people at every level of an organization—regardless of how good the founders themselves are. I would much rather see average founders with brilliant people unleashing that brilliance throughout a company than tremendously talented founders who are unwilling to surround themselves with people who might outshine them.

I like to say that B players hire C players in order to make themselves seem like A players. But if a B player hires A players, then they're really not a B player anymore. They're an A player, too. You will never be outshined by great people fighting for you. Brilliance is not zero-sum. Within a particular industry, we can get caught up in competing for market share and forget that an even more effective growth strategy is to expand the overall market instead. I don't need your DTC food business to fail in order for mine to succeed, and in fact your success will make more customers eager to find great products, secure in the knowledge that great products are out there—and we can both crush it.

◉　◉　◉

I want to end this chapter by sharing the story of one of the greatest successes I have ever helped to unlock, proof that by recognizing and fostering the talents of others, you can make a real impact in people's lives and on the world.

Aidan Kehoe is the founder of SKOUT CyberSecurity, helping

businesses around the globe solve their security issues. He grew up in circumstances not so dissimilar from mine, but across the Atlantic in Ireland. He emigrated to the United States when he was twenty-three years old, knew one person in Florida, had no money and no visa, and started out as a restaurant dishwasher. The owner of the restaurant saw something in him, and let him open up an outdoor bar for him in exchange for a work visa. Aidan did exactly what I did at McDonald's, making himself indispensable in a role that may not have been his dream, but was the opportunity he had been given. Aidan leaned heavily on his endearing Irish brogue and a bartender's penchant for great storytelling. Before long, he ended up plucked from the bar by the visionary builder and golf course owner Michael Pascucci, hired to work at the world-class Sebonack Golf Club (its course designed by golfing legend Jack Nicklaus) in Southampton, a playground for wealthy New Yorkers a couple of hours east of Manhattan.

Aidan, an entrepreneur at heart, soaked up the wisdom of the club members around him, sought mentorship, and built his network, eventually launching an insurance brokerage on his own and finding his way to RSE. I watched over the years as Aidan identified an even bigger opportunity than selling insurance: cybersecurity. He ran through the same process he had when starting his brokerage, consulting anyone who would give him a few minutes of their time in order to identify an unmet need within the industry. As it turned out, he found one. Hackers were increasingly targeting small and midsize businesses—easy marks that couldn't afford costly precautions and were being ignored by bigger criminal networks. Ransomware incidents skyrocketed in the years leading up to the birth of SKOUT, and Aidan pounced on the opportunity to help these smaller companies.

With the backing of the Pascucci family, Aidan launched his business and became a self-styled expert in cybersecurity, as the CEO of SKOUT. Despite his lack of formal training, he identified with small business owners and could speak their language. When their files were taken hostage, small business owners didn't want to talk to someone working in a call center overseas. They trusted Aidan, and he became a valuable resource. But Aidan knew that building the business was going to drain cash for years during the ramp-up. He needed to be part of an investment company with deep pockets, and the constitution to stomach losses. He convinced me and Stephen to buy the nascent firm from him outright.

Looking back, honestly, Aidan could have probably convinced me to invest in anything, because what he most convinced me of was his own hidden genius that needed to be unlocked. The more I got to know him, the more I found myself turning to him for help working through the most complex fact patterns. His gift was being able to see through the noise and understand what was really going on. He was and is earnest, scrupulously honest, humble, and supremely self-aware—but he lacked the skills to scale a business. His deep empathy was usually an asset, but when it came to tough personnel choices, Aidan chose to work around the weak links and shoulder more and more of the load himself in order to compensate. A classic Martyr. But, as I've said, Martyrs can be taught and are often well-intentioned. What did I do? I brought in Dr. Laura Finfer.

I wanted Dr. Finfer to help unlock Aidan's power. To her, what made Aidan special was his willingness to grow, learn, and improve. She spoke to fifteen of Aidan's employees to get an understanding of what was happening at the company, and put together a ten-page report that was brutal in its honesty. There were problems with communication, with people's roles being properly defined, with the vision of the company, and so much more. Dr. Finfer felt the challenges in the report might be insurmountable, and that Aidan just wasn't going to end up the right leader to take his organization to the next level.

But Aidan shocked both of us with the intensity of his response. After a week to digest the report, he sat in a conference room with me and Dr. Finfer and downloaded the findings with such openness and transparency that it was uncomfortable. He didn't want to run out of that room, though the emotions were so raw that I did. When he finished downloading, he excused himself for a moment so that he could walk into the conference room next door, where there was a senior leadership team meeting taking place.

"You might as well all pass this around and read it, since nothing in here is going to surprise any of you. I've got a lot of work to do."

He tossed the report in the center of the table and walked out. I have never seen a mic drop like that in my career. Dr. Finfer had never seen such a bold move either. On the one hand, she thought it was politically unsophisticated—who leaves themselves so vulnerable to their team?—and yet on the other hand, so powerfully brilliant. By admitting your weaknesses—indeed, by showing them to your team, in black and white on the page—you are acknowledging to them that you are not perfect, and they aren't either. You are owning your flaws instead of hiding them. He asked his team to hold him accountable to fix everything on the list. Aidan admitted that he needed help, and he committed to change.

"The report rocked my world in a big way," Aidan remembers. "I never got such professional and accurate feedback about myself—but what was great is that it was able to become a road map for how to get better. I literally had it in front of me every single day, with a plan to address each of the problems and challenges it presented. I understood that I needed to grow at a faster rate than my company was growing, or else the company would be limited by me and my capabilities."

Sharing the report with his team was Aidan's way of burning the boats. Once they saw him at his worst, there was no turning back. He was all in on transforming his behavior and his business. His team knew from that point forward how much he cared. "Whatever you think you're hiding," Aidan remembers me telling him, "everyone else already knows. So if people know it already, why wouldn't I share it? I wanted to put my hand up and say, I know I'm not perfect, but I will do my best to get better. And then, when other people in the company saw that I was really open to talking about how I needed to improve, they were able to have the same conversations about themselves." It became a virtuous cycle of self-awareness and massively impactful improvement.

But that makes it sound too easy. After Dr. Finfer's report, it was an incredibly difficult journey for Aidan. He was facing a lot of challenges at home—his eldest son had been diagnosed with autism spectrum disorder, and his daughter was now facing health challenges of her own—and at the same time we had taken on new investors who were mercilessly holding Aidan's feet to the fire. Buyer's remorse is a nasty form of acid reflux. These investors felt like Aidan had brought them in at an inflated valuation, and they were determined to extract their commensurate pound of flesh. They were subjecting Aidan to unrelenting pressure.

I had warned Aidan that his team would be no match for sophisticated investors. The leader of the investment firm was a wonderful visionary who signed on for the same reasons we did, to back the jockey, but he was flanked by technocrats—under-indexing on feelings, short on empathy, all about the numbers—and I knew from experience that they would grind Aidan down. Of course, they were just doing their job. Private equity technocrats are suspicious of humans who over-index on the soft skills, so Aidan needed to assemble an ambidextrous team capable of speaking Excel to investors and human to customers. Easier said than done.

Aidan called me one night, at his lowest. He had sent me a photo of his daughter wrapped up in an EKG monitor, undergoing an overnight sleep study to look for the cause of her seizures. "My daughter was in the hospital," Aidan remembers, "and our new investors were really unhappy. We had employees leaving, we were struggling with sales, my world was collapsing, I hadn't slept in weeks, and we were in a business that was so intense in the first place, with clients panicking over security breaches. I called Matt and told him that I couldn't do it anymore, and that I would leave at the end of the year."

I stepped out of the dinner and paced outside. Aidan was crying through his words. "I think I'm done," he said. "I'm not cut out for this, and I'm so sorry I've failed you."

"I've been around long enough to know when someone's done," I told him, "and you are not even close. When you're done, I will call you and tell you. In the meantime, you need to take a break. Your daughter is in the hospital, you are up all night every night. You need to shut down now!"

It was a seminal moment for the business, and for Aidan personally. "Once you surrender, there's a release after," Aidan explained later. "I knew it was going to be okay. I was so emotionally invested in the company, in its success, and in the people working there, I just wanted to make sure I didn't let anyone down." After that conversation, he did it. Over the course of the next six months, Aidan rebuilt his entire executive team, adding two senior leaders who were absolutely fantastic, the most important hires he had ever made, a CFO and a head of sales I knew would change the trajectory of the whole company. In addition, he reinvented the business model, changed the way communications at the company worked, improved his own personal health, and eventually found a pot of gold at the end of the rainbow.

Two years after he hit bottom, in 2021 SKOUT CyberSecurity was purchased by Barracuda Networks, at a price well into nine figures before the business's fifth anniversary. Aidan is walking away with enough money to last him the rest of his life and beyond.

One of the new leaders we had recruited wasn't set to get paid for a year after the deal closed, to make sure he didn't leave. At Aidan's behest, I worked to get the deal changed and get him a check up front. He deserved it. The whole team deserved it. Aidan's turnaround was the most unbelievable business accomplishment I had ever witnessed.

Dr. Finfer agrees. "In my world," she told me, "executive coaching is effective when the person is intelligent, self-aware, and motivated. Aidan was all three—and that's seventy-five percent of the battle right there. The rest is guidance from those who can supply new ideas or new ways of looking at things." Dr. Finfer supported Aidan on that journey. So did I, and so did lots of the people he worked with. Aidan did so much work, but it was truly a team effort to turn the ship around.

◉　◉　◉

Sharing Aidan's story brings me so much joy. I didn't realize when I first started out how much reward I would find in unlocking the potential of others, proof positive that altruism enhances your own sense of well-being.[4] Professor Carolyn Schwartz of the University of Massachusetts Medical School has found that helpers are happier and less depressed than those who don't fall into that category.[5] We're rewarded with a "warm glow" that has been identified in the brain MRIs of people acting in the service of others.[6]

I love to marvel at what others can do, and I love to find ways to help them bring those talents to the world. A big part of my journey has been to find ways to devote more time to this part of my life. How can I not live my life doing that for others, whenever I'm able to?

Burning the boats can put you in a position to find what stirs the most powerful feelings within you. You push further and further, you find what resonates in your soul, and you build a life doing more of it. What's the end game? The best part is that you never have to decide. You just keep on going.

CHAPTER 9

MANIFEST
YOUR BOLDEST
DREAMS

———————

I grew up hooked on baseball cards, and for some reason I can't quite remember, I idolized one player above all the rest, the Montreal Expos (and later Chicago Cubs) outfielder Andre Dawson, aka The Hawk. A monster hitter and equally impressive fielder with a mantel full of awards, and ultimately induction into the Baseball Hall of Fame, Dawson had such a smooth swing that he made hitting 438 career home runs (forty-sixth most all-time as I write this) look effortless. They say you should never meet your heroes, or at least expect to be disappointed when you do, but I'm pretty sure Andre Dawson would prove to be an exception based on what has happened since his retirement from baseball in 1996.

In what has to be one of the most unusual professional juxtapositions among celebrities, in 2003, he started running a funeral home in Miami, Florida, and has been there ever since. As profiled by ESPN and others, he does whatever task is required of him, driving a hearse one day, and greeting mourners the next. "You don't know where God is going to lead you," he has said, "and this never would have—in my wildest imagination—been something I would have thought that I'd be doing. But I feel like maybe this is my calling."[1]

◎ ◎ ◎

You think about his story, and maybe it doesn't feel like the same kind of Burn the Boats journey I've been talking about throughout this book. For you, it might not be—and for me, it might not be, either. I don't want to run a funeral home. I honestly can't imagine doing so. But Andre Dawson's journey isn't mine. I give him a ton of credit for being able to put aside the status and fame of his professional sports career and chase fulfillment. And in that way, his story makes exactly the point I wanted this book to conclude with: burning the boats is about owning the journey. It's about giving yourself the best opportunity to divine the path that's right for you, manifesting your dreams no matter what they are, and seeing them through no matter how far-fetched, silly, or implausible they might seem.

Micah Johnson climbed up the professional baseball ladder just like Andre Dawson. After a stellar stint in the minor leagues, he made the White Sox opening day lineup as the team's second baseman in 2015, recording a hit his second time up. But it wasn't to last. Over the next four seasons, it was up and down for Johnson, across six different organizations, spending much of his time back in the minor leagues. After the 2018 season, he retired at just twenty-eight years old. But that's not the end of his story. While playing baseball, he discovered a passion for art, and started painting, whenever he could find the time. "My teammates saying they liked my art was the affirmation I needed to give me the confidence to pursue it," he told me. And he pursued it with the same energy he'd pursued his sport. "I'd seen the results of hard work, the sacrifices over decades in order to reach the levels I did in baseball. I knew the same thing would apply to my art. I would get better and better, as long as I kept working at it," he says. Johnson had a solo art exhibition at Atlanta's Woodruff Arts Center in 2017—while he was still playing professional baseball—and began working on commissions for his fellow players, drawing portraits and even a tattoo for one teammate. He could have continued bumping around the league, hoping for another chance at baseball stardom. Instead, he chose to retire and focus his energy full-time on his art, confident that he would only continue to improve.

In 2019, with no job and no sales, Johnson discovered NFTs and jumped in with both feet. His young nephew asked him if astronauts could be Black, which launched him on an artistic mission that he knew could be far bigger than baseball: he would create art to inspire children to dream. Johnson committed everything to this endeavor. He moved from North Carolina to New Hampshire with his girlfriend and infant daughter during the pandemic, working all-nighters in his art studio to craft the perfect collection. And over the past year, he has generated more than $2 million dollars in sales, built around his Black astronaut character, Aku, who has since become the first NFT property optioned by a television studio. He's not done yet. "I haven't reached the tipping point," Johnson says. "My goal is to reach millions of kids around the world, to inspire them to understand that they can be anything, no matter their circumstances, and no matter what they have to overcome."

Johnson has made far more money as an artist than he did as a ballplayer, a second act that's simply astonishing, and proof that when you think you've reached the apex of your career, you might just be standing in the nadir of your destiny.

◎ ◎ ◎

Laurie Segall was a CNN journalist for almost a decade, covering tech companies like Facebook and Apple beginning in 2008. "I started there right out of the recession," she remembers, "when there was no startup beat. The iPhone had just come out, and suddenly it wasn't cool to go to Wall Street anymore. I was drawn to these creators, these out-of-the-box thinkers who were entering the tech scene. I was interested not just in their products and companies, but in who they were as people, and in covering not just technology but where it intersects with humanity and society."

Laurie went on to become senior technology correspondent, interviewing tech leaders from Salesforce's Marc Benioff to Uber's Dara Khosrowshahi and talking to Mark Zuckerberg more than any other reporter. But she saw cable news changing as people moved away from traditional sources of content, and she craved being in the driver's seat. "I had always been a self-starter," she says, "from initially getting my job off a pitch to create a beat that didn't exist, to launching CNN's first streaming show, and I decided that I didn't want to wait for permission to move fast.

"I saw a YouTube video of a rabbi talking about how lobsters grow," Laurie continues, "and how they need to go through a period of discomfort, they need to shed their shell. And it clicked for me. That's what I needed to do. I needed to create my own media company instead of just reporting on what others were doing. I went to [former CNN head] Jeff Zucker and told him I wanted to leave. He asked me to stay on in some capacity, but I knew I wasn't going to succeed unless I was all in. I had to cut the cord. Jeff had been my mentor, and I trusted him, and I was so flattered that he wanted me to stay, but I said to him, 'Jeff, let me tell you how lobsters grow.' And I did it."

In 2019, Laurie launched a production company, Dot Dot Dot, focused on telling stories about the intersection of technology and humanity. "I left the job a million journalists would have killed for, but I knew I wanted to create." Her leap was not without fear. "I can say this because I've been in media my whole career," she explains. "We make this process seem so easy after the fact. We put people who burn the boats on the covers of magazines after they've become wildly successful—but failure, and the roller coaster of ups and downs, is part of every journey. I loved journalism, I loved what I did, and I was great at it, but it wasn't enough. How long can you sit with the feeling that it's not enough? How long can you let yourself wonder if you have the courage to be afraid before you actually decide to do it? It was scary, and it's scary for everyone, and maybe we just don't talk about the fear enough."

I couldn't say it better myself. I got to know Laurie and was blown away by her courage and her ambition. As we talked, we both realized that her future was destined to involve more than just storytelling and content creation. As I write this, she is in the process of pivoting Dot Dot Dot into the cross-platform media property that is going to bring the metaverse—Web 3.0, NFTs, the future of the Internet—to the masses. Her deep relationships in the tech space will allow her to not just tell stories, but help all of us create and build in the new online world, connecting users to the NFT marketplace, to cryptocurrency, and to the blockchain, and becoming the destination for people to learn about, access, and benefit from the vast new opportunities out there. Laurie and her company will become the gateway to the metaverse.

All of this could only have happened by leaving CNN and going out on her own. "I didn't have any idea how to create a business," she admits, "but I know from being a reporter: if you don't know how to do something, you ask someone who does. I think women especially have this fear that if you don't know how to create a business, you can't create a business—but there have been so many incredible women who have done it, and I'm just so privileged to be trying to follow in their footsteps. The independence I've gained, the opportunity to figure out my own vision instead of having to get my ideas approved by someone else, it has just been the hardest and most rewarding thing I've ever done."

◎ ◎ ◎

Laurie makes a crucial point about the independence she gained from escaping a world where she had to get her ideas blessed by others. This is the real secret of a life and career you're excited to attack each morning: you need to find the path that allows you to fully be yourself, express yourself, and unleash your power in its fullest form. When I was filming my television pilot, I ended up getting to experience a kind of joy I hadn't even realized I was missing. For so many years, across so many endeavors, I'd been self-censoring, holding back part of myself because there were others I felt I needed to defer to or gain buy-in from. I was playing from a place of fear, trying to shine less than the full wattage I was capable of, mindful of the Tall Poppy Syndrome I explained in chapter 2. In other words, I was trying not to get my head cut off.

Now, as the "talent" at the center of the project, I was empowered to be fully myself—and that freedom was fascinating to explore. As Curt Cronin would say in the context of a battlefield, I took the safety off. It's hard to achieve greatness if you're spending mental energy trying to rein yourself in. When I talk about going all in on your dreams, it's not just about eliminating backup plans and hedges—it's also literally about putting all of yourself into the endeavor, and not holding back.

Sometimes the journey to those dreams is onward and upward, but sometimes it isn't. Sugared + Bronzed is a successful sunless tanning and all-natural hair removal chain run by a couple, Courtney Claghorn and Sam Offit, who started with one location when they were twenty-three years old, and built the business up over nearly a decade to ten locations across the country. The profit margin was substantial, and I could see their path to massive growth.

While I was doing diligence on the business, another investor came in and wanted to buy a majority of the company. Courtney and Sam were faced with a choice: Do they cash out, and reap the reward of their hard work, or do they keep pushing to get even bigger, and make an even greater score? There's not a right or wrong decision when you're weighing the possibility of walking away with enough money for your lifetime, and your children's lifetime, versus continuing to try to grow it. It depends in large part on the details, but also on who you are and the kind of life you want to live.

"I think as entrepreneurs we don't always look at the negative and consider the risk," Courtney told me, "and that really made me think about how risky we were being by having all of our eggs in one basket. I think now that we've sold a majority stake, we have less 'do or die' pressure, and the ability to think more clearly about life and business. We were able to buy an amazing home and create a sanctuary. And now we can think more clearly about what we want our next business endeavor to be, how to help other startups find their success, and I can do a lot more charity work. All in all, I'm really happy."

Who could blame her? I mean, for so many people, that's their dream. That's why they start a business in the first place. They want to eventually find that freedom and relieve that pressure.

If I were them, I might have sold, I might not have sold. I sell companies at the same time as we buy companies. While working on this book, my team sold SKOUT. We bought Magnolia Bakery. We're constantly making deals. But here's the lesson of the book: as soon as I do anything, I'm instantly looking at my situation and figuring out what's next.

Not everyone is lining up to turn in their baseball glove (and million-dollar salary) for a mop to clean a funeral home. Not everyone would quit a job as on-air talent for CNN. But that's the point. These are *their* journeys. Yours is going to be different, as you find your own gifts, your own passions, your own callings. Yours will be uniquely yours, mine is uniquely mine, and I didn't write this book to tell you the right path. I wrote it to tell you how to find that path, and how to follow it for an impactful life.

What can you do that no one else can? What have your life experiences led you to, and how can you bring those experiences to life in the world? How do you want to spend your days, and what legacy do you want to leave?

The Joy Is in the Journey

There are nearly a million Google results when searching for the postmarathon blues. And science has in fact proven that marathon runners feel a tremendous emotional letdown after the race is over.[2] There's an inevitable melancholy when you reach something you've been training and planning for. The anticipation outweighs the accomplishment. The pursuit is what gives you joy, and the actual act—whether a marathon or closing the big deal at work—

can never live up to the anticipation. Kaitlin Woolley and Ayelet Fishbach, whose research on the power of discomfort I mentioned in chapter 4, are also the authors of a paper titled "The Experience Matters More Than You Think," finding in their research that how we feel when actually performing an activity matters more than how we think we'll feel beforehand, or how we remember it afterward.[3]

Even Olympians feel this same effect.[4] Win or lose, they feel psychologically depleted when they return home, and are prone to serious depression—especially if they don't have a plan for what comes next. The dirty little secret of a successful life is that you can never actually get to a happy place to stop working, stop trying, stop aiming for more. Success and contentment are built on perpetual pursuit. Achieving at even the highest level doesn't mitigate this. There has been a tremendous amount of research done around the letdown people feel after big achievements. As has been written in *Harvard Business Review*, "To be fully engaged, we need to experience an ongoing sense of growth on the job."[5] That's why Michael Jordan retired from basketball at the peak of his success and why Jon Stewart left *The Daily Show*. "I think there are moments when you realize that [being great at something is] not enough anymore," Stewart said, "or that maybe it's time for some discomfort."[6]

"I was actually scared to get tenure," HBS professor Francesca Gino told me. "I had seen colleagues achieve it and then go through these moments of depression. They were working so hard toward something, and then it stopped, and it wasn't what they expected. We think that things like winning the lottery will have a huge effect on our happiness, but when it happens, we adapt really quickly. Events we see as so important don't end up making that big of a difference. Instead, it's important to make progress toward something. I actually tried to reframe the idea of tenure in my mind, not as a destination, but as a milestone in a larger journey of having impact on the world. I had to avoid seeing it as the goal in itself."

You can be proud of what you accomplish—you can look back and say, "I can't believe I've gotten this far"—but then your next step has to be looking ahead and realizing how much further you still might be able to go.

◎ ◎ ◎

Joshua Becker is a former pastor who has become a bestselling author writing about minimalism. He has found such joy in sharing the gospel of decluttering, and how emptying your life of the possessions you do not need can lead to great satisfaction.[7] I can't say that I'm fully on board with his minimalist philosophy—I love fast cars—but where I couldn't agree more is in the idea that things, whether tangible or the kinds of accomplishments we dream about achieving, don't bring nearly the reward we expect.

Becker writes about how the emptiness of sports is felt most in victory.[8] "When you win," he says, "the pursuit of the goal is removed. There is no one left to defeat. There is no obstacle left to overcome . . . But it doesn't change your life in any way. In fact, work begins again in the morning."[9]

◎ ◎ ◎

There are people who push back when I talk to them about burning the boats. They tell me that burning the boats sounds like a recipe for a life of perpetual discontent.

"Simmer down, Matthew," they say. "Why do all of this work, constantly stretching for the next achievement, when you could simply bask in the glory of what you've already done and live a life of leisure?"

The answer is that of course burning the boats is hard, but hard is what keeps us happy. The joy isn't in the life of leisure, it's in the struggle, the pursuit, the purpose. It's hard, and that's why it's rewarding, and that's why it's worth doing.

Just ask Marc Lore. He could have retired after selling Diapers .com. But he went on to start Jet, and it led to an even bigger exit. Now he's onto even more—with Wonder, with the Timberwolves, and with his city of the future.

Or ask my friend Bobbi Brown. She sold the right to use her name to sell beauty products when she launched her makeup line decades ago—and so she couldn't take it with her when she left her parent company Estée Lauder in 2016. For years, she wore a necklace with the date that her noncompete agreement would end. As soon as it did, she launched a new brand, Jones Road, wanting to go direct-to-consumer for the first time—and has become a TikTok star at age sixty-five.

Or ask Gary Vaynerchuk. "I don't need the outside validation," he tells me, "because I'm in it for the game. I'm thrilled with success, thrilled with fancy things, but they're such a distant second and third to my complete obsession over the game and the process. How I treat business is that the losses will come, but they just motivate me the next time around. I'm just grateful to play the game, and to get to do what I do every day."

◉ ◉ ◉

John Skipper was the president of ESPN, cochairman of Disney Media Networks, and then head of the British sports media company

DAZN Group, before deciding to launch a venture of his own, Meadowlark Media, a content production studio he started with sportswriter and podcast host Dan Le Batard in 2021. John's experience running a multibillion-dollar media company highlights that the joy of the journey doesn't necessarily mean that bigger is better, and that nothing can replace the freedom to work with people you value, on projects that keep you learning and growing.

"After twenty-seven years at an established leader," he explains, "running DAZN gave me the chance to be a disruptor, and see the industry from a completely different perspective, getting exposure to a far more international business landscape, and seeing what it was like to experiment with entirely new business models."

Beyond that, launching his own studio—in his mid-sixties—added new excitement and new rewards. "I've learned so much," he says. "I had never started a business before. And now, I can do what I want to do, say what I want to say, and work with amazing people. ESPN had an obligation to do the thing that worked the best for the business, but that sometimes meant that if someone was a talented jerk, we had to put up with it. Here, not so much. And that makes it so much more fun. I get to work with people who are genuinely humane and decent—and creatively interesting on top of that."

The right journey doesn't always have to mean constantly scaling up from a revenue perspective. I said earlier that the size of an opportunity doesn't necessarily correspond with the energy required. The corollary there is that the size doesn't necessarily equate with how rewarding it is, either. "People think they need to be on top of the pyramid, but if you're happy doing it, that's what's important," John says. "I was running a company with billions of dollars in revenue, and now I have twenty employees . . . but it's so much more rewarding because it's my own. You don't always have to go upward in terms of money. Do really interesting things instead." As I write this, Meadowlark Media has just signed a multiyear first-look deal with Apple to produce documentary content and unscripted series for Apple TV. Knowing John, I can't wait to see what develops.

Live Dreams Concurrently

Those football players I talk to about their postplaying careers fall into a predictable trap. "Don't bother me with all this stuff now," they say. "I'm focused on playing, so let me finish doing that, and then I'll deal with the rest of my life." But we all fall into that trap sometimes, don't we?

I can't take that on, I'm too busy.

Let me finish this project, and then I'll have the space to take on the next.

I'll start my business once things slow down at work.

I'll have time to pursue my passions . . . after I retire.

These are all rationalizations that maintain the same status quo. But the time will never be right. You can't predict how things will unfold, and you can't schedule your triumphs. The world will not wait for you. To live a life of perpetual growth, you have to leverage what you are doing today to move you closer to what you want to do tomorrow—even if that means doing two, three, four, seventeen things at once. The world doesn't care if you are already busy.

Insights will not wait, and instincts will not take a back seat until a better time comes along. There will never be a better time than today. You will always be busy—or, at least, you *should* always be busy.

And you know what? Things are actually a lot easier to accomplish if you don't wait for the right time. Your point of greatest leverage is when you're busiest, when you have exciting projects going on, a job in the executive suite, heat behind your company, deals in the works, people you're engaged with. That's when you pitch them the next big idea, not when everything else has concluded and you're just spinning your wheels. Not when you're desperate for someone to say yes so that you have a new purpose and something to do. There's a saying poker players are fond of that applies just as much to the game of life: scared money never wins. You have to take advantage of those fleeting moments when things are going well by launching your new ventures then, long before you actually need to. The problem with leverage is that when you're desperate for it, it's too late to create it.

You always have to be open to opportunity, even if the time is wrong. You need to "save space for grace" as Curt Cronin likes to say. It's a beautiful way of conveying that you don't need to have all the answers mapped out before you embark on a big move. You are only required to take the first tentative steps in the direction of your ambition. Beyond that, trust that the universe will augment your effort as needed. You need to be open to allowing ideas, people, and serendipity into your life.

My eighty-two-year-old partner Stephen Ross lives this philosophy. He owns the Dolphins, he rebuilt the west side of Manhattan— but why stop there? He's recently decided to reimagine Palm Beach as a post-COVID, work-from-anywhere society, he brought a Formula One race to Miami, and he built a 1,200-acre golf course, just for good measure. Stephen commissioned a painting by artist Peter Tunney that hangs in his headquarters, emblazoned with these words: "I'll be busy for the rest of my life." He sure will be—and he loves every minute of it.

Find the Point of Greatest Impact

If there's one disappointment that drives me in life, it's the knowledge that things could have been so much better for me and for my mother if only someone had offered us a helping hand when we were at our lowest. If only someone would have swooped in and recognized our suffering, made sure I was able to get to school, made sure she had the medical care she desperately needed, made sure we had food, made sure our apartment was safe and clean . . . my childhood would have been so different.

Michael Rubin, CEO of Fanatics, understands what it means to provide help to kids who are struggling. With his company's success, he started REFORM Alliance, an organization bringing awareness to inequities in America's criminal justice system. Backed by more than $50 million—including a $10 million donation from Twitter's Jack Dorsey—the group helps families hurt by unfair probation and parole laws and advocates for system change. In December 2021, he and rapper Meek Mill brought twenty-five kids to have an NBA "Christmas experience" on the court with Mill and fellow rapper Lil Baby in Philadelphia before a 76ers game.[10] "Every kid here has a mom or dad that's currently in prison or has been in prison for a technical violation," Rubin said. "They didn't commit a crime, but went to prison." The kids played a scrimmage on the court, and watched the Sixers play the Heat from courtside seats. "We wanted to give them the best day of their life," Rubin said.[11]

◉　◉　◉

My friend Curtis Martin was a running back for eleven seasons in the NFL and is in the Pro Football Hall of Fame. He grew up in circumstances that make my childhood look easy. His grandmother was found stabbed to death in her bedroom when Curtis was nine years old. For two years, the murderer was still on the loose—and Curtis and his mother lived in fear that he would come for them next, since their address had been published in the newspaper. In inner-city Pittsburgh, Curtis lost two dozen friends to street violence growing up, including his best friend, shot to death in front of Curtis's eyes while the two of them were walking down the street. He didn't even begin playing football until his senior year of high school, and yet pretty soon every school in the country was after him. But he felt purposeless and unfulfilled until he found religion and realized: football could give him a platform, a voice, a way to help others and bring meaning to his own life.

For him, football has always been a means to an end, a way to do good. On his one day off from football each week, every Tuesday, he'd make his way around New York City and spend time with different homeless people he'd met over the years, sitting with them, talking to them, seeing them as human beings. At the other end of the spectrum, he'd convene some of the most famous people in the world in clandestine meetings and create a safe place to share their troubles. He wanted to bring light into the lives of as many struggling individuals as he could. Curtis's childhood torment could have made him bitter and angry, but instead it made him incredibly empathetic, giving, and wise. He's an example of how to find ways to use what we're good at to change people's lives and lift others up, even the most unfortunate.

* * *

I know what it means to feel so powerless in trying to find a way to a better life. I burn the boats because I long to find myself in a position to give others the help that I never got. That's really where it all ends up for me. I see the point of greatest impact, and know that I can build toward being able to help more and more people get through the worst.

In the years since my mother died, I set up a scholarship fund at Queens College in her honor, the Linda J. Higgins Empowerment Scholarship, awarding it to several single mothers each year. I know how hard it was for her to balance motherhood and getting an education, and I wanted to give others the advantages my mom never had. These women have overcome the most impossible odds to end up standing onstage, diplomas in hand.

In 2019, when I gave the commencement address at the school, I had the scholarship recipients stand up. Just like my mother had done with me when I was ten years old, they brought their kids to campus that afternoon and I was transported back to that same patch of dirt I played on thirty years earlier. It is one of the only happy memories of my childhood. The rest I've blocked out.

"Tameka and Rosanna," I said to them. "Like my mother, you overcame the most impossible odds to be standing here. You did not make excuses. You did not become a victim. And you never, ever gave up."

Those scholarship winners are so inspiring. I talk to them every year and try to contribute beyond the money. One recent get-together was absolutely gut-wrenching. A single mother who had emigrated from Latin America recalled how one evening she had no babysitting coverage for her eleven-year-old daughter and so she brought her to campus. The professor wouldn't let her sit quietly in the back of the classroom, as she thought it would be some kind of nonsense breach of decorum. The mom told the group how she sat her daughter on the floor outside the door, told her to read quietly— and then broke down. Her daughter, this strong little firecracker, hugged her and said, "No, no, Mommy, it's okay. I'll be fine. I'm so proud of you. You can do it!"

Another recipient, Ekaterina Kalmanson, fled Russia years ago, trying to escape a violent husband. She came here without speaking a word of English, and never thought she would go to college. Finally, she applied—and then she was diagnosed with breast cancer. On the day she got that diagnosis, she received a letter in the mail from Queens College offering her the scholarship in my mother's name. There she was, crying on the phone to me—the scholarship was the only thing that made it possible for her to go.

She told me that she reread my commencement speech so she could draw strength from my mother. "If your mother could do it," she told me, "then so can I."

My mother always predicted her life would mean nothing and that her memory would be discarded. I couldn't bear for that to be the outcome. After she died, the mayor asked me if there was anything special we could do to honor her. It was a very kind gesture, and I told him there was in fact one last dying request she had. In her final days in her apartment, she begged me to drive her around the Queens College campus again. It was really her only place of joy. At the time, I was too busy getting ready for the new job, and now, after her death, I was tormented by it. And so the mayor arranged for her casket to be driven through the campus one final time.

Now these scholarships make me feel like I am helping my mother rewrite a new ending to her own story. Her legacy did not come to an end alone in that sad apartment on Springfield Boulevard. She lives on in these strong, defiant women—and I am her messenger.

❋ ❋ ❋

I ran for president of Queens College, back when I was a student, and I was beaten terribly. It was my first real failure. My opponent was the late José Peralta, a kind, decent man. That campaign for president launched José into a lifetime of public service, and he went on to have a tremendous career in the New York State Assembly and the New York State Senate. His running mate for class president was Alan van Capelle. When Alan graduated in 1997, 60 percent of all Americans opposed the idea of marriage equality. Alan could have accepted the status quo, but instead, he did something. He became the leader of the advocacy group Empire State Pride Agenda. He fought to change hearts and minds, and when that didn't work, he fought to change politicians.

After a marriage equality bill was narrowly defeated in the New York State Senate in 2009, Alan campaigned for his old Queens College running mate, José Peralta, to join the State Senate. José won, and two years later, he cast one of the deciding thirty-three votes to make marriage equality the law in New York State.

I share this story to say that we all have the power to make meaningful change through our actions. Do not sit idly by. If you open your eyes wide enough, you'll see that something is happening in the world right now that we find acceptable today—but will be ashamed of tomorrow. You can pick your cause, and it doesn't really matter what it is, as long as it sparks something within you. And then you can find a way to fix the system, one step at a time, one boat at a time, looking for those points of maximum impact and doing everything you can to move the world in the right direction.

◉ ◉ ◉

My friend Darren Rovell is an example of how small things, small nudges, can completely change someone's life. Darren was a reporter at ESPN for years, but his superpower was as an information-arbitrage genius. He would buy memorabilia from auction houses—either small ones that didn't get publicity, ones that had buried interesting items too deep in their catalogs, or ones that didn't effectively explain an item's story—that he knew were undervalued. The items would be worth more on the day Darren bought them simply because he was great at telling their stories. He would resell the items on related anniversaries—the anniversary of the date of a particular concert or sporting event, for instance—for huge multiples of what he had originally paid.

As one example, for years Darren invested in Warren Buffett, noticing a disconnect between the love expressed for the man known as the Oracle of Omaha and the lack of collectors. It paid off in 2022, when Darren sold his most grand piece for millions, more than two hundred times what he paid for it: the largest-known Buffett signature (a foot and a half long) on a sheet of eighteen uncut, uncirculated dollar bills from the Kansas City Treasury. This was how Darren's mind worked, making connections that others didn't see, and figuring out how to turn them into compelling narratives that would move people. That's what made him such a valuable reporter.

I could see that the highest and best use of Darren's skills would require autonomy so his mind could roam. Using his unusual pattern-recognition skills as a reporter was not going to set him free. It would be so much more valuable to use them in a business context in which he had an ownership stake. So I encouraged Darren to make the moves I knew he had inside him, and that I knew he longed to make.

But it wasn't easy to build up the courage to burn a big, prestigious boat like ESPN. He had a hard time consolidating the gains he'd made in his career there, locking in the accomplishment of being a reporter and moving on to further aspirations. I wanted him to start an investment fund and put his genius to work, or at least get in on the ground floor at a young company and be able to use his unique skills to help them find success. I saw in him such talent that was ready to be unleashed.

And then we at RSE wrote a check to help build a young sports gambling company. I realized this was it: if Darren could run content for the brand, and take an equity stake in the business, it could change his life. It was a perfect fit. "I wasn't ready to go full entrepreneur," Darren remembered, "but I also wasn't comfortable with the people who had control over my career. I felt like they were good at winning meetings, but weren't good at the execution. By going to a startup, I had fewer bosses and for the first time in my life, I felt like I was truly controlling my business destiny."

His deal had him front and center when it came to content and branding and gave him a stake in the company. He burned the boats, and it changed his life. The company was sold less than three years after Darren joined, and he walked away with enough money to write his next ticket. "I have been doing what I love every day for the past twenty-one years," he explains. "But the fact that I made the decision to leap is the best decision I ever made."

◉   ◉   ◉

My friend Julianne Hough is another example of someone deciding to move their life in a more fulfilling, more rewarding direction by finding their point of greatest potential impact. Building on her experience as a dancer, singer, and actress—a multiple-time winner and then judge on *Dancing with the Stars*—Julianne wanted to bring dancing to the masses. She launched KINRGY, a wellness platform that provides people with a means to stay mentally and physically fit through dance-driven workouts that incorporate movement, strength work, breath work, visualization, and meditation. KINRGY started out as a set of in-person classes but moved online during the COVID-19 pandemic, with Julianne and a set of trained, carefully selected guides helping thousands of users and subscribers reach their peaks.

"Dance, for me, has always been my superpower," she told me, "and I believe it's innately everyone's. Around the world, people dance for celebration, they dance for crops, they dance for fertility, they dance for healing. It's a universal language." Julianne sees dance as the quickest way that someone can change their state of mind, with movement linked to emotional connection, and she wanted to bring that power to the public. She had a realization that she was taking from the world—but instead she wanted to give, and decided to use her passion to create the business.

"When are you going to bring *Dancing with the Stars* to the masses?" people kept asking her, and she sought to give that same kind of holistic, fully immersive experience to people at scale, to help them feel as if anything is possible. Julianne understood her skills and began to build a team to fill the gaps, people who understood how to turn her gifts and her ideas into a business. That's how KINRGY was born, and Julianne has been able to see herself now not just as a dancer and a celebrity, but as someone who can help the world achieve their dreams. A year after the company's founding, Julianne was in front of my students, guest lecturing in my course at HBS—not as a TV star, not as an actress, not as a singer, but as the founder of a great business and the leader of a movement. With KINRGY, she has started a true next act.

There Is No Final Port

The more territory we conquer, the more capacity we have to help others, to serve and give back, and the more capacity we have to improve our lives and our futures.

But how do you do it? When you put down this book, how do you actually start burning the boats? Most growth is hindered, and ultimately most businesses falter, because we focus solely on finding the right answers instead of questioning whether we're asking the right questions. There are only a few more questions you need to ask yourself, as you absorb the lessons of this book and get ready to launch your next journey:

---

* What am I uniquely positioned to do that no one else can?

* What insights do I see that no one is acting on?

* What makes me special, and how can I leverage that to the greatest extent possible?

* What, in my heart of hearts, do I really *want* to do?

You don't have to have everything figured out, and if you think you have it all figured out, I guarantee that you will fail. The leading sign of lack of self-awareness is complete confidence in your plan and your ability to execute it. Problems beget solutions. Put yourself in a bind to which you have no answers and surprise yourself with the depth of your ingenuity and problem-solving skills.

* * *

When I say there is no final port, I think some people feel a visceral objection. They think I'm saying they can never relax, never rest, never say they're finished. That's not quite the message I'm trying to convey. As you take your journeys, you may indeed find an island where you want to build a home, stay awhile, set up camp, and live your life free of the pressure of constantly achieving something new. You're recharging, and you're allowed to recharge. We all need to recharge. But eventually, you're going to feel those pangs again. You can't stay in one place forever. Unless you're an unusual person, wired differently than almost everyone I meet, staying still won't bring you the same joy as continuing to strive, and to go all in on new adventures.

The greatest regret people have on their deathbeds is that they never pursued their boldest dreams. As I was finishing this book, I had breakfast with Scott Tannen, the founder and CEO of Boll & Branch, a luxury home goods retailer that I've seen grow from the inside. Tannen himself is the perfect embodiment of so many of the ideas in this book. He had already had a huge exit, founding and selling Candystand.com, one of the world's largest online gaming sites, but when he and his wife, Missy, were renovating their home, they had an epiphany.

Looking at home decor, Scott and Missy noticed that the market was missing a luxury brand that was actually living the values of the customers it was trying to sell to. He saw an opportunity to reinvent the supply chain, working directly with makers around the world in an ethical, fair way—and seven years later the company has raised more than $100 million.

"We couldn't believe that there wasn't a brand or product that was clearly 'the best bedding to get,'" Scott told me. "So we made one."

It was an insight others could have had, but hadn't, "a can't-miss that a whole lot of people, for a whole lot of time, missed," Scott says.

Over breakfast that morning, Scott happened to mention that after a long search, he'd finally found a firm able to drive their social media strategy effectively. He paid $10,000 and the firm generated $300,000 of revenue, at an 80 percent margin. It was unbelievable, he told me, and admitted they'd been through a lot of failed attempts before they found this agency. When he said the firm's name, it immediately rang a bell, because it was the very same firm—Village Marketing—that I remembered hearing about countless times over the past few years. I told Scott that I had to meet the founder and figure out if we could use her across my entire portfolio.

When I got on a call with Vickie Segar, who started the firm in 2013, she reminded me that it wasn't the first time we'd met. She had been the marketing director at Equinox from 2010 until 2013, and had just left when we initially talked about a job—one of the very first job openings at Jesse Derris's then-nascent PR firm. Back then, Vickie had a vision for how marketing should be done, and felt like no one was listening. "There was no question that consumers were spending an increasing amount of time on social media," Vickie explains, "but they weren't spending time with brands, they were spending time with people. In fact, while most brands continued to try to force potential consumers onto their owned social media pages, I wanted to meet consumers where they already were, inserting brands into conversations their customers were having with others.

"The insight that consumers were spending time on social with people over brands was obvious to me," Vickie continues, "but seemingly not to everyone. The existing agency model wasn't built to work with influencers, wasn't receptive to it, and left the door wide open for smaller players like me to own the category."

It was the same feeling I had when I first met Gary Vaynerchuk. Vickie had incredible insight, and really understood her domain. I tried desperately to persuade her to join our team. I knew Derris would be huge, and that she was exactly the kind of genius we needed. And then she turned us down.

Vickie remembers that she turned down the job because she knew that this was her one chance to go out on her own and see if she could make it. Now, talking to her eight years later, she had done it. She was employing 150 people, with $14 million in annual revenue, and—balancing all that while having two young kids at home—she had become the very best in this niche of the industry. She would have been my employee, but now she was a tremendously successful founder.

"As a female in the startup space a decade ago," Vickie explained to me, "starting a family—or taking a maternity leave of any kind—was outwardly discouraged. I started my own company because, very simply, I needed to create an environment where I could be the mom I wanted to be, while maintaining the career I felt so passionate about. I needed flexibility. I also knew I had an opportunity to help pave the way for other women, which led me to start an all-female company that has had a flexible work environment from its inception."

It's such an inspiring success story—a successful business, and, even more important, a successful life. In February 2022, she sold the firm to the world's largest advertising company, WPP, creating financial freedom for herself and her family—coincidentally, just months before Jesse sold his firm, too. That one moment when she chose to believe in herself rather than become our employee completely changed the trajectory of her life.

◉ ◉ ◉

And that's really the goal, isn't it? For burning the boats to bring you true satisfaction, there needs to be a *why?* behind it—a goal that makes all the striving worth it. The joy is absolutely in the journey, but you still need to be propelled by a purpose larger than personal enrichment or ego gratification. The pursuit of excellence can be a strong motivating force, for sure, but if there's not something more, the victories can start to feel hollow.

For me, it all comes back to my childhood. I'm driven to build a platform—and the funds to back it—in order to help ameliorate the kind of suffering my mother and I endured. It breaks my heart just writing this, but the last thing my mother said to me as I walked out the door that morning on the way to City Hall was that she promised to eat applesauce from then on. She wanted to lose the weight. She wanted to live. She told me she wanted to take an airplane for the first time and sit by the ocean. On her last day on earth, she still had dreams, and she desperately wanted another chance to make the changes that maybe could have saved her life. I didn't know it that morning, but it was too late.

It's not too late for the rest of us. Burning the boats is a recipe to leave no dream unfulfilled, no ambition denied. We all need to give ourselves a chance to realize the ceiling of our talents, to find the limits that we'll never quite reach, to know ourselves and to appreciate our power to make things happen. There is simply no higher use of my life than to help others on those journeys. That lesson I learned as a kid, that no one was coming to save us, while true, was not a foregone conclusion. We all have choices to make. Do we intervene, or do we look away? Even a small gesture can alter the trajectory of someone's life, if perhaps just by supplying hope in darkness. Now I can be that ray of light for someone else who desperately needs it.

Back when I met with Father Leonir, we talked about my journey, and he told me that I wasn't really able to heal from the trauma of my childhood because I was spending my energy fruitlessly trying to go back in time and save my mother from succumbing to her own suffering. I was never going to be able to heal her or that little boy by her side—but what I *could* do was save others who were drowning. "Go to the river," Father Leonir said. That's how I would find my path to peace.

◉　◉　◉

And that's how I found myself on a stage in Central Park in September 2021, with the privilege of speaking to a crowd of 60,000 people on the Great Lawn about how we could all make a difference. For the past three years, an interfaith offshoot of the Catholic Church called the Global Solidarity Fund has been quietly raising money to support migrants and refugees around the world and strengthen the impact of faith-based organizations that serve hundreds of millions of people. Migrants tug at me. When we see horrific images of mass migration on TV, we should ask not *why are they coming here?* but rather *what are they running from?* How bad must it be, and how desperate must you feel to flee your homeland—and how resourceful and hardworking must you have to be to make that journey? I've been involved in the GSF, trying to give back and enlist others to this mission. On that stage, I announced that we were launching a campaign to raise $100 million for food, vaccines, and job training—and that we'd already raised the first $28 million toward that goal.

My mandate was to transmit Pope Francis's vision of equality to everyone listening, regardless of their own personal religious beliefs, and get them to feel the message of global solidarity. In the middle of a rock concert . . . in a park . . . in forty-seven seconds! I was told that I had to stay on script, tightly timed, going onstage soon after Prince Harry and Meghan Markle. I was nervous, but as I ascended the stairs to the stage, I saw the beautiful Manhattan skyline rise up to meet me, the buildings along Fifth Avenue, where some of the wealthiest people in the world live and work, towering over us. At that moment, I thought about someone idly sipping exquisite tea in those buildings overlooking Central Park, contrasted with Father Leonir in a war zone rendering aid to a family fleeing murder and rape. I instinctively knew that I needed to go off script to connect with the audience. I needed to burn the boats for Father Leonir and Pope Francis.

"You see those buildings over there in Central Park right behind you?" I asked the audience, who turned their heads while the camera shifted to show the millions more watching around the world. The teleprompter went into a frenetic tailspin. "I did not grow up there. I grew up in a place called Queens, New York. Now, like a lot of people in New York, I grew up really poor and relied upon public services, and there were a lot of times when I didn't know where my next meal was coming from, and I'm grateful for all the support I had. Yet I remember in my most desperate times when my stomach was empty, it was so often met with a full heart and a box full of food from my local Catholic food pantry. That's why I'm here tonight . . ."

I apologized later for the extra forty-two seconds. A month later, I was afforded the honor of a lifetime—a private audience with Pope Francis at the Vatican. Pope Francis upended tradition when he was elected the Vicar of Christ on Earth in 2013, eschewing all the worldly trappings of the office—not least of which the regal Palace quarters—choosing instead to live permanently in guest housing and drive around Rome in a 1984 Renault.

There was an underlying message to his revolutionary approach. Soon after his election, the Pope visited Rome's Casal del Marmo prison and washed the feet of twelve inmates. "The person who is most high among us must be at the service of others," explained Pope Francis. "To wash your feet, this is a symbol, a sign that I am at your service."[12]

I watched him walk into the unassuming room in the Vatican, all of us privileged to be there gathered in a circle. Pope Francis went one by one and engaged each of us, making us feel like we were the only person in the world. I told him that I was inspired to come because of his compassion, that I had grown up poor, and had benefited from my local parish food pantry. I was here—raising money and trying to help the church—in order to return the favor.

He explained how the opposite of indifference is solidarity, and how we all need to give, not just from a distance but intimately. "Bring the poor close to you," he said. "Go to the periphery, not just of your body, but of your soul." With those words, I was transported back in time, remembering how toward the end of her life, my mother so desperately wanted someone to wash her hair, so she could feel just a little bit human again, but she was met with disgust at the local salon because she couldn't bathe herself anymore. She wanted so much to be seen. Money helped, but human contact was what she really craved. Solidarity. Hope. Connection.

◉ ◉ ◉

I've tried to connect in these pages. I've tried to connect with the founders and partners I work with, and the people I come across in life who could use my help. My visit with Pope Francis will stick with me forever, especially the words he ended the meeting with, the perfect words to send you off to burn some boats of your own: "Be courageous."

I know how simple it sounds, but how hard it actually is. When I was leaving the Jets, people told me I was making an impossibly risky, impossibly stupid move. They said I wouldn't get my calls answered, and I'd have nothing without the team. I told them, no—the Jets aren't the platform, I am my own platform.

You are your own platform. Your brilliance is the platform. Own what you are great at and never look back.

Be courageous.

◉ ◉ ◉

I was on vacation not long ago in Lake George, New York. We rented a boat, and there was the most adorable wooden boathouse on the lake, around for more than half a century. I started talking to one of the owners, a descendant of the man who had first built the entire enterprise—the boathouse, and all of the boats. There was a gorgeous wooden boat docked in a slip off to the side, lovingly maintained and seemingly frozen in time. It looked like something that belonged on a canal in Venice.

"What's the story with that one?" I asked.

"Ah, that boat is very special."

Sixty years ago, the boathouse had burned to the ground. A

news dispatch from May 5, 1957, confirmed the story: "Smith's Boat House at Bolton Landing burned. Fire companies from Bolton Landing, Lake George, Chestertown, and Warrensburg worked at the scene for over five hours to extinguish the blaze."

The original owner was working that day when the fire erupted. The old logs framing the boathouse were a tinderbox. He knew the structure could be replaced, but he feared the fire would engulf the boats, and destroy everything he had spent his life working toward. He raced to push many of the boats out into the lake, but was running out of time. In an instant, he had an epiphany. With an inferno blazing all around him, he ran inside the repair shop and pulled an axe off the wall. He stood over the remaining prized boat, and began swinging wildly at the hull. If he sank the boat, the engine would flood, but the rest of the boat would be spared the flames. Then when the fire was extinguished, he could raise the boat, replace the parts, and rebuild his business.

If you take anything away from the lessons here, I hope it's my abiding belief in your infinite capacity to just figure it out. Trust me, when your back is against the wall, and there's seemingly no way out, you will find a way.

Instead of burning those boats, you might just have to sink them instead.

ACKNOWLEDGMENTS

I've always imagined my improbable life as a series of handoffs in one never-ending relay race. Starting with my first job in Queens, New York, there was always that one person who saw where I was going and not where I came from, picked up the baton, and carried me to the next leg. Diane Cohen, Alan Gershuny, Congressman Gary Ackerman, Michael Shenkler, Michael Nussbaum, David Oats, Cristyne Lategano-Nicholas, Colleen Roche, Sunny Mindel, Lou Tomson, Kevin Rampe, Michael McKeon, Governor George Pataki, John Cahill, Lisa Stoll, Jay Cross, Woody Johnson, Len Schlesinger, Jeff Frost, Holly Jacobs, Clay Newbill, Rob Mills, Mark Burnett, Barry Poznick, Mark Hoffman, and of course, my partner, my mentor, and surrogate uncle Stephen Ross. At different crossroads over my career, all of you valued my potential over pedigree and paved the way for each new professional breakthrough. There are many more who believed in my ability more than I did. I carry you in my heart with gratitude every day.

I hope you find this book uncomfortably raw and vulnerable at times. I am indebted to all of the extraordinary visionaries from every walk of life whose stories animate what it means to Burn the Boats. Aidan Kehoe and Mike Tannenbaum in particular, thank you for holding nothing back and letting me share your unrelenting commitment to self-improvement.

I'm grateful to all of the readers who went through unpolished versions of this manuscript. You made the end result infinitely better with sharp insights, gentle feedback, and loving encouragement that *Burn the Boats* could change lives: Claudia Lezcano del Campo, Susanne Norwitz, Dave Warren, Eric Van Wagenen, Elyse Propis, John Ciorra. Vanessa Ballesteros, your comments broadened the *Burn the Boats* aperture to better speak to those denied the opportunities afforded to me over the years.

How did I get on *Shark Tank* or my own TV pilot? My agent Reed Bergman saw in me an unexpected TV personality and made it happen.

To my incredibly dedicated team at RSE Ventures, is there anything you can't do? We are a team of ants that can shoulder many times our body weight. Your ability to navigate any situation gave me the brain space I needed to write this book and phone it in when necessary. Uday Ahuja, Corrine Glass, Ljena Dedvukovic, thank you for your steady leadership of our exceptional team. Jessica Rizzo, without you there is no RSE, and your unshakeable positive energy over the last decade is a gift to all of us. Lou Majano, thank you for your help coordinating the endless details that writing a book requires, and arranging over fifty interviews!

Burn the Boats owes its existence to my big-thinker literary agent, Michael Palgon, who shaped this book through a series of caffeine-infused marathon whiteboard sessions. My love of books began with Beverly Cleary, so to join the imprint she called home— William Morrow—fills me with pride and nostalgia. Mauro DiPreta at HarperCollins immediately saw the potential of *Burn the Boats* to change lives, and went all in on this first-time author to bring it to life. Thank you to Andrew Yackira for making this book better with each successive edit. Carol Lehmann, you are a true artist who produced a book cover so powerful and arresting it is impossible to overlook. Jeremy Blachman was my partner in every aspect of creating *Burn the Boats*. Through countless sessions over the course of a year, we kept digging deeper into the ideas in these pages and then mined for stories and subjects to accentuate each concept. It's hard to imagine someone capable of caring more about your book than even you do, but that's how it felt to work with Jeremy.

To my beautiful children, the hardest part about writing this book was keeping you completely out of it, just as I have kept you out of the public eye all these years. It is the one inauthentic part of *Burn the Boats* that feels like a lie, because I want the world to know that you are my entire life. My wise fifteen-year-old son, thank you for the page turn. You will notice every one of your brilliant edits have been incorporated (and yes, there will be a test).

My mother, Linda, died with $100 in her bank account, but I inherited the most valuable gift a parent can give a child: limitless faith in my ability to figure anything out. Every preposterous plan was met with irrational support. The blueprint for *Burn the Boats* was sketched a long time ago on our kitchen table. Much of my childhood was sanitized in this book, and my brothers Todd, Timmy, and Tommy also paid a heavy price for our upbringing that I do not attempt to capture in these pages. But I want you to know that I see you. Todd, you have been my consigliere since we were kids. Everyone needs someone who knows the whole story. For me, that is you.

Finally, my dear wife, Sarah. How did we get so lucky? You are all things at once—my best friend, my soulmate, my North Star when I can't find my way and my coconspirator when I don't want to. There is no one I admire more.

This book is dedicated to you.

NOTES

INTRODUCTION

1. Hoff, Rabbi Dr. Naphtali. 2017. "Learn to Burn Your Boats." Jewishlinknj .com. November 9, 2017. https://jewishlink.news/features/21533-learn-to -burn-your-boats.
2. "The Annotated Art of War (Parts 11.38-40: No Way Back)." n.d. Changingminds.org. Accessed August 11, 2022. http://changingminds .org/disciplines/warfare/art_war/sun_tzu_11-8.htm.
3. Bishop, Greg. 2011. "Channeling Churchill, Ryan Inspires His Team." *New York Times*, January 7, 2011, sec. Sports. https://www.nytimes.com /2011/01/08/sports/football/08ryan.html.

CHAPTER 1: TRUST YOUR INSTINCTS

1. Emerson, Ralph Waldo. 1993. *Self-Reliance and Other Essays*. Mineola, New York: Dover Publications.
2. Jasper. 2019. "Airbnb Founder Story: From Selling Cereals to a $25B Company." *Get Paid for Your Pad*. August 9, 2019. https:// getpaidforyourpad.com/blog/the-airbnb-founder-story/.
3. "Stephen Ross." n.d. *Forbes*. Accessed August 31, 2022. https://www.forbes .com/profile/stephen-ross/?sh=4df40b506220.
4. Williams, Keith. 2016. "The Evolution of Hudson Yards: From 'Death Avenue' to NYC's Most Advanced Neighborhood." Curbed NY. December 13, 2016. https://ny.curbed.com/2016/12/13/13933084/hudson -yards-new-york-history-manhattan.
5. Schulman, Pansy. 2019. "New York Citadel: A Future History of Hudson Yards." https://digitalcommons.bard.edu/cgi/viewcontent .cgi?article=1286&context=senproj_s2019.

6. Skid, Nate, and Jonathan Fazio. 2021. "How Abhi Ramesh Built a $1 Billion Start-up Called Misfits Market." CNBC. May 23, 2021. https://www .cnbc.com/video/2021/05/23/how-abhi-ramesh-built-a-1-billion-start-up -called-misfits-market.html.

7. Wilco, J. R. 2011. "The Stonecutter's Creedo." Pounding the Rock. December 27, 2011. https://www.poundingtherock.com/pages/the -stonecutters-creedo.

CHAPTER 2: OVERCOME YOUR DEMONS AND ENEMIES

1. Nishant, Niket. 2021. "Impossible Foods Raises $500 Mln in Funding Round Led by Mirae." Reuters, November 23, 2021, sec. U.S. Markets. https://www.reuters.com/markets/us/impossible-foods-raises-500-mln -latest-funding-2021-11-23/.

2. Connor, Andrea. 2017. *The Political Afterlife of Sites of Monumental Destruction: Reconstructing Affect in Mostar and New York.* United Kingdom: Taylor & Francis.

3. Wolfson, Elizabeth. 2017. "The 'Black Gash of Shame'—Revisiting the Vietnam Veterans Memorial Controversy." *Art21 Magazine.* March 15, 2017. http://magazine.art21.org/2017/03/15/the-black-gash-of-shame-revisiting -the-vietnam-veterans-memorial-controversy/#.YvU8TezMLoZ.

4. Kapp, Matt. 2016. "Of Stone and Steel: The Story behind the 9/11 Memorial." *Vanity Fair.* September 9, 2016. https://www.vanityfair.com /news/2016/09/the-story-behind-the-911-memorial.

5. Jensen, Michael, Torsten Twardawski, and Nadja Younes. 2021. "The Paradox of Awards: How Status Ripples Affect Who Benefits from CEO Awards." *Organization Science* 33 (3). https://doi.org/10.1287/orsc.2021.1475.

6. Billan, Dr. Rumeet, and Todd Humber. n.d. "The Tallest Poppy: Successful Women Pay a High Price for Success." Viewpoint Leadership, Women of Influence, Canadian HR Reporter, Thomson Reuters. Accessed August 11, 2022. https://static1.squarespace.com /static/5760345a044262a766b7a699/t/5bc4aa0f4785d3ab4d047fd7 /1539615256731/TPS+Whitepaper.pdf.

7. Billan and Humber.

8. Kross, Ethan, Emma Bruehlman-Senecal, Jiyoung Park, Aleah Burson, Adrienne Dougherty, Holly Shablack, Ryan Bremner, Jason Moser, and Ozlem Ayduk. 2014. "Self-Talk as a Regulatory Mechanism: How You Do It Matters." *Journal of Personality and Social Psychology* 106 (2): 304–24. https://doi.org/10.1037/a0035173.

9. Jordt, Hannah, Sarah L. Eddy, Riley Brazil, Ignatius Lau, Chelsea Mann, Sara E. Brownell, Katherine King, and Scott Freeman. 2017. "Values Affirmation Intervention Reduces Achievement Gap between Underrepresented Minority and White Students in Introductory Biology Classes." Edited by Jeff Schinske. *CBE—Life Sciences Education* 16 (3): ar41. https://doi.org/10.1187/cbe.16-12-0351.

10. Logel, Christine, and Geoffrey L. Cohen. 2011. "The Role of the Self in Physical Health." *Psychological Science* 23 (1): 53–55. https://doi.org /10.1177/0956797611421936.

11. *National Geographic.* 2015. "The Power of Positivity | Brain Games." www.youtube.com. June 22, 2015. https://www.youtube.com /watch?v=kO1kglop-Hw&t=1s.

12. Hendricks, Jaclyn. 2021. "Rex Ryan's 'Toe Expert' Joke Causes 'Get Up' Cast to Completely Lose It." *New York Post.* December 13, 2021. https:// nypost.com/2021/12/13/espn-get-up-cast-loses-it-over-rex-ryans-toe-expert -joke.

13. Wenders, Wim, dir. 2018. *Pope Francis: A Man of His Word.* Focus Features.

14. Vatican News. 2019. "Pope Francis Reflects on Meaning of Death." YouTube Video. YouTube. https://www.youtube.com /watch?v=fjhoVsUloUI.

CHAPTER 3: TAKE THE LEAP

1. Ruiz, Eric M. 2016. "Meet Sarah Cooper, the Ex-Googler behind the Cartoons That Have Captured the Internet." *Observer.* October 4, 2016. https://observer.com/2016/10/meet-sarah-cooper-the-ex-googler-behind -the-cartoons-that-have-captured-the-internet/.

2. Johnson, Eric. 2018. "For Comedian Sarah Cooper, a Job at Google Was Plan B." Vox. January 10, 2018. https://www.vox.com/2018/1/10/16871786 /sarah-cooper-comedian-google-dick-costolo-kara-swisher-recode-decode -podcast.

3. Shin, Jihae, and Katherine L. Milkman. 2016. "How Backup Plans Can Harm Goal Pursuit: The Unexpected Downside of Being Prepared for Failure." Papers.ssrn.com. Rochester, NY. April 10, 2016. https://ssrn.com /abstract=2538889.

4. M, Marvis. 2020. "I HATE PLAN B - Arnold Schwarzenegger - the Most Inspiring Speech Ever." www.youtube.com. December 9, 2020. https:// www.youtube.com/watch?v=uGHI58Fhrgk.

Notes

CHAPTER 4: OPTIMIZE YOUR ANXIETY

1. Diamond, David M., Adam M. Campbell, Collin R. Park, Joshua
    Halonen, and Phillip R. Zoladz. 2007. "The Temporal Dynamics Model
    of Emotional Memory Processing: A Synthesis on the Neurobiological
    Basis of Stress-Induced Amnesia, Flashbulb and Traumatic Memories,
    and the Yerkes-Dodson Law." *Neural Plasticity* 2007: 1–33. https://doi
    .org/10.1155/2007/60803.

2. Woolley, Kaitlin, and Ayelet Fishbach. 2022. "Motivating Personal Growth
    by Seeking Discomfort." *Psychological Science* 33 (4): 9567976211044685.
    https://doi.org/10.1177/09567976211044685.

3. Hood, Julia. 2001. "Higgins Steers Kozmo with Political Gusto." Prweek
    .com. PR Week Global. March 5, 2001. https://www.prweek.com
    /article/1238055/analysis-profile-higgins-steers-kozmo-political-gusto-matt
    -higgins-sees-symmetry-political-pr-dot-com-pr-demand-strong-conviction
    -willingness-brave.

4. McCallum, Jack. 2019. "Have You Heard the One about My Crippling
    Depression?" *Boston* magazine. December 2, 2019. https://www
    .bostonmagazine.com/arts-entertainment/2019/12/02/gary-gulman/.

5. McCallum, 2019.

6. Wilstein, Matt. 2020. "The 10 Best Stand-up Specials to Stream While
    Quarantined." *The Daily Beast*, March 17, 2020, sec. Entertainment.
    https://www.thedailybeast.com/10-best-stand-up-specials-to-stream-under
    -coronavirus-quarantine.

7. Posnanski, Joe. 2009. "Zack Greinke Is in Total Control." *Sports Illustrated*.
    April 28, 2009. https://www.si.com/more-sports/2009/04/28/zack
    -greinke.

8. Wulf, Steve. 2015. "The Mastery and Mystery of Zack Greinke." ABC News.
    October 15, 2015. https://abcnews.go.com/Sports/mastery-mystery-zack
    -greinke/story?id=34499251.

9. Plaschke, Bill. 2013. "Zack Greinke Gets through Anxious Moments." *Los
    Angeles Times*. February 15, 2013. https://www.latimes.com/sports/la-xpm
    -2013-feb-15-la-sp-0216-plaschke-greinke-20130216-story.html.

10. Helder, T. Van, and M. W. Radomski. 1989. "Sleep Deprivation and the
    Effect on Exercise Performance." *Sports Medicine* 7 (4): 235–47. https://doi
    .org/10.2165/00007256-198907040-00002.

11. Kozan, Kayla. n.d. "Huge List of CEOs That Meditate at Work | 2020."
    Peak Wellness. Accessed August 11, 2022. https://peakwellnessco.com
    /ceos-that-meditate-at-work/.

12. Seppälä, Emma. 2015. "How Meditation Benefits CEOs." *Harvard Business Review*. December 16, 2015. https://hbr.org/2015/12/how-meditation-benefits-ceos.

13. Novak, Viveca. 2011. "Bum Rap for Rahm." FactCheck.org. January 13, 2011. https://www.factcheck.org/2011/01/bum-rap-for-rahm/.

CHAPTER 5: EMBRACE EACH CRISIS

1. Fredrickson, Barbara L., Michele M. Tugade, Christian E. Waugh, and Gregory R. Larkin. 2003. "What Good Are Positive Emotions in Crisis? A Prospective Study of Resilience and Emotions Following the Terrorist Attacks on the United States on September 11th, 2001." *Journal of Personality and Social Psychology* 84 (2): 365–76. https://doi.org/10.1037/0022-3514.84.2.365.

2. Panja, Tariq. 2022. "Rare Champions League Rights Sale Produces Two Winners." *New York Times*, February 3, 2022, sec. Sports. https://www.nytimes.com/2022/02/03/sports/soccer/champions-league-relevent-uefa.html.

3. "Year of Wonders 1665–1667." n.d. National Trust. https://www.nationaltrust.org.uk/woolsthorpe-manor/features/year-of-wonders.

4. Freke, Timothy. 2002. *Tao*. Harry N Abrams.

5. Daniels, Cora. 2004. "The Man Who Changed Medicine." Money.cnn.com. November 29, 2004. https://money.cnn.com/magazines/fortune/fortune_archive/2004/11/29/8192713/index.htm.

6. Schwartz, Barry. 2006. "More Isn't Always Better." *Harvard Business Review*. June 2006. https://hbr.org/2006/06/more-isnt-always-better.

CHAPTER 6: BREAK THE PATTERNS THAT STAND IN YOUR WAY

1. Greenberg, Jason, and Ethan R. Mollick. 2018. "Sole Survivors: Solo Ventures versus Founding Teams." SSRN Electronic Journal. https://doi.org/10.2139/ssrn.3107898.

2. Howell, Travis, Christopher Bingham, and Bradley Hendricks. 2022. "Don't Buy the Myth That Every Startup Needs a Co-Founder." *Harvard Business Review*. April 20, 2022. https://hbr.org/2022/04/dont-buy-the-myth-that-every-startup-needs-a-co-founder.

3. Reilly, Claire. 2018. "Juicero Is Still the Greatest Example of Silicon Valley Stupidity." CNET. September 1, 2018. https://www.cnet.com/culture/juicero-is-still-the-greatest-example-of-silicon-valley-stupidity/.

4. Lanxon, Nate. 2009. "The Greatest Defunct Web Sites and Dotcom

Disasters." CNET. November 18, 2009. https://www.cnet.com/tech /computing/the-greatest-defunct-web-sites-and-dotcom-disasters/.

5. "Theranos." 2016. Web.archive.org. June 22, 2016. https://web.archive .org/web/20160622193253/https://www.theranos.com/test-menu.

6. Katz, Ariel. 2021. "The Theranos Fiasco Shows How Much Startup Advisory Boards Matter." TechCrunch. October 10, 2021. https:// techcrunch.com/2021/10/10/the-theranos-fiasco-shows-how-much -startup-advisory-boards-matter/.

7. Kuran, Timur, and Cass Sunstein. 2007. "Availability Cascades and Risk Regulation." The University of Chicago. https://papers.ssrn.com/sol3 /papers.cfm?abstract_id=138144.

CHAPTER 7: CONSOLIDATE YOUR GAINS

1. Del Rey, Jason. 2021. "Walmart's E-Commerce Chief Is Leaving to Build 'a City of the Future.'" Vox. January 15, 2021. https://www.vox.com /recode/2021/1/15/22232033/marc-lore-walmart-leaving-jet-city-future -capitalism.

2. Souhan, Jim. 2021. "New Owners Have Some Wild Ideas — like Turning Timberwolves into Winners." *Star Tribune*. September 28, 2021. https:// www.startribune.com/timberwolves-alex-rodriguez-marc-lore-wild-ideas -jim-souhan/600101481/.

3. Alsever, Jennifer. 2021. "Why Tech Billionaire Marc Lore Wants to Build a Utopian City." *Fortune*. September 1, 2021. https://fortune .com/2021/09/01/billionaire-marc-lore-utopian-city-equitism/.

4. Gould, Jennifer. 2021. "Jet.com Founder Marc Lore Has Fleet of Trucks Ready to Deliver Bobby Flay to You." *New York Post*. December 14, 2021. https://nypost.com/2021/12/13/jet-com-founder-marc-lore-has-fleet-of -trucks-ready-to-deliver-bobby-flay-to-you/.

5. Geng, Joy J., Bo-Yeong Won, and Nancy B. Carlisle. 2019. "Distractor Ignoring: Strategies, Learning, and Passive Filtering." *Current Directions in Psychological Science* 28 (6): 600–606. https://doi.org/10.1177 /0963721419867099.

6. Braverman, Harry. 1998. *Labor and Monopoly Capital: The Degradation of Work in the Twentieth Century*. New York: Monthly Review Press.

7. Kasra Design. 2020. "Dwayne Johnson - Back against the Wall | Collage Animation." Vimeo. November 23, 2020. https://vimeo .com/482895699.

CHAPTER 8: SUBMIT TO THE GREATNESS OF OTHERS

1. Cook, John. 2011. "Jeff Bezos on Innovation: Amazon 'Willing to Be Misunderstood for Long Periods of Time.'" GeekWire. June 7, 2011. https://www.geekwire.com/2011/amazons-bezos-innovation/.

2. "'A Voice for the Underdog and Underprivileged.'" n.d. Www.pulitzer .org. Accessed August 11, 2022. https://www.pulitzer.org/article/voice -underdog-and-underprivileged.

3. Bloomberg. 2020. "Ark's Cathie Wood Has 'No Regrets' on Tesla Call." www.youtube.com. December 18, 2020. https://www.youtube.com /watch?v=ORrZMaX8VQc.

4. Weinstein, Netta, and Richard M. Ryan. 2010. "When Helping Helps: Autonomous Motivation for Prosocial Behavior and Its Influence on Well-Being for the Helper and Recipient." *Journal of Personality and Social Psychology* 98 (2): 222–44. https://doi.org/10.1037 /a0016984.

5. Farino, Lisa. 2017. "New Research Shows That Helping Others May Be the Key to Happiness. – G.O. Community Development Corporation." G.O. Community Development Corporation. April 25, 2017. https://www .go-cdc.org/2017/new-research-shows-that-helping-others-may-be-the-key -to-happiness/.

6. Santi, Jenny. 2015. "The Science behind the Power of Giving (Op-Ed)." Livescience.com. December 1, 2015. https://www.livescience.com/52936 -need-to-give-boosted-by-brain-science-and-evolution.html.

CHAPTER 9: MANIFEST YOUR BOLDEST DREAMS

1. Keating, Peter. 2020. "The Baseball Hall of Famer Who Runs a Funeral Home." ESPN.com. May 28, 2020. https://www.espn.com/mlb/story /_/id/29224947/the-baseball-hall-famer-runs-funeral-home-andre-dawson -second-act.

2. Scott, Ellen. 2018. "Why You Feel Down after Running a Marathon." *Metro.* June 15, 2018. https://metro.co.uk/2018/06/15/get-post-marathon -blues-7633314/.

3. Woolley, Kaitlin, and Ayelet Fishbach. 2015. "The Experience Matters More than You Think: People Value Intrinsic Incentives More inside than Outside an Activity." *Journal of Personality and Social Psychology* 109 (6): 968–82. https://doi.org/10.1037/pspa0000035.

4. Florio, John, and Ouisie Shapiro. 2016. "The Dark Side of Going for Gold."

Notes

The Atlantic. August 18, 2016. https://www.theatlantic.com/health /archive/2016/08/post-olympic-depression/496244/.

5. Friedman, Ron. 2015. "Staying Motivated after a Major Achievement." *Harvard Business Review.* February 3, 2015. https://hbr.org/2015/02 /staying-motivated-after-a-major-achievement.

6. Friedman, 2015.

7. Becker, Joshua. 2012. "About Becoming Minimalist." Becoming Minimalist. May 8, 2012. https://www.becomingminimalist.com /becoming-minimalist-start-here/.

8. Becker, Joshua. n.d. "The Emptiness of Sports Is Most Felt in Victory." www.becomingminimalist.com. Accessed August 11, 2022. https://www .becomingminimalist.com/emptiness/.

9. Becker, "The Emptiness of Sports Is Most Felt in Victory."

10. Young, Jabari. 2021. "Fanatics Owner Michael Rubin Put His $18 Billion Empire aside to Focus on Families Affected by Unfair Justice System." CNBC. December 24, 2021. https://www.cnbc.com/2021/12/24/fanatics -owner-michael-rubin-reform-alliance-hosts-76ers-experience.html.

11. Young, 2021.

12. Parham, Robert. 2013. "Pope Francis Models Humility in World That Practices Humiliation." Good Faith Media. April 2, 2013. https:// goodfaithmedia.org/pope-francis-models-humility-in-world-that-practices -humiliation-cms-20624/.

INDEX

Index

Index

ABOUT THE AUTHOR

Matt Higgins is a self-made serial entrepreneur with deep operating experience that spans multiple industries over his twenty-five-year career. Higgins holds dual roles as cofounder and CEO of the private investment firm RSE Ventures. His business-building acumen also earned him a spot as a recurring guest Shark on ABC's *Shark Tank* during seasons ten and eleven. He is a prolific investor in the direct-to-consumer space and leveraged this expertise to become an executive fellow at Harvard Business School, where he coteaches the course "Moving Beyond DTC." A lifelong New Yorker, Higgins was appointed press secretary for the New York City mayor's office at age twenty-six—the youngest in history—managing the global media response during the 9/11 terrorist attacks before ultimately becoming chief operating officer of the Lower Manhattan Development Corporation. After transitioning to the private sector, he spent fifteen years in senior leadership positions with two National Football League teams, starting as EVP of business operations for the New York Jets before serving as vice chairman of the Miami Dolphins for nearly a decade. Higgins received the Ellis Island Medal of Honor in 2019, joining the ranks of seven former US presidents, Nobel Prize winners, and other leaders for his work to improve society. He is also a longstanding board member of Autism Speaks, advocating for scientific research and greater acceptance of neurodiversity.